BANK CONTROL OF LARGE CORPORATIONS
IN THE UNITED STATES

BANK CONTROL
OF LARGE
CORPORATIONS
IN THE
UNITED STATES

DAVID M. KOTZ

University of California Press
Berkeley · Los Angeles · London

University of California Press
Berkeley and Los Angeles, California

University of California Press, Ltd.
London, England

Copyright © 1978 by
The Regents of the University of California

First Paperback Printing 1980
Second Cloth Printing 1979
ISBN 0-520-03937-8 paper
ISBN 0-520-03321-3 cloth
Library of Congress Catalog Card Number: 76-24585

Printed in the United States of America

Contents

List of Tables   vii

Preface   ix

1. The Problem of Corporate Control   1
   The Managerial Thesis   2
   Owner Control   6
   Financial Control   8

2. The Meaning of Control   14
   Control Distinguished from Managing   16
   The Basis of Control   18

3. The Evolution of Financial Control Over Large
   Corporations Since 1865   23
   The Rise of Banker Control: 1865-1914   24
   War, Prosperity, and Banker Power: 1915-1929   41
   Decline of Banker Power: 1930-1945   51
   Resurgence: 1946-1974   60

4. The Extent of Financial Control Over the 200 Largest
   Nonfinancial Corporations, 1967-1969   72
   The Sample of 200 Corporations   72
   Control Categories   75
   Rationale for the Working Definitions   79
   Groups of Financial Institutions   84
   Data Sources   89
   Problems in Applying the Working Definitions   93
   Overall Results   96
   Results by Assets and Size Group   101
   Results by Sector   105

Types of Financial Institutions   108
The Most Powerful Financial Institutions   110
Financial Control and Owner Control   113
Comparison of Larner's Results to These Results   116

5. The Exercise of Financial Control and Its
   Significance   119
   The Means of Exercising Financial Control   120
   The Implications of Financial Control for Market Behavior   130
   The Economic and Social Significance of Financial Control   140

Appendices
A. The Sample of 200 Corporations   151
B. Classification of the 200 Largest Nonfinancial
   Corporations by Type of Control, 1967-1969   157
C. Financial and Owner Control Among Industrial
   Companies, by Industry   192
D. Companies Controlled by Groups of Financial
   Institutions   196

Selected Bibliography   201

Index   207

Tables

1. The Share of Financial Institutions in Total Corporate Stock Outstanding   65
2. The Ten Largest Commercial Bank Trust Departments, 1974   70
3. Summary of Control over the Top 200 Nonfinancial Corporations   97
4. Summary of Control over the Top 200 Nonfinancial Corporations, by Assets   102
5. Summary of Control over Nonfinancial Corporations with Asset Rank 11 through 200   103
6. Financial and Owner Control over the Top 200 Nonfinancial Corporations, by Size Group   104
7. Financial and Owner Control over the Top 200 Nonfinancial Corporations, by Sector   106
8. Financial Control over the Top 200 Nonfinancial Corporations, by Type of Controlling Financial Institution   109
9. Financial Control over the Top 200 Nonfinancial Corporations, by Source of Control   110
10. Financial Institutions Controlling More than One Company among the Top 200   111
11. Number and Assets of Companies among the Top 200 Controlled by the Four Groups of Financial Institutions and by Cleveland and Chicago Financial Institutions   112
12. Larner's Control Results for the 141 Largest Nonfinancial Corporations Excluding Utilities, 1963   117
13. My Control Results for the 141 Largest Nonfinancial Corporations Excluding Utilities, 1967-1969   117
A-1. The 200 Largest Nonfinancial Corporations Ranked by Assets at Year-end 1969   151

B-1. Classification of the 200 Largest Nonfinancial
     Corporations by Type of Control Excluding
     Control by Groups of Financial Institutions,
     1967-1969   159
B-2. Changes in the Classification of the 200 Largest
     Nonfinancial Corporations Resulting from the
     Inclusion of Control by Groups of Financial
     Institutions, 1967-1969   185
B-3. Alphabetical Index to Table B-1   188
C-1. Financial and Owner Control among Industrial
     Companies in the Sample, by Industry   193
C-2. Industry Categories in Table C-1 and Standard
     Industrial Classification Categories   194
D-1. Companies Controlled by the Chase Group   196
D-2. Companies Controlled by the Morgan Group   197
D-3. Companies Controlled by the Mellon Group   199
D-4. Companies Controlled by the Lehman-Goldman,
     Sachs Group   199
D-5. Companies Controlled by Chicago Financial
     Institutions   200
D-6. Companies Controlled by Cleveland Financial
     Institutions   200

Preface

The United States is presently going through its third major period in this century of widespread popular concern about the concentration of economic power. The first was the so-called Progressive Era of 1900-1916, which closely followed the emergence of the giant corporation. The second came during the Great Depression of the 1930s, as many blamed big business for the economic crisis.

The past decade has witnessed a new outpouring of books and articles about the concentration of economic power in the United States. This is a natural reaction to the series of unsettling events that Americans have experienced recently — an unpopular Asian war, corporate and political scandals, double-digit inflation, widespread unemployment. The most popular type of study in this vein focuses on a particular individual, family, corporation, or industry. Thus, Howard Hughes and J. Paul Getty, the Rockefeller family and the duPont family, ITT and ATT, the oil industry and the auto industry have all received a thorough going over.

This book is concerned with economic power in the United States, but it does not focus on any individual person or corporation. Starting from the assumption that the giant corporation is the central economic institution in modern U.S. capitalism, it explores the question, "What group in U.S. society holds predominant power over the giant corporation?" The thesis presented is that bankers have re-emerged, after a period of partial eclipse during the Great Depression and World War II, as the major group that controls large corporations. This dominant group, of course, does not include the small-town banker; rather, it is restricted to a small number of giant, well-established banks, principally in New York City, and secondarily in Pittsburgh, Chicago, Cleveland, and a few other major cities. The power held by the leading bankers should be of

concern to economists interested in the market behavior of
large corporations, to anti-trusters interested in the sources of
market power, and to anyone else interested in the concentration of economic power in present-day capitalism.

Most of the analysis in this book centers on the levers of
power which banks and other financial institutions hold over
large corporations. The focus is on the relationships among
institutions. Such a focus is convenient for analyzing the power
of the banks. However, it may obscure the fact that institutions
such as banks and corporations are inanimate entities, having no
will of their own apart from that of the human beings who
control them. When we ask who controls the large corporation,
we are really asking which of the various sections of the capitalist class — bankers, industrialists, merchants, etc. — is the dominant one. Or, have the capitalists as a whole lost control of large
corporations to the hired corporate managers, as proponents of
the Managerial Thesis claim? Thus, real relationships among
groups of people lie behind apparent relationships among
institutions.

This work is a revised version of my doctoral dissertation in
economics, submitted at the University of California at Berkeley in 1975. I received help from many individuals in preparing
the original dissertation and in revising it for publication. I owe
a great debt to Robert Fitch for interesting me in the subject of
bank control over large corporations. He overcame my initial
resistance to the idea that banks might be very powerful, and he
introduced me to the basic sources of information on the
subject. Professor Robert Aaron Gordon of the University of
California, Berkeley, helped me turn a rough idea into a man-
ageable outline for research, and he continued to make helpful
suggestions and comments throughout the research and writing
stages. Professor Benjamin Ward also provided helpful suggestions, as well as encouragement. Other professors and graduate
students at the University of California, Berkeley, provided
useful comments. Of course, any shortcomings in this work are
my own responsibility.

Without the work of the late Representative Wright Patman,
and the House Banking and Currency Committee's Subcommittee on Domestic Finance, which Patman chaired, this study
could not have been undertaken. Representative Patman's Subcommittee produced investigations of the major banks which
both provided the best raw data for students of bank control

and stimulated other governmental agencies to do investigations of their own. I also am indebted to the Subcommittee on Reports, Accounting, and Management of the Senate Government Operations Committee for providing me with useful information. I would also like to thank the staff of the New York Stock Exchange library for providing me with extremely efficient access to a large number of corporate proxy statements.

DAVID M. KOTZ

Washington, D.C.
1976

CHAPTER ONE

The Problem of Corporate Control

In the typical unincorporated business firm, the owner both supplies the capital and directs the company's operations. Control of the privately owned business is normally held firmly by the owner. In the corporate business firm the roles of capital supplier and director of operations are divided among several groups: shareholders, bondholders, directors, and officers. The original intention, as embodied in law, was that control over a corporation be held ultimately by the body of shareholders and exercised through the elected board of directors. However, in practice it is possible for someone other than the body of stockholders to have control over the firm.

The corporate form of organization spread rapidly in the later decades of the nineteenth century. By 1900 it was predominant in railroads, public utilities, mining, and manufacturing. This development set off struggles for control over business firms among various individuals, groups, and institutions. The chief contenders for control have been individual stockholders, financial institutions, and the corporate management itself.

Before going any further it is necessary to explain what is meant by the term "control." In chapter 2 this problem will be examined at length. For now, control will be defined as the power to determine the broad policies guiding a firm. This is distinguished from the day-to-day managing of a firm, although it is possible that the same person or persons have control over, and carry out the day-to-day managing of, a given firm.

What difference does it make who controls corporations? A firm operating in a hypothetical perfectly competitive market must behave according to the dictates of profit maximization or cease to exist. The goals and preferences of whomever controls the firm do not have any consequences for firm behavior in the long run. However, that is not true of a firm that has a significant degree of market power. If the controller of a firm with market power cares ultimately about the firm's growth rate of sales, the social usefulness of its product, or the extent of reliance on external finance, as well as, or instead of, caring about profits, then the firm's market behavior is affected. Furthermore, if several firms that compete with each other or are customers of one another are controlled by the same agency, this affects the degree of market power that is present in the industries concerned.[1]

The question of who controls large corporations has implications that go beyond market behavior. The distribution of economic and political power, the predominant social values, the types of social and economic changes and reforms that are likely and possible — all of these are strongly influenced by the nature of control over large corporations. A society whose major productive units are controlled by their professional, non-owning managers should differ in the above dimensions from one in which millions of shareholders had true control over productive enterprise. Both would differ from a society in which a small number of financial institutions dominated the private economy.

THE MANAGERIAL THESIS

For several decades the view most widely held among economists about who controls the major nonfinancial corporations has been the managerial thesis. First popularized by Adolf A. Berle and Gardiner Means in the early 1930s, the managerial thesis holds that large corporations have passed through several stages since the late nineteenth century, culminating in the modern "managerial corporation."[2] According to this view, the nineteenth century corporation at first looked much like its noncorporate predecessor. One person or small group functioned as the entrepreneur, owning most of the stock and directly exerting managerial authority. The names of some of the great corporate entrepreneurs of that period are still familiar: Rockefeller, Vanderbilt, Carnegie. As corporations became larger, majority control grew more difficult and costly. It became more common for an individual or group to hold control

1. For a more detailed discussion of these questions, see chapter 5.
2. Adolf A. Berle and Gardiner C. Means, *The Modern Corporation and Private Property*, rev. ed. (New York, 1968).

through a large minority stockholding, rather than an absolute majority.

In addition to big stockholders, managerialists admit a secondary source of power over the early corporation. Financial institutions were sometimes able to exert at least some influence over large corporations, according to this view, through their role as suppliers of capital to the corporation.

By the 1920s, the managerialists claim, control by big stockholders and bankers over large corporations had begun to recede. Real control was passing to the individual corporation's board of directors and senior officers. These managers normally owned at most a small fraction of the corporation's stock, yet they were able to become self-perpetuating and responsible only to themselves, as the managerial corporation reached maturity and predominance in the post-World War II period.

Two developments are thought to have been particularly important in bringing about the ascendence of the managerial corporation. First, after the entrepreneurial founders of many large corporations died, their stockholdings were dispersed among numerous heirs, who often were interested only in receiving income from the fortune, not in exercising control. The increasing absolute size of the major corporations made continued stockholder control by one individual more difficult. In some cases wealthy families sold off their concentrated stockholdings in return for the benefits of diversified wealth. As Berle and Means put it, "the position of ownership has changed from that of an active to that of a passive agent."[3] Ownership had become separated from control.

Second, managerialists argue that the giant corporations which were founded in the late nineteenth and early twentieth centuries became so profitable that they were increasingly able to generate most or all of the financing they needed out of internal funds. Therefore, financial institutions lost their power over nonfinancial corporations. Financial institutions were now relegated to the role of modest intermediaries, supplying funds where requested, giving financial advice, and so forth. It is thought that management control emerged in the vacuum left by the decline of stockholder and financial power.

The managerial thesis has achieved impressively widespread acceptance. Most neoclassical economists, moderate critics of

3. *Ibid.*, p. 64.

orthodoxy such as John Kenneth Galbraith, and even most Marxist economists have accepted at least the broad outlines of the thesis. But there is significant disagreement about what implications the managerial corporation has for corporate behavior and economic analysis.

The influence of the managerial thesis is partly due to the impressive empirical findings of its proponents. Berle and Means classified a corporation as management controlled if no stockholder owned as much as 5 percent of the stock, and under joint management-minority control if the largest holding was between 5 percent and 20 percent. They found 44 percent of the 200 largest nonfinancial corporations (ranked by assets), representing 58 percent of the assets of the top 200, to be management controlled.[4]

Robert J. Larner attempted to update Berle and Means' classification of the top 200 nonfinancial corporations of the late 1920s to the year 1963.[5] Using the figure of 10 percent of the stock held by one stockholder as his dividing line between management and owner control, he found 83.5 percent of the top 200 nonfinancial corporations, representing 84 percent of the assets, to be management controlled.[6] Larner concluded that Berle and Means' prediction that the management-controlled corporation would achieve overwhelming predominance among major nonfinancial corporations had come true by the early 1960s.

The post-World War II period has produced a voluminous literature on the implications of the managerial corporation. Robert Aaron Gordon suggested that corporate managers would retain profit maximization as their major goal but would be likely to also strive for other, potentially conflicting goals, such as maximizing the size of the firm or serving broader social goals.[7] Carl Kaysen argues that the managerial corporation seeks growth and change, relying on internal financing to carry

4. *Ibid.*, p. 109. The remainder were held to be controlled by a minority or majority stockholder or through a legal device.

5. Robert J. Larner, "Ownership and Control of the 200 Largest Nonfinancial Corporations," *American Economic Review* (September 1966). See also Larner, *Management Control and the Large Corporation* (Cambridge, Mass., 1970).

6. Larner, *Management Control*, p. 12. The more widely cited 1966 article by Larner presented slightly different results: management control involved 84.5 percent of his sample by number and 85 percent by assets.

7. Robert Aaron Gordon, *Business Leadership in the Large Corporation* (Berkeley, 1961), p. 237. However, Gordon does not totally discount the influence of big stockholders and financial interest groups.

out its plans.[8] Rather than trying to maximize profits for the stockholders, Kaysen contends that "management sees itself as responsible to stockholders, employees, customers, the general public, and perhaps the firm itself as an institution."[9] One consequence of the shift of power from stockholders to managers is that now "there is no attempt to push off onto workers or the community at large part of the social costs of the enterprise. The modern corporation is a soulful corporation."[10]

John Kenneth Galbraith views the corporate soul in a different light.[11] The twin desires of corporate managers for growth and the exercise of technological expertise result, in his view, in a society dominated by household gadgets, moon rockets, and militarism, while art and general culture suffer.

Some writers have developed mathematical models for the managerial corporation. Robin Marris translates the managers' personal goals of income, security, power, and prestige into an objective function that has two independent variables: the corporation's growth rate and "valuation ratio." The latter variable is the ratio of the market value of the corporation's equity securities to the corporation's net assets at book value; it represents security against take-over raids.[12] The consequences for market behavior include a faster growth rate, lower profit rate, and a higher retention ratio than would be found for a firm operated to maximize returns to the shareholders. Similar models, although with some variations, have been proposed by William Baumol[13] and Oliver Williamson.[14]

Finally, there is a large group of economists who, while accepting the predominance of the management-controlled corporation, do not think that any important changes in economic

8. Carl Kaysen, "The Social Significance of the Modern Corporation," *American Economic Review* (May 1957), p. 315. See also Kaysen, "Another View of Corporate Capitalism," *Quarterly Journal of Economics* (February 1965).

9. Kaysen, "Social Significance," p. 313.

10. *Ibid.*, pp. 313-14.

11. John Kenneth Galbraith, *New Industrial State* (Boston, 1967).

12. Robin Marris, *The Economic Theory of 'Managerial' Capitalism* (Glencoe, Ill., 1964), pp. 260-65.

13. William Baumol, *Business Behavior, Value, and Growth* (New York, 1959); and "On the Theory of Expansion of the Firm," *American Economic Review* (December 1962). In Baumol's dynamic model a firm will shift price and output in response to changes in fixed costs.

14. Oliver Williamson, *The Economics of Discretionary Behavior* (Englewood Cliffs, N.J., 1964); and "Managerial Discretion and Business Behavior," *American Economic Review* (November 1963). Williamson's managerial firm responds differently to changes in a profits tax or lump sum tax than would a profit maximizing firm.

theory are required solely as a consequence of the separation of control from ownership. Shorey Peterson argues that market constraints, shareholder pressure, and business custom enforce traditional profit-maximizing behavior on the managerial corporation.[15]   Robert Solow argues that the threat of take-over, along with other factors, prevents managers from exercising much discretion.[16]   Paul Baran and Paul Sweezy contend, on a somewhat different basis, that managers' desires for rising wealth and status lead them to pursue long-run profit maximization.[17]

This traditionalist interpretation of managerial capitalism is not very persuasive. If largely unpropertied managers have control over large firms with significant market power, then departures from classical firm behavior seem quite likely. One who questions the managerialists' conclusions might instead take a second look   at the empirical evidence on just who is in control.

OWNER CONTROL

A few studies have challenged the managerial thesis by presenting evidence for the continuing primacy of owner control among large nonfinancial corporations. The most comprehensive was the Temporary National Economic Committee's Monograph No. 29, which was based on extensive information on stockholdings in the top 200 nonfinancial corporations (ranked by assets) in 1937-1939.[18]   Employing a more flexible rule than most other studies for determining whether a corporation was controlled by a stockholder, the Temporary National Economic Committee study classified only 30.5 percent of the top 200 nonfinancial corporations, representing 40 percent of the total

15. Shorey Peterson, "Corporate Control and Capitalism," *Quarterly Journal of Economics* (February 1965).

16. Robert Solow, "The New Industrial State or Son of Affluence," *The Public Interest* (Fall 1967).

17. Paul Baran and Paul M. Sweezy, *Monopoly Capital* (New York, 1966), pp. 39-40. However, for Baran and Sweezy, profit maximization does not lead to efficient use of resources or welfare optima, but rather to an irrational, destructive economic and social order.

18. U. S., Temporary National Economic Committee, *Investigation of Concentration of Economic Power,* Monograph No. 29, "The Distribution of Ownership in the 200 Largest Nonfinancial Corporations," 1940. (Hereafter cited as T.N.E.C. Monograph No. 29.) The data were obtained by direct correspondence with the companies being studied.

assets of the 200, as having "no visible center of control." [19] These results were widely cited at the time as disproving the managerial thesis. However, the Temporary National Economic Committee's results were for "immediate control," which classifies a nonfinancial corporation controlled by another nonfinancial corporation through stock ownership as owner controlled. In comparing the Temporary National Economic Committee results with Berle and Means' results for immediate control, one finds that they are very close to each other. [20] The Temporary National Economic Committee study may be regarded as validating the estimates of Berle and Means and, therefore, strengthening their conclusions. [21]

Don Villejero did a study in 1961 of 232 of the 250 largest industrial corporations (ranked by assets), concluding that 61 percent of them were controlled by a "community of interest" based on stock ownership. [22] However, his "community of interest" combines the stockholdings of all the corporation's directors and officers, a few major stockholders, and some associated financial institutions. His conclusions amount to an assertion that if managers, big stockholders, and financial institutions associated with a corporation all worked together, they could exercise control — a claim which does not affect the managerial thesis.

In 1967 Robert Sheehan published a study of owner control among the top 500 industrial corporations (ranked by sales). [23] Using a 10 percent stockholding as the lower limit for owner control, he found 30 percent of the top 500 were owner controlled by an individual or family, although the proportion for the top 100 was only 11 percent. Direct comparison is difficult, but it appears that Sheehan's results are consistent with Larner's findings for the top 200 nonfinancial corporations.

19. *Ibid.*, app. XI. A 10 percent stockholding was sufficient for minority control, but a 5-10 percent holding could suffice if the stockholding group was well represented in management.

20. According to Berle and Means, 32.5 percent of the top 200 nonfinancial corporations, representing 44 percent of total assets, were immediately management controlled.

21. This fact was pointed out in an unpublished article by Michel De Vroey, "The Measurement of the Separation of Ownership and Control in Large Corporations. A Critical Review." (April 1971).

22. Don Villejero, "Stock Ownership and the Control of Corporations," *New University Thought* (Autumn 1961, and Winter 1962).

23. Robert Sheehan, "Proprietors in the World of Big Business," *Fortune* (15 June 1967).

One is left with the conclusion that advocates of the continuing importance of owner control among the largest nonfinancial corporations have not successfully challenged the empirical basis of the managerial thesis.

FINANCIAL CONTROL

A third view about the nature of control over large corporations, which is called the financial control thesis, emphasizes the role of financial institutions as centers of control. According to this view, as large corporations emerged in the United States in the forty years following the Civil War, bankers increasingly replaced individual stockholders as the controllers of large nonfinancial corporations. The basis of the bankers' power was their control over sources of capital that the growing corporations needed. The financial control thesis was widely accepted in the early part of the twentieth century, when the name J. P. Morgan was a household word.[24]

In the first two decades following World War II, the financial control thesis found few adherents, as the managerial thesis, in its many variants, came to predominate. Marxist economists had been among the most active (though by no means the only) proponents of the financial control thesis; in the 1940s Paul Sweezy, probably the most influential Marxist economist in the United States, took the position that the central role of banks had ended. He argued that the powerful position of bankers was a temporary phenomenon associated with the initial appearance of the large corporation. Sweezy wrote in 1942:

> Bank capital, having had its day of glory, falls back again to a position subsidiary to industrial capital, thus reestablishing the relation which existed prior to the combination movement . . . The dominance of bank capital is a passing phase of capitalist development which rough-

24. There is a voluminous literature on the financial control thesis for the pre-World War II period. For example, see Rudolf Hilferding, *Das Finanzkapital,* Wiener Volksbuchhandlung (Wien, 1923); John Moody, *The Truth About the Trusts* (New York, 1904), and *Masters of Capital* (New Haven, 1919); Louis D. Brandeis, *Other People's Money and How the Bankers Use It* (New York, 1914); Lewis Corey, *House of Morgan* (New York, 1930); Ferdinand Pecora, *Wall St. Under Oath* (New York, 1968) (originally published in the 1930s); and U. S., Congress, House Banking and Currency Committee *Report of the Committee Appointed Pursuant to H. R. 429 and 504 to Investigate the Concentration of Money and Credit,* 62nd Congress, 2nd Session, 1913 (Pujo Committee report).

ly coincides with the transition from competitive to monopoly capitalism.[25]

In the 1960s there was a revival of interest in the financial control thesis. Statistical data on the use of external finance by large corporations, which had been available but had gone largely unnoticed since the late 1950s, indicated that no long-run decline had occurred in the relative reliance on external finance by large corporations between 1900 and the 1950s.[26] This seemed to weaken one pillar of the managerial thesis — the view that large corporations generated the capital funds they needed internally.

Second, a number of writers commented on the growing blocks of stock held by bank trust departments, investment companies, and other institutional investors. Daniel Baum and Ned Stiles wrote in 1965 that institutional investors were accumulating substantial, though as yet unexercised, power over corporate managements.[27] Even Adolf A. Berle, in his later writings, suggested that the stage of management control may be giving way to a stage of control by fiduciary institutions.[28]

A few Marxist writers continued to press the financial control thesis in the post-World War II period. Victor Perlo argued that large corporations are clustered into several major and minor groupings, with the great commercial banks at the control centers of these "interest groups."[29] S. Menshikov did a study of corporate control in the early 1960s, relying on interviews with bankers and businessmen and on studies of director interlocks and financing relationships.[30] He concluded that financial control was still the major form of control over large corporations.

25. Paul M. Sweezy, *The Theory of Capitalist Development* (New York, 1942), p. 268. See also Sweezy, "The Decline of the Investment Banker," *Antioch Review* (Spring 1941). In the former work Sweezy argued that the term "finance capital," orginated by Hilferding and widely use by Marxists, suffered from the connotation of banker dominance. Sweezy suggested, "This being the case, it seems preferable to drop it [finance capital] altogether and substitute the term 'monopoly capital' " (*Theory of Capitalist Development*, p. 269). This suggestion turned out to be quite successful.

26. See chapter 3.

27. Daniel J. Baum and Ned B. Stiles, *The Silent Partners: Institutional Investors and Corporate Control* (New York, 1965).

28. Adolf A. Berle, *Power Without Property* (New York, 1959), p. 59.

29. Victor Perlo, *Empire of High Finance* (New York, 1957).

30. S. Menshikov, *Millionaires and Managers* (Moscow, 1969).

All of the above studies suffered from a lack of information about the stock that financial institutions hold as institutional investors. Commercial bank trust departments are the largest institutional investors, managing stock investments for personal trust funds and for corporate pension funds. Bank trust departments are not required to make public any information about their investments. When regulated companies, such as the railroads and airlines, report the identities of their leading stockholders to their regulatory agencies, the blocks of stock held by financial institutions remain hidden behind a wall of "nominee names." That is, financial institutions usually hold stock not in the institution's name but in the name of various nominees, such as "Kane and Company" and "Cudd and Company."

Thus, outsiders could only make guesses about the stockholdings of bank trust departments until 1968. In that year the Subcommittee on Domestic Finance of the House Banking and Currency Committee, chaired by the late Representative Wright Patman, published a study of commercial bank trust department holdings of the stock of large nonfinancial corporations.[31] The Subcommittee found that commercial bank trust departments managed about $160 billion in stock during 1968.[32] It found that 147 of the 500 largest manufacturing and mining corporations (ranked by sales) had 5 percent or more of their common stock held by a bank trust department, in 1967.[33] The Patman Report concluded that "the major banking institutions in this country are emerging as the single most important force in the economy."[34] The Subcommittee warned that growing bank control may result in restraints of competition and poses serious conflict of interest problems.[35]

The Patman Report appeared to weaken the managerial thesis further. The assumption that large stockholdings in nonfinancial corporations had been dispersed over time was a major underpinning of the managerial thesis. The Patman Report showed that many large blocks of stock in nonfinancial corpora-

31. U. S., Congress, House Banking and Currency Committee, Subcommittee on Domestic Finance, *Commercial Banks and their Trust Activities*, 90th Congress, 2nd Session, 1968. (Hereafter cited as *Commercial Banks and their Trust Activities*; it will also be referred to it by its popular title, "The Patman Report.") For a detailed description of the data contained in this report and the other government reports described in this chapter, see chapter 4.

32. *Ibid.*, vol. 1, p. 47.

33. *Ibid.*, p. 3.

34. *Ibid.*, p. 5.

35. *Ibid.*, p. 1.

tions, held by commercial bank trust departments (and usually voted by the bank), had previously gone undetected.

The Patman Report caused a further growth of interest in the financial control thesis. Two more government studies followed. The Securities and Exchange Commission's *Institutional Investor Study Report* compiled information on stockholdings by financial institutions that is in some respects more comprehensive, in other respects more limited, than the Patman Report data.[36] The Securities and Exchange Commission's report concludes that "large institutions, particularly banks, have the potential economic power to exert significant influence over many companies whose securities comprise their portfolios, particularly large companies." However, the report argues that institutional investors "tend to be reluctant to exercise their power, particularly in an open and public way."[37]

Two subcommittees of the Senate Government Operations Committee published a study entitled *Disclosure of Corporate Ownership* in 1973.[38] Based on a voluntary questionnaire submitted to 324 large corporations by Senator Lee Metcalf, this study published data on the leading stockholders in the 163 corporations that responded, focusing on banks' stockholdings.

In 1970 a series of three articles appeared by Robert Fitch and Mary Oppenheimer, entitled "Who Rules the Corporations?"[39] Based partly on the Patman Report, the authors argued that the major New York banks had achieved a position of dominance over large nonfinancial corporations. They claimed that the banks use their power to make nonfinancial corporations borrow excessively, and that the banks are partly responsible for the decline of the railroads and the problems of the power utilities.

The Fitch and Oppenheimer articles set off a debate among Marxist economists. Paul Sweezy, James O'Connor, and Edward Herman wrote critiques of the financial control thesis, arguing that there is no convincing evidence that the banks control large

36. U. S., Securities and Exchange Commission, *Institutional Investor Study Report,* House Document 92-64, (referred to the House Committee on Interstate and Foreign Commerce), 1971. (Hereafter cited as *Institutional Investor Study Report.*)

37. *Ibid.,* pt. 8, pp. 124-25.

38. U. S., Congress, Senate Government Operations Committee, Subcommittees on Intergovernmental Relations, and on Budgeting, Management, and Expenditure, *Disclosure of Corporate Ownership,* 93rd Congress, 1st Session, 1973 (hereafter cited as *Disclosure of Corporate Ownership.*)

39. Robert Fitch and Mary Oppenheimer, "Who Rules the Corporations?" pts. 1,2,3, *Socialist Revolution,* vol. 1, nos. 4-6.

nonfinancial corporations.[40]   Fitch defended his position in several later articles.[41] Unfortunately, this debate seems to have left most followers of the controversy somewhat confused about the role of banks and even about what precisely are the issues in the controversy.

The government studies discussed above provide a mass of data about bank stockholdings in large nonfinancial corporations. However, no clear picture emerges from them, or from the other studies cited, of the degree of power that banks possess over large corporations — only a general impression that banks might be more powerful than had been realized. Thus, the challenge which the financial control thesis presents to the managerial thesis remains only an implicit one.

There is a need for a systematic study and evaluation of the financial control thesis, taking advantage of the data that have become available in the above-mentioned government reports, as well as the other scattered sources of information that can be found. In this work I attempt to provide such a study. Chapter 2 discusses what it means for a person or institution to "control" a corporation. Chapter 3 places the financial control thesis in historical perspective, by tracing the changing relationships between financial institutions and nonfinancial corporations from the Civil War to the present. Chapter 4 presents a study of control over the 200 largest nonfinancial corporations (ranked by assets), for the years 1967-1969. This study utilizes three main control categories: owner control, financial control, and no identified center of control.[42] In determining whether a corporation was controlled by a financial institution, account was taken of stockholdings, creditor relationships, and director ties.

Chapter 4 reveals that a significant proportion of the 200 largest nonfinancial corporations are under financial control. Chapter 5 examines the means that financial institutions use to exercise their control over nonfinancial corporations and explores the implications of financial control over large nonfinancial corporations. Financial control has important implications

---

40. Paul M. Sweezy, "Resurgence of Financial Control: Fact or Fancy?," *Monthly Review* (November 1971); James O'Connor, "Question: Who Rules the Corporations? Answer: The Ruling Class," *Socialist Revolution*, vol. 2, no. 1; Edward Herman, "Do Bankers Control Corporations?," *Monthly Review* (June 1973).

41. Robert Fitch, "Reply," *Socialist Revolution*, vol. 2, no. 1; and Fitch, "Sweezy and Corporate Fetishism," *Socialist Revolution*, vol. 2, no. 6.

42. The category of "no identified center of control" is similar to Berle and Means' category "management control."

for the market behavior of business firms, involving the degree of competition in individual markets, the nature of buyer-seller relationships, the tendency of firms to engage in mergers and acquisitions, and the nature of financial markets. No less important, financial control has consequences for the "reformability" — the potential "soulfulness," in Kaysen's terminology — of the large corporation; for the degree of concentration of economic and political power; and for our understanding of the nature of the dominant economic class under modern capitalism. The financial control thesis raises an important challenge to the widely accepted managerial thesis.

CHAPTER TWO
The Meaning of Control

It is important to be specific about what is meant by "control" over a corporation. A definition commonly found in the literature is "the power to select (or reject) the board of directors of a corporation".[1] Since we use the term "management" to refer to the board of directors and senior officers of a corporation, and since the board of directors selects the senior officers, the above definition of control amounts to the power to select the management of a corporation.

This definition may be suitable for a study of the degree of power associated with ownership. The ultimate source of power available to a big stockholder is to vote his stock for an alternative slate of directors, and to convince other stockholders to do likewise. However, it is not adequate for an investigation of financial control. Using this definition is likely to result in overlooking other methods of exercising influence. For example, a bank may exert influence over a corporation by putting pressure on the management, rather than by selecting management personnel.

One implication of the above definition is that a corporation having no large stockholder will appear to be controlled by its management. Joe Bain, a leading expert on industrial organization, points out that in the case of such management-controlled corporations, one may ask about the managers, "Are they simply professional managers with a primary or sole obligation to the shareholders of the corporation, or are they perhaps representatives of or obligated to interests not officially identified with the corporation by ownership?"[2] Thus, Berle and

---

1. A definition of this type is used in Joe S. Bain's textbook, *Industrial Organization*, 2nd ed. (New York, 1968), p. 71, and in Adolf A. Berle and Gardiner C. Means, *The Modern Corporation and Private Property*, rev. ed. (New York, 1968), p. 66.

2. Bain, pp. 71-72.

Means classified United States Steel Corporation as management controlled in 1929, since no large stockholding group was identified, yet R. A. Gordon found U.S. Steel to be under "a strong and continuing influence" by the Morgan banking interests in the 1920s and 1930s.[3]

As was mentioned in chapter 1, the definition of control used in this study is "the power to determine the broad policies guiding a corporation."[4] This definition has the disadvantage of being less precise than the previous definition, and as a result, is more difficult to apply to specific situations. It is a more appropriate definition, however, to use for a study of control by financial institutions, since such control is often exercised by pressure on management.

What are "the broad policies guiding a corporation"? By this is meant the goals of the firm,[5] the general strategy for achieving those goals, and the policy for distributing the fruits of corporate activity among various claimants. In terms of the usual categories of business decision-making, these "broad policies" refer primarily to the following four policies:

1. Goals of the firm.
2. Expansion policy (including mergers and acquisitions).
3. Financial policy.
4. Policy for distribution of profits.

Each of the above four policies has important effects on the firm's economic performance and directly affects the interests of any groups that might contend for control. Other policies that a controlling group might want to determine directly include labor policy, pricing policy, marketing policy (including purchasing and sales), and organizational structure. However, one would expect such policies normally to be left to the management's discretion. Furthermore, less important aspects of the previous four policies would be left to management's discretion.

3. Robert Aaron Gordon, *Business Leadership in the Large Corporation* (Berkeley, 1961), p. 207.

4. This definition was used in U. S., Congress, House Banking and Currency Committee, Subcommittee on Domestic Finance, *Commercial Banks and Their Trust Activities*, 90th Congress, 2nd Session, 1968, vol. I, p. 22, and Temporary National Economic Committee, *Investigation of Concentration of Economic Power*, Monograph No. 29, "The Distribution of Ownership in the 200 Largest Nonfinancial Corporations, 1940," pp. 99-100.

5. By the goals of the firm, I mean the following: a) what variables (such as profits or sales) should be maximized, if any? b) what importance do "social service" type variables, such as product quality or usefulness, have as ends in themselves, if any?

There are many individuals, groups, and institutions whose welfare is significantly affected by the policies of any large business corporation. Besides stockholders, management, and associated financial institutions, the list would include middle and lower level employees, competitors, customers, suppliers, associated law firms, and the government. Each of these groups and institutions has at least some influence on corporate policies. In a sense, the power to determine the basic policies of a corporation is shared by many groups. To say that a single group has control over a corporation means constructing a model in which all groups having any power over the corporation, except for the one singled out as being in control, are regarded as forming part of the environment within which the controlling group operates. It is useful to construct such a model for any economic entity which one group has much more power over than does any other single group.

For large corporations in which each of two or three groups has a significant and roughly equal degree of power, it is more realistic to alter the model of control slightly. In such cases, each of the two or three groups will be regarded as having "partial control" over that corporation. When a corporation is partially controlled by several groups, the corporation's basic policies may result from a compromise among the groups; or each group may have dominant authority concerning a particular basic policy.

CONTROL DISTINGUISHED FROM MANAGING

It will be helpful to distinguish control from "managing." The term "managing" is used here rather than "management" because the latter term refers to a group of people. "Managing" means the activities of directing and administering a business. It includes the initiation and approval of decisions and coordination of the firm's operations.

In the large corporation the activities that constitute managing are distributed among the various levels of the corporate hierarchy: outside directors, senior officers, and their subordinates. In some cases an outsider participates in managing by initiating a proposal or approving or vetoing a proposal made by the corporate management. The way in which the activities of managing are distributed among the different levels of management (and possible outsiders) varies from one firm to another. However, the important decisions affecting the firm's choice of goals and objectives, its expansion policy, financial policy, and policy for distribution of profits — the "broad policies guiding the corporation" — are subject to approval by the top corporate authorities: the chief executive officer, the board of directors, or a key board committee.[6]

In contrast to managing, which is an *activity*, control is a *power*. It is the power to affect the managing of a corporation, since the promulgation of the broad policies guiding a corporation is part of managing. More specifically, control is the power to determine the outcome of that part of managing which involves setting the broad policies guiding the corporation.

There are three ways that a controlling group's power may be translated into policy making. First, representatives of the group may serve as part of the corporation's management, where they are in a position to set policies. For example, a big stockholder may serve as chairman of the finance committee, or may name a close business associate to serve in that post. Second, a controlling group may pressure the management to follow certain policies. The controlling group's power to exert such pressure may derive from the ability to replace the management if its advice is rejected, or from the ability to harm the interests of the management. An example of the latter would be a financial institution's sale of a large quantity of a corporation's stock, resulting in a significant decline in the stock price.

The third way that a controlling group's power may be translated into policy making is a passive one. The management of a corporation, being aware of the power of the controlling group, may pursue policies that it believes will satisfy the controlling group, without that group exerting any active pressure. For example, a corporate management may pursue a cautious expansion policy and conservative financial policy because the financial institution that is its main creditor is known to strongly favor a conservative course.

A controlling group that is satisfied with the policies being followed by the management may have no motivation to intervene. Only if the corporate management should go beyond certain bounds may the controlling group relinquish its passive role and become active. Given that the material interests of any controlling group are greatly affected by the broad policies followed by the corporation, it seems reasonable to assume, even if the controlling group does not appear to actively

6. Gordon, pp. 91-94.

exercise its power over the corporation, that the corporation's policies are nevertheless those that the controlling group wants the corporation to follow. That is why control, defined as a power rather than as an activity, is an important category. Indeed, it is often easier and more reliable to obtain evidence on the power of groups associated with a corporation and then to make inferences about who ultimately determines policy, than it is to find direct evidence about who ultimately is determining policy.

The above does not imply, however, that there is no need to ask whether a particular controlling group actively exercises its power. In recent years, spokesmen for financial institutions have often insisted that they do not exercise the power they hold over corporate managements. Chapter 5 will consider the exercise of financial control over nonfinancial corporations.

An ambiguity about the definition of control used here involves the cohesiveness of possible controlling groups. For example, the entire body of stockholders of a corporation could be regarded as having the power to determine the broad policies guiding the corporation — if they could act in concert. One would not consider the entire body of stockholders to be a control group for the large corporation because this group is so large and diverse, and most members of it have such a small stake in the company, that common action in opposition to management is highly unlikely. Thus, owner control is restricted to cases where one individual, a family, or a group of business associates owns a large block of stock in a corporation.[7] Chapter 4 will discuss the meaning of a group of financial institutions for purposes of control. The relevant criteria for defining such a group are close association and common interests of the members.

THE BASIS OF CONTROL

As was mentioned in chapter 1, three categories of groups have been contenders for control over the large nonfinancial corporation since its rise to importance in the late nineteenth century: individual stockholders (owner control), financial institutions (financial control), and the senior officers of the nonfinancial

---

7. The cohesiveness of a family can be called into question in some cases. For example, the duPont family today has several branches that appear to act independently.

corporation (management control).[8] The basis of the individual stockholder's power is, quite obviously, his possession of the rights associated with ownership of stock, particularly the right to vote for directors. The basis of the senior officers' power is, first of all, their strategic location. They actually make the decisions, and, if left to their own devices by an absence of stockholders' or financial institutions' power, may become the controlling group by default. Control of the proxy machinery may enable the management to perpetuate itself in power. Proponents of the managerial thesis point to the specialized knowledge about the company's operations which the top management develops as another source of its power relative to that of other groups. The force of personality that a chief executive officer may possess has been cited as an additional source of power for the officers.

What sources of power over nonfinancial corporations do financial institutions possess? Since this question involves the central subject of this study, it requires careful analysis. One such source of power is control over common stock. When a financial institution is the holder of record of a large block of a corporation's stock — even if the financial institution is not the beneficial owner of the stock — this may be a source of power over the corporation, for two reasons.[9] First, if the financial institution has the right to vote the stock, which is usually the case, it can vote against management proposals, and it can initiate or join a proxy fight to replace the existing board. Second, apart from the exercise of the voting power associated with stock, an institution can sell its holding suddenly, which would depress the price of the stock and hence harm the interests of management and other stockholders; or it could sell its holding to a group attempting a take-over.

The ability to take such actions, associated with control over the voting and sale of stock, are the ultimate bases of the

8. A fourth source of control over large nonfinancial corporations is other nonfinancial corporations, as when nonfinancial corporation A owns a substantial percentage of nonfinancial corporation B's stock. However, in such cases I regard nonfinancial corporation B as controlled by whomever controls nonfinancial corporation A. Thus, this study will deal with ultimate control, rather than immediate control. For a discussion of ultimate versus immediate control, see chapter 4.

9. The stockholder of record is the person or institution listed on the corporation's books as the stockholder. The beneficial stockholder is the person or institution entitled to ultimately receive the financial benefits of stockownership. For example, when a bank trust department holds stock in trust for a wealthy individual, the bank trust department is the holder of record and the wealthy individual is the beneficial stockholder.

power that is possessed by a big stockholder. The power associated with control over voting the stock is the more significant of the two. The selling of stock is a source of power only as a threat. Once it is carried out, that power is gone. Voting power, however, has the advantage of continuing after use.

Financial institutions may also derive power over nonfinancial corporations from their role as suppliers of capital.[10] Commercial banks make short-term and medium-term loans to corporations, and through their trust departments they buy new corporate bonds. The most important purchasers of corporate bonds are life insurance companies, which absorbed almost half of the bonds issued by nonfinancial corporations between 1956 and 1965.[11] Investment banks indirectly supply capital by acting as wholesalers or retailers of corporate bond and stock issues. A commercial bank may also be an indirect supplier of capital, by acting as "lead bank" of a consortium to provide a major loan.[12]

A corporation taking out a big loan or floating a new bond issue often must accept certain written restrictions on its activities, intended to ensure that the borrower will be able to make the interest payments and repay the principal. These "protective provisions" may affect financial policy, mergers and acquisitions, and distribution of profits. For example, a bank granting a term loan often places limits on dividend payments or future borrowing.[13] If lenders or investment banks have compelled a borrowing corporation to accept such restrictions, then the financial insitutions have exercised a measure of influence over that corporation for the duration of the obligation. However, the specificity of such a written agreement limits its significance as a control device. As long as the borrowing corporation complies with the document, the institution can exert no further influence on the basis of the agreement.

More important than such written agreements is the informal power sometimes possessed by a potential supplier of funds, or by a major creditor, over a corporation that is in financial difficulty. The ultimate source of such power is the

10. The capital supplier role was the original basis of financial control when it rose to importance in the late 19th century. However, today the holding of stock is a more important basis of financial control. See chapter 4, table 9.

11. Raymond Goldsmith, *Financial Institutions* (New York, 1968), p. 140.

12. For example, Manufacturers Hanover Trust played the role of lead bank for Chrysler Corporation in the late 1960s.

13. See Elvin F. Donaldson and John K. Pfahl, *Corporate Finance*, 2nd ed. (New York, 1963), p. 548.

threat of forcing the corporation into receivership. On the basis of that threat, a financial institution may obtain substantial informal power over a corporation, including the right to name officers and directors or dictate certain policies. If a corporation does go into receivership, financial institutions may be able to obtain control directly, although the 1939 Chandler Amendments to the Federal Bankruptcy Act have limited the power of financial institutions to do so.[14]

A corporation that requires a large supply of external funds, even if it is financially sound, may have to yield a certain amount of informal influence to a big lender or investment bank. Many entrepreneurs refuse to borrow much money for that very reason. If the need for funds is particularly urgent — for example, to move into a new, highly attractive market, or to replace obsolete facilities — then the likelihood of strong financial influence or control resulting is greater.[15] The ultimate source of the power obtained by financial institutions in such situations is the threat of denying further funds, which could prevent the corporation from carrying out its plans. The degree of competition among financial institutions is an important factor here. The practice among investment banks of establishing "traditional relationships" with particular large corporations, which other investment banks respect, magnifies the influence that investment banks can exert.[16]

Some writers have viewed director interlocks between financial institutions and nonfinancial corporations as a third source of power over the corporation. There are two problems with this view. First, the observation that one person sits on the boards of both a financial institution and a nonfinancial corporation ignores the question of which institution the person really represents, if either. For example, the president of corporation A may serve as a director of corporation B and financial

14. However, it still occurs today. When Fifth Avenue Coach Lines of New York ended a four-year receivership in June 1972, the new directors were sponsored by Devon Securities, an investment bank. The new chairman and president was a Devon partner. (*Wall St. Journal*, 6/16/72, p. 2.)

15. For example, it was announced in May 1971 that John M. Place, a long-time officer of Chase Manhattan Bank, had been named as the new president and chief executive officer of Anaconda Copper, although most observers had expected a top Anaconda mining engineer to get the position. *Fortune* magazine explained this appointment as a result primarily of Anaconda's need for large infusions of capital to develop new copper sources, to replace those lost to nationalization in Chile, such losses having represented two-thirds of Anaconda's capacity. (*Fortune*, 5/71, p. 33.)

16. Traditional investment banker relationships are weaker today than they were several decades ago. See chapter 3.

institution C; this interlock between corporation B and financial institution C may be a coincidence, not involving any other relationship between the two companies. To solve this problem, the concept of "director representation" is used in place of director interlock. When a director interlock is found between a financial institution and nonfinancial corporation, an attempt is made to discover what institution the common director represents, usually assuming that he represents the institution that employs the person. The presence on a corporation's board of a representative of a financial institution, rather than just a director interlock between the two institutions, is the relevant datum for this study.

There is a more serious difficulty involved in viewing director interlocks as a source of financial power. Even if we know that a director represents the financial institution, his position on the board is not in itself a *source* of power over the corporation. One director cannot determine policy, nor can two or three, unless their wishes are backed up by something else, such as a big block of the corporation's stock being held by the financial institution he represents. Director representation may be an indication that a relationship of control exists, and also a method of exercising such control; however, director representation does not in itself constitute a source of power. Whether director representation constitutes a reliable indicator of financial control over a corporation depends on such factors as the number of representatives; whether the representatives hold important positions on the board of the corporation, such as chairman of the board or member of the finance or executive committee; and the coexistence of actual sources of power over the corporation held by the financial institution.

The power that financial institutions may have over nonfinancial corporations results from a combination of the above factors. It is those factors that must be considered in determining whether a particular financial institution has full or partial control over a particular corporation. The relative importance of the above factors and the exact way each operates have varied in different historical periods. So too has the resultant power of financial institutions over nonfinancial corporations. The next chapter undertakes an historical examination of the power relations between financial institutions and large nonfinancial corporations since the Civil War.

CHAPTER THREE

The Evolution of Financial Control Over Large Corporations Since 1865

The past century may be divided into four periods. The first goes from 1865 to 1914, during which time financial control first emerged and became an important phenomenon. The second period, from 1915 to 1929, witnessed the growth of new institutional and geographic centers of financial power. The third period, encompassing the Great Depression and World War II, saw a significant decline in the power of financial institutions. The fourth period, from 1946 to 1974, witnessed a resurgence of financial institutions.

In sketching the three periods from the end of the Civil War through World War II, several questions will be considered. What is the extent of control by financial institutions over large nonfinancial corporations? Which types of financial institutions, and which particular financial institutions, are most important as centers of control? How is financial control accumulated and exercised? What types of nonfinancial corporations are most often controlled by financial institutions? What are the major economic consequences of financial control?

Since the remainder of this work will analyze financial control in the later part of our fourth historical period, in this chapter the fourth period will be treated somewhat differently from the three preceding ones. For the post-World War II period only the most important developments affecting the degree of power that financial institutions possess over large corporations will be analyzed. The results of these developments for financial control over nonfinancial corporations — how widespread it is, what types of large corporations are most frequently controlled by financial institutions, what financial institutions and financial groups have become most important, how financial control is exercised, and the economic and political significance of financial control today — are the subjects of the remaining chapters.

THE RISE OF BANKER CONTROL: 1865 TO 1914

At the close of the Civil War the American economy was one of small, local enterprises. The railroad builders had already adopted the corporate form of organization, which, in a few decades, would facilitate the emergence of giant business enterprises of regional and even national scope. However, in 1865 even most railroads were still local corporations, each owning no more than a few hundred miles of track.[1]

In one respect the early corporation was not very different from its predecessor, the proprietorship. An individual or small group normally exercised full control over the corporation, through ownership of a majority of the stock. The legal form of ownership had changed and was vested in a transferable security, but the relationship between ownership and control was at first not greatly different from an extended partnership. Although ownership of the common stock of railroads was not yet widely dispersed, the bonds issued by the railroads did find a substantial market both in the United States and abroad.

In an abstract economic model it is often assumed that purchases and sales take place effortlessly and directly. In actual history complex institutions may develop to facilitate market transactions, particularly those involving a large number of participants and large sums of money. As the sale of new corporate securities began to attract a large number of participants and involve large sums of money, a specialized institution developed to facilitate the process: investment banking. An investment bank is an intermediary in the sale of new securities. The investment bank may underwrite a new security issue, which means that it agrees to purchase, at a fixed price, any securities that the issuer is unable to sell after a certain date. Or the investment bank may initially purchase the security issue and then resell the securities to the ultimate purchasers or to other intermediaries.

By 1870 there were a number of firms, chiefly in New

---

1. Edward G. Campbell, *The Reorganization of the American Railroad System* (New York, 1938), p. 11.

York, Boston, and Philadelphia, that specialized in investment banking. Most were private banks whose humble origins in the early and middle 1800s were that of dry goods or clothing merchants.[2] At the time of the Civil War investment banks handled mainly state and Federal government securities and railroad bonds. Their initial role was that of modest intermediary, between those in need of capital and those having some to invest. They sometimes provided financial advice as well, when it was sought. However, the rapid and uneven growth of the American economy in the succeeding decades would soon transform the leading investment bankers from modest intermediaries into powerful agents of control over American business.

Active Investment Banking and the Railroads

The decades that followed the Civil War witnessed a rapid extension of the railroad system of the United States. Between 1865 and 1893 total railroad mileage grew more than five-fold, from less than 35,000 miles in the former year to 176,000 in the latter.[3] The rapid increase in rail mileage was accompanied by the consolidation of small, local railroad corporations into great systems, beginning with Cornelius Vanderbilt's expansion of the New York Central Railroad, primarily by mergers, into a line stretching from the Atlantic seaboard to Chicago and west by 1869. During the years 1880 through 1888 nearly two-thirds of the railroad companies in the United States were absorbed by the remaining third.[4]

Both extension and consolidation required financing. To raise the necessary capital the railroad companies made increasing use of the services of investment banks. By the 1880s the leading investment banks came to acquire a position of influence over the railroads, and representation of investment banks on railroad boards of directors became common.[5]

2. Drexel, Morgan and Company (renamed J. P. Morgan and Company in 1895), Kuhn, Loeb and Company, and other leading private banks of the late 19th century originated in dry goods or clothing trade. Their early merchant activities often involved extending credit to manufacturers until the product was sold. The business of underwriting the sale of new securities was not a long step from underwriting the sale of clothing. The great private bankers of Europe, such as the Rothschilds and the Barings, had similar origins. See John Moody, *Masters of Capital* (New Haven, 1919), pp. 4-6; and Vincent P. Carosso, *Investment Banking in America: A History* (Cambridge, Mass., 1970) chap. 1.

3. Campbell, pp. 9, 11.

4. *Ibid.*, pp. 11-12.

5. Carosso, p. 33. However, some of the most powerful investment bankers chose not to sit on corporate boards. Jacob Schiff of Kuhn, Loeb and Company was an example. "So far as Schiff was concerned he preferred, as a rule, that his firm

The exercise of influence over the policies of corporations whose securities they sponsor is called "active" investment banking. The basis of power over corporations, which enabled investment banks to assume an "active" role, was control over sources of capital that the railroads needed in large amounts. A major reason why the leading investment banks accumulated substantial influence was the practice among investment banks of respecting one another's established investment banking relationships. Had the investment banks competed vigorously for the business that the railroads had to offer, the investment banks' influence would have been greatly reduced. Competition among investment banks would have permitted a railroad to reject the advice of its investment bank, knowing that it could turn to other investment banks for its capital needs. The practice of respecting established investment banking relationships developed in the late 1860s, although it did not become an absolute rule right away.[6]

A substantial portion of the capital used to build and consolidate American railroads between the Civil War and the 1890s came from Europe, particularly England. By the late 1880s English investors had bought more than $2 billion worth of American railroad securities. The Union Pacific, the Great Northern, and the Northern Pacific were largely built with English, Dutch, and German capital.[7]

A small number of leading investment banks achieved a virtual monopoly over access to European capital sources during this period. The leading investment banks had close ties with either English or German capital. Drexel, Morgan and Company (renamed J. P. Morgan and Company in 1895) and Kidder, Peabody and Company maintained ties with English capital. Kuhn, Loeb and Company and J. W. Seligman and Company

---

should not be so represented (on boards of directors). He felt that by personal conference and advice he could do as much as through formal representation." (Cyrus Adler, *Jacob Schiff: His Life and Letters* (London, 1929), vol. 1, p. 27.

6. Carosso, p. 27. The Pujo Committee Report of 1913 stated: "No railroad system or industrial corporation for which either of the houses named (Morgan and Company and seven other banks) has acted as banker could shift its business from one to another. Where one has made an issue of securities for a corporation the others will not bid for subsequent issues of the same corporation." — U. S., Congress, House Banking and Currency Committee, *Report of the Committee Appointed Pursuant to H. R. 429 and 504 to Investigate the Concentration of Control of Money and Credit*, 62nd Congress, 2nd Session, 1913, p. 133 (hereafter cited as House Committee on Banking and Currency, *Report. . .*)

7. Campbell, p. 13.

were close to German capital sources.[8] European capitalists investing in the American railroads knew that they were taking a risk. They were investing in a distant country of which they did not have great knowledge. It is not surprising that they chose to operate through a handful of established investment bankers whom they regarded as trustworthy. This situation placed substantial power in the hands of these few investment bankers. It is widely believed that the investment bankers used the power conferred on them to urge the railroads to pursue a conservative course of action and avoid risky undertakings that might endanger the bondholders' interests.[9]

Although the 1880s saw the development of substantial investment banker power over railroad companies, forces were at work that would result in much more thorough banker control by the 1890s. One such factor was the competition among railroads in the 1870s and 1880s. Competing railroads often built parallel roads between two cities. By 1884 there were five independent lines operating and two more being built between Chicago and the East Coast; John Moody estimated that three would have been sufficient for the business.[10] Throughout the United States tracks were built at a furious rate, apparently far in excess of what the demand could support.[11] Parallel building and overextension led to frequent rate-cutting. The railroads would now and then arrange pools to set prices, but agreements proved short-lived. Competition and disastrous price wars would break out again. These practices made the major American railroads financially insecure by the late 1880s.[12]

The unrestrained competition among railroads was not the only factor leading toward financial difficulty. A second was

8. All of the leading investment banks of the late 19th century were either "Yankee" (Anglo-Saxon) or German Jewish. The Yankee houses had ties with English capital, and the Jewish houses with German capital. See Carosso, chap. 1; and Barry Supple, "A Business Elite: German-Jewish Financiers in the 19th Century United States," *Business History Review*, XXXI (Summer 1957).

9. See Carosso, p. 33. For a general discussion of the conservative investment banker versus the risk-taking entrepreneur or promoter, see below, pp. 33-34; see also E. G. Nourse and H. B. Drury, *Industrial Price Policies and Economic Progress* (Washington, D. C., 1938), pp. 145ff.

10. Moody, *Masters of Capital*, p. 25.

11. "By the early eighties about twice as many railroad lines had been built as the country could profitably employ, and there had been issued about four times the amount of securities that the country could pay interest or dividends on." (*Ibid.*, p. 24.) See also Campbell, chap. 2.

12. Moody, *Masters of Capital*, p. 25.

the predatory practices of certain railroad capitalists. Jay Gould, Daniel Drew, and James Fisk were notorious for buying control of a railroad, looting its assets, and selling out before the damage became generally known. An outstanding example involved Gould's control of the Union Pacific in the late 1870s. He bought up a series of unused, worthless railroad lines which, when combined together, paralleled the Union Pacific's main route. He then prevailed upon the Union Pacific board, which he controlled through stockownership, to buy the parallel route at a high price. The resulting damage to the Union Pacific's stock value did not harm Gould, since he had secretly sold his holdings. Gould made an estimated ten million dollars from the transaction.[13]

Such predatory activities illustrate a weakness in the corporate form of organization, from the point of view of social rationality. The ease of transfer of corporate stock makes the looting of a corporation very tempting. A controlling stockholder may be able to make money more rapidly by stealing from a corporation — indirectly, stealing from the many stockholders and creditors — than by operating the corporation at maximum profitability.[14]

Both predators such as Jay Gould and more traditional enterpreneurs had brought the railroads to the brink of bankruptcy by the late 1880s.[15]   At this point the leading investment bankers moved to save the railroads, their bondholders, and their own businesses as well. J. P. Morgan called the heads of all the major western railroads to a meeting at his private library in December 1889. Morgan and a few other investment bankers sought to impose an agreement on the railroads to act collectively instead of individually. A board would be set up to regulate railroad rates, with the power to impose fines on violators. Most of the railroad men present accepted the terms under pressure.[16]   Morgan established a similar agreement between the Pennsylvania Railroad and the New York Central Railroad, which specified that the two roads would "avoid wasteful rivalry" in the future.[17]

13. Matthew Josephson, *The Robber Barons* (New York, 1934), pp. 196-201.
14. Such activities are more heavily circumscribed by law today; but, nevertheless, they still occur.
15. For a thorough discussion of the practices that undermined the railroads' financial status, see Campbell, chap. 2-4.
16. Lewis Corey, *The House of Morgan* (New York, 1930), pp. 166-72; and Carosso, pp. 38-40.
17. Corey, p. 172.

These efforts to restrain the rugged individualism of the railroad entrepreneurs through voluntary agreements did not prove to be very successful. However, by the late 1880s the financial position of a few railroads, such as the Santa Fe, became so bad that their investment bankers were able to assume direct control.[18] A few years later, in 1893, a financial panic struck, and the shaky railroads collapsed. Soon more than half of the railroad mileage in the United States was in receivership.[19] This afforded an opportunity to effectively impose the policies that the investment bankers had been urging in vain.

As one railroad after another failed, investment bankers, particularly Morgan and Company, assumed the role of reorganizing the bankrupt companies. Only the leading investment bankers had the access to capital and the confidence of investors necessary to successfully undertake the reorganization of large railroads. According to Moody, by 1898 Morgan was the dominant figure in railroading, having "largely reorganized the railroad system of America." He had control of the South Atlantic seaboard lines, the Erie, the Reading, the Northern Pacific, the Baltimore and Ohio, and many others.[20] Kuhn, Loeb and Company was the second most important banker, as far as control of railroads was concerned.[21]

Although the ultimate basis of the investment bankers' power in this period was their control over capital sources, in many cases they came to control, and sometimes own, the common stock of the railroads as well. Investment bankers were sometimes paid for their services partly in stock. For example, Kidder, Peabody and Company, together with the Barings, accumulated a majority of the Santa Fe's voting stock in 1889. When they moved to reorganize the nearly bankrupt line that year, their voting power enabled them to elect their slate of directors, which included two partners in Kidder, Peabody.[22]

In cases where an investment bank undertaking a railroad reorganization did not own a majority of the railroad's stock, the device of a voting trust was usually employed. The investment banker would insist that all of the railroad's stock be placed in a trust, with voting power over the stock vested in trustees named by the banker. A voting trust would commonly

18. Carosso, pp. 34-36.
19. Moody, *Masters of Capital*, p. 27.
20. *Ibid.*, pp. 31-32. See also Campbell, chap. 5.
21. Kuhn, Loeb and Company reorganized the Union Pacific in 1897, among others. See Carosso, pp. 33ff.
22. Carosso, pp. 35-36.

last for five, and sometimes ten, years. J. P. Morgan often used a voting trust to assure full control, after his attempt to reorganize the Baltimore and Ohio in 1887 had failed when the controlling interests voted his representative out.[23]

Through a voting trust Morgan and the other leading investment bankers were often able to maintain control of a railroad after it had begun making profits again. After the voting trust expired, Morgan usually kept a representative on the finance committee of a railroad, to see that the policies he favored would be continued.[24]

What were the economic consequences of the rise of investment banker control over the railroads? There were four interrelated economic consequences which were the most significant. First, the investment banks encouraged consolidation of the railroads into giant systems, both before the 1890s and during the period of reorganizations. Second, the investment bankers succeeded in reducing competitive behavior among the railroads. As Carosso puts it, "Their purposes . . . were to bring order and stability to an industry sorely in need of it, promote cooperation and harmony among competitors, and restore the investors' confidence in railroad securities."[25] Their assumption of full control in the 1890s enabled them to go a long way toward accomplishing that purpose. The vigorously competing railroad entrepreneurs, as well as the railroad predators such as Gould, were brought under control by the investment bankers. Henceforth, when sharp competition broke out between railroads, it usually involved a struggle between rival financial groups rather than rival entrepreneurs.[26]

The third consequence, which follows from the first two, was the establishment of a monopolistic rate structure. A commissioner from the Interstate Commerce Commission reported in 1903, "Five years ago, the crying evil in railway operations was [rate] discrimination . . . in its place comes that other danger which always attends monopoly, the exaction of an unreasonable charge."[27]

Fourth, the process of allocation of capital within the railroad industry had become much more centralized. A small

23. Moody, *Masters of Capital*, p. 29.
24. Carosso, pp. 40-41; and Campbell, p. 148.
25. Carosso, p. 38.
26. For a discussion of competition between financial groups, see below, pp. 38-39.
27. Carosso, p. 41.

number of major railroad systems were controlled by a small number of investment bankers. This represented an unprecedented concentration of economic power. J. P. Morgan and a few other investment bankers had substantial power to determine which railroads would expand and which would not, which areas of the country would be chosen for expansion, and how many railroad lines would be built between two given cities. The investment bankers were not free agents, and were subject to numerous external forces; but they were becoming the key points of decision making in the rapidly growing economy.

The Development of Large Industrial Corporations and Financial Control

Railroads were not the only companies that grew rapidly in the decades after the Civil War. Stimulated by the improving transportation system and the discovery of new technologies, the modern factory with its power-driven machinery was replacing the small workshop. Young entrepreneurs were building large companies in steel, petroleum refining, meat packing, electrical equipment, and other industries.

Before the 1890s few industrial companies had adopted the corporate form of organization, remaining as partnerships. The great banking houses had not yet taken an interest in financing industrials, regarding them as too risky.[28] During the 1890s a significant number of industrial companies began to go public.[29] The railroads were bankrupt, and few were growing very rapidly; the investment banks could no longer ignore the growing, capital-hungry industrials. They began to handle the securities of industrials and to establish a position of influence over them.

As with the railroads, the investment bankers used their influence to encourage consolidation and discourage competition. J. P. Morgan played the decisive role in the merger that combined the Edison General Electric Company and the Thompson-Houston Company, the two largest manufacturers in the young electrical industry, to form the General Electric Company in 1892.[30] Morgan unceremoniously forced the president of Edison General Electric, Henry Villard, to retire upon

28. *Ibid.*, pp. 43-44.
29. For example, in the early 1890s Proctor and Gamble, P. Lorillard, and Westinghouse Electric converted from partnerships to corporations.
30. Forrest McDonald, *Insull* (Chicago, 1962), pp. 50-51.

formation of General Electric; soon afterward the engineer-founders of Thompson-Houston were forced out as well.[31] Two Morgan partners were on the board of the new company.[32] The bankers had prevailed over the self-made entrepreneurs and inventors who had created the industry.[33]

Morgan's formation of General Electric was a few years ahead of its time. Before 1898 most industrial mergers were the work of individual entrepreneurs, promoters, and brokers. Beginning with J. P. Morgan's formation of Federal Steel in 1898, the leading investment bankers played the major role in financing industrial mergers and also in financing the on-going activities of manufacturing companies.[34]

The formation of the United States Steel Corporation illustrated the impact of investment bankers on manufacturing. The steel industry had been highly competitive from its inception in the 1870s. The Carnegie Steel Company, an integrated producer, was the strongest company in the industry. Andrew Carnegie, an individualistic, independent entrepreneur, continually attempted to undercut his rivals, rejecting the "community of interest" principle favored by the investment bankers. In 1898 Morgan entered the warring industry by consolidating three basic steel companies to form Federal Steel, and then forming two more companies making finished steel products.[35] Morgan's companies temporarily forced Carnegie to accept a pooling arrangement, but he soon began competing again.[36] In 1901 Morgan bought out Carnegie and most of the remainder of the steel industry to form United States Steel. Morgan personally named the first directors of the company, and he continued to have veto power over new directors at least through 1913.[37]

The triumph of banker control in the steel industry resulted in consolidation and reduced competition. Upon its formation United States Steel produced over 60 percent of American iron and steel output.[38] High steel prices were encouraged not just

31. *Ibid.;* Josephson, p. 384.

32. John W. Hammond, *Men and Volts* (New York, 1941), p. 195.

33. The exception was Charles Coffin, the president of Thompson-Houston. He accepted Morgan's leadership and was given the presidency of General Electric. See Hammond, pp. 195-96, and McDonald, pp. 50-51.

34. Carosso, pp. 44-45.

35. Corey, pp. 249-55.

36. *Ibid.,* pp. 250, 264-65.

37. U. S. Congress, House Banking and Currency Committee, *Investigation of Concentration of Control over Money and Credit, Hearings,* 62nd Congress, 2nd Session, 1913, p. 1025.

38. Corey, p. 276.

by the market power of the new company and its practice of "community of interest" but also by its overcapitalization. The tangible assets of United States Steel at the time of its incorporation were estimated at $682 million, yet $1321 million in bonds and stock were sold to the public.[39] Enormous promoters' profits were made in this consolidation. The high interest and dividend burdens imposed by overcapitalization encouraged high steel prices. Overcapitalization was the rule for other banker-promoted consolidations. The *American Banker* estimated that 25 percent of the total capital of the companies formed by merger in 1899 represented "pure inflation."[40]

The development of United States Steel over the next three decades illustrates the caution and conservatism of bank-controlled corporations. The company became known for slowness in adopting new methods, its major concern being the protection of its present investment.[41]

The conservative, anticompetitive bias of investment bankers may be explained as the result of two factors. First, a banker's success requires getting other people to entrust their money to him. It requires the establishment of a series of close connections with various institutional and individual sources of capital. While a rising entrepreneur or promoter may be willing to risk everything for the chance of acquiring great riches, the banker must avoid the losses that will sometimes occur in risky undertakings, for fear of losing the trust of his depositors and contacts.

The second reason for the banker's conservatism is his interest in a large number of corporations. The leading investment banks financed many actually or potentially competing companies. A cost-cutting innovation might promise great rewards to an individual entrepreneur, but the increased profits may come partly at the expense of competing companies. An investment banker with an interest in a large number of companies thus may be expected to prefer a monopolistic policy of "safe profits for all" rather than "profits for some at the expense of others."

However, the investment banker cannot completely avoid responding to the temper of the times. A prolonged economic boom often gives rise to a period of speculative fever. Individual promoters begin to make enormous profits from speculative

39. *Ibid.*, p. 273.
40. *American Banker*, LXV (3 January 1900), p. 9 (cited in Carosso, p. 46).
41. "U. S. Steel: The corporation," *Fortune* (March 1936), pp. 63,170, 173.

activities. A desire to share in such large profits spreads among investors. Smaller financial institutions find it irresistible to join in. Finally even the leading financial institutions may be unable to avoid becoming involved in financing risky, speculative activities. Both pressure from an investment banker's clients for rising profits and the banker's own desire to partake in the high speculative profits will have an effect. However, the established financial institutions do not generally initiate such speculative periods.

As with the railroads in the 1880s, the investment bankers' power over industrial corporations derived from their control over access to capital. Entrepreneurs who were willing to accept their leadership would see their companies grow to monopolistic positions; those who refused it risked stagnation or even loss of the company. However, some entrepreneurs were able to maintain their independence of Wall Street, the most notable being John D. Rockefeller and his associates. Indeed, the profits of their Standard Oil Trust were in the process of creating a new financial group with power rivaling that of Morgan.

Financial control over some companies was a stable, long-term phenomenon, as in the case of United States Steel.[42] However, in other cases full financial control would last for a relatively short period of time. This often happened when financial control resulted from temporary financial difficulty encountered by a corporation. For example, in 1910 the rapidly growing General Motors Company, then only two years old, found that it had over-invested in fixed plant and inventories and was forced to raise a large amount of capital quickly.[43] An investment banking syndicate headed by Lee, Higginson and Company, J. W. Seligman and Company, and Central Trust Company of New York acquired control through a five-year voting trust agreement, in exchange for underwriting a $15 million note issue. When the agreement expired in 1915, the banks relinquished control.[44]

In this period the leading investment bankers avoided the

42. See Robert A. Gordon, *Business Leadership in the Large Corporation* (Berkeley, 1961), pp. 202-7.
43. Lawrence H. Seltzer, *A Financial History of the American Auto Industry* (Boston, 1928), pp. 225-26.
44. *Ibid.*, pp. 166-73. The five year period of banker control was characterized by caution and retrenchment. Several lines of autos were discontinued and others were consolidated. No dividends were paid on the common stock. This contrasts to the policy of rapid expansion under entrepreneur William C. Durant prior to 1910. In 1915 Durant returned, with duPont backing. See Seltzer, chap. 4.

securities of light manufacturing and retail trade companies. Beginning in 1906 two small New York investment banks, Goldman, Sachs and Company and Lehman Brothers, began to handle the securities of such companies, starting with Sears, Roebuck and United Cigar Manufacturers. The two investment banks had an agreement to work together, and rarely did either handle an issue individually. They grew rapidly and established a position of influence over a number of light manufacturing and retail trade companies.[45]

Groups of Financial Institutions

During this period several distinct groupings emerged among New York financial institutions, based on close institutional and personal relationships. These groups of financial institutions included not only private banks whose main business was investment banking, but also commercial banks. The distinction between these two institutions became somewhat blurred after 1900 when national banks, whose primary business was commercial banking, began to engage in investment banking.[46]

The Morgan group was based on an alliance between Morgan and Company and the First National Bank of New York. George F. Baker, the president and chief stockholder of the latter from 1874 through 1912, had been a close friend and associate of J. P. Morgan since 1873.[47] Three partners in Morgan and Company were directors of the First National Bank in 1912, and two leading Morgan partners had been executives of the First National Bank before joining Morgan and Company. Morgan and Company was the second largest shareholder in the First National Bank, after George F. Baker.[48] After 1900 the First National Bank engaged in investment banking in addition to its commercial banking business, and by 1914 its importance as an investment bank was comparable to that of Morgan and Company and Kuhn, Loeb and Company.[49]

Morgan and Company and the First National Bank of New York together controlled three more New York banks in 1912: Bankers Trust, Guarantee Trust, and the National Bank of

45. Carosso, pp. 82-83.
46. *Ibid.*, p. 97. In 1902 the Comptroller of the Currency began restricting investment banking activities by national banks. This led some national banks to set up security affiliates to handle their investment banking activities.
47. House Banking and Currency Committee, *Report. . .*, pp. 66, 80.
48. *Ibid.*, p. 81.
49. Carosso, p. 100.

Commerce. Morgan and Company organized Bankers Trust in 1903 and held control by means of a voting trust at least through 1912. A majority of the stock of Guarantee Trust was purchased by Morgan and Company and associates in 1910. The National Bank of Commerce had twelve director interlocks with Guarantee Trust in 1912.[50]

Alliances with commercial banks were important to enable Morgan and Company to provide financing for companies it controlled. A second type of financial institution particularly important in this regard was life insurance companies, which had become important in capital markets in the 1880s.[51] The life insurance companies held great pools of long-term capital that could be used to purchase bond and stock issues underwritten by investment bankers. They could also be used to buy a controlling stock interest in other corporations. Investment bankers and promoters began to contend for control over the leading life insurance companies in the 1890s. At that time New York Life became closely affiliated with Morgan and Company.[52] In 1910 Morgan and Company bought a majority of the stock of Equitable Life. Morgan paid almost a thousand times earnings for the stock, but it was a good investment, for the control it brought over the disposal of policyholders' assets.[53] By 1910 Morgan had control of the three largest life insurance companies, since he controlled Mutual Life as well.[54]

The House of Morgan and its associated financial institutions had control over a large number of nonfinancial corporations by 1912. These included at least ten great railroad systems, three street railway corporations, United States Steel, General Electric, American Telephone and Telegraph, International Harvester, and Western Union. In addition, Morgan had close affiliations with many more corporations.[55] Morgan partners held seventy-two directorships in forty-seven large corporations, and the First National Bank of New York officers held forty-six directorships in thirty-seven large corporations.[56]

50. House Banking and Currency Committee, *Report. . .*, pp. 57-60.
51. Raymond Goldsmith, *Financial Institutions* (New York, 1968), p. 164. From the 1880s through World War I life insurance companies put about two-fifths of their funds into corporate bonds and stock.
52. Moody, *Masters of Capital*, pp. 126-28.
53. House Banking and Currency Committee, *Report. . .*, p. 83.
54. Moody, *Masters of Capital*, p. 150.
55. Corey, p. 354; House Banking and Currency Committee, *Report. . .*, pp. 60-71.
56. House Banking and Currency Committee, *Report. . .*, p. 89.

Kuhn, Loeb and Company also had control or influence over numerous corporations by 1912. Aside from its strong position in railroads, it was the dominant force in Westinghouse Electric.[57]

As was mentioned above, one major entrepreneur who succeeded in remaining completely independent of banker influence was John D. Rockefeller. In building his Standard Oil Trust he followed a policy of steadily accumulating cash. "They were their own bankers from the start and were in a position . . . to snap their fingers at Wall Street and Lombard Street," comments Moody.[58] The enormous profits of the Standard Oil Trust made this policy possible.

In 1891 James Stillman became president of the City Bank of New York (later re-named the National City Bank). Stillman was a close friend of William Rockefeller, the brother of John D. Rockefeller. Standard Oil money began to flow into the City Bank, and in two short years it became the largest bank in New York, having been half the size of several others in 1891.[59] The Stillman-Rockefeller alliance, operating through the City Bank, put the growing Standard Oil cash assets to work, establishing control over many corporations.

Stillman, William Rockefeller, and their associates organized the Amalgamated Copper Company (predecessor of Anaconda Copper). They obtained control of the Consolidated Gas Company of New York (predecessor of Consolidated Edison).[60] They provided financial backing for E. H. Harriman, an aggressive railroad empire builder, enabling him to establish control over the Union Pacific Railroad and several other railroads.[61] By 1914 the National City Bank had an investment banking business comparable to that of Morgan and Company, Kuhn, Loeb and Company, and the First National Bank of New York.[62] The officers of the National City Bank held thirty-two directorships in twenty-six large corporations.[63]

57. *Ibid.*, pp. 78-80. When Westinghouse Electric ran into financial difficulty in 1908, New York bankers forced George Westinghouse, the inventor and company's founder, to retire, and Kuhn, Loeb and Company took control. Harvey O'Connor, *Mellon's Millions: The Life and Times of Andrew W. Mellon* (New York, 1933), p. 55.

58. Moody, *Masters of Capital*, p. 54.

59. *Ibid.*, pp. 63-64.

60. House Banking and Currency Committee, *Report. . .*, p. 75.

61. *Ibid.*, p. 74; Moody, *Masters of Capital*, p. 66.

62. Carosso, p. 100.

63. House Banking and Currency Committee, *Report. . .*, p. 90.

By 1914 a few powerful groups of financial institutions had formed outside the Northeast. The most important one centered around the Mellon National Bank of Pittsburgh. The Mellon banking family financed the Carnegie Steel Company in the decades after the Civil War, and by 1914 had achieved control over numerous Pittsburgh area companies in steel, coal, and railroads.[64]   Their most important holdings, however, were Gulf Oil, the largest independent oil company, and the monopolistic Aluminum Company of America. The Mellons were primarily commercial bankers rather than investment bankers. They achieved control by providing loans to struggling new companies in exchange for a large portion of the stock.[65] However, the financial resources of the Mellons were nowhere near that of the Morgan or Stillman-Rockefeller group at this time.

The rise of financial control had played a role in eliminating the old-style competition between entrepreneurs in many industries. However, financial control of industry was not absolute. Many individual entrepreneurs and promoters remained. Some had close ties with a group of financial institutions. Others were relatively independent. Furthermore, rivalries between groups of financial institutions sometimes led to competition between companies they controlled. This was particularly true before the middle of the first decade of the twentieth century.

An example was the attempt by Harriman to establish a route linking the Union Pacific Railroad to Chicago, enabling it to compete directly with the Morgan-dominated lines. This effort by Harriman led to a battle for control of the Northern Pacific Railway in 1901. Harriman, backed by Stillman-Rockefeller money, attempted secretly to buy control of the Northern Pacific, which was then run by Morgan-backed James J. Hill. The battle for the Northern Pacific's shares drove the price up to $1000 a share, causing a minor financial panic on Wall Street. Morgan finally offered a "community of interest" solution, giving Harriman and William Rockefeller positions on the Northern Pacific board.[66]   Harriman had been willing to

64. O'Connor, chap. 4.

65. This method was used by the Mellons to establish control of Gulf Oil and the Aluminum Company of America (then the Pittsburgh Reduction Company). See O'Connor, chap. 5,6.

66. For a full account, see Corey, chap. 26, or Moody, *Masters of Capital*, chap. 6.

fight it out, but his financial backers forced a settlement, illustrating Harriman's dependence on them.[67]

After 1907 the overt rivalry between the Morgan group and the Stillman-Rockefeller group largely ceased. In 1909 Morgan and Company became a large stockholder in the National City Bank; in 1912 J. P. Morgan, Jr., was a director of the National City Bank.[68]   However, the two groups retained their separate identities and interests.

Reforms

The rise of financial control was occasioned by the rapid development of large-scale enterprise and its associated separation of ownership and control. Financial control in turn facilitated the further growth of firms through expansion and consolidation and encouraged a further decline in competition through a policy of community of interest. By the turn of the century the concentration of economic power in Wall Street and the decline in competition had produced a strong popular reaction. Whereas in Europe the rise of concentration and financial control strengthened the popular sentiment for socialism, in the United States the reaction primarily took the form of support for a return to the small business economy of the early nineteenth century.

Between 1905 and 1914 a number of government actions were taken against the growth of monopoly and financial control. In 1905 the Armstrong Committee in New York State exposed the abuse of life insurance companies by financial groups. A regulatory law passed by New York State in response made it more difficult for bankers to manipulate life insurance assets for speculative purposes.[69]

The Supreme Court broke up a number of trusts, including the Standard Oil and Tobacco trusts, in 1911. However, these dissolutions had little immediate effect, since the various component companies continued to be run by the same men, with little if any competition.[70]   The Rockefellers, for example, maintained control of the parts of the Standard Oil Trust at least into the 1930s.

67. Corey, p. 301.
68. *Ibid.*, p. 355; House Banking and Currency Committee, *Report. . .*, p. 71.
69. Carosso, pp. 124-26.
70. Moody, *Masters of Capital*, p. 153.

The establishment of the Federal Reserve System in 1913 weakened the New York banks somewhat. Heretofore the New York banks had been the reserve depositories for smaller banks around the United States. Now the Federal Reserve System took over that function.

Section seven of the Clayton Act of 1914 made it illegal for a corporation to acquire the stock of another where the result would be a substantial reduction in competition. Section eight forbade interlocking directorates among large banks and trust companies. This law made it somewhat more difficult for the bankers to carry out their community of interest policy.

Probably the most important event along these lines was the House Banking and Currency Committee's investigation of "the concentration of money and credit" in 1912-1913. Known as the Pujo Committee investigation, after Congressman Arsène Pujo, it interrogated the great financiers of the day. J. P. Morgan steadfastly denied that he possessed any power:

> Q. You do not think you have any power in any department of industry in this country, do you?
> A. I do not.
> Q. Not the slightest?
> A. Not the slightest.[71]

Other financiers were more forthright. Although none of the Committee's recommendations was adopted, the hearings focused unfavorable publicity on the leading bankers. Apparently in response to the hearings, in 1914 J. P. Morgan, Jr., who had succeeded his father as head of the firm upon his father's death in 1913, announced that he and his partners would resign from the boards of twenty-seven corporations.[72]

The above investigations and reforms caused some difficulties for the great bankers. They forced them to attempt to disguise their power. However, they did not seriously weaken the edifice of financial control itself. Not until the 1930s, when

---

71. House Banking and Currency Committee, *Report...*, p. 137. See also "Letter from J. P. Morgan and Company to the Subcommittee of the Committee on Banking and Currency..." (25 February 1913). In an argument that at least stands the test of time, Morgan and Company insisted that the laws of supply and demand determine the allocation of credit, leaving the Morgan firm the mere servant of these forces.

72. Carosso, p. 179. However, they retained thirty-three directorships, including at least one representative on the board of each important corporation under control or influence by Morgan and Company (Corey, p. 419).

some of the Pujo Committee recommendations were belatedly adopted, did government actions substantially affect financial control over industry.

WAR, PROSPERITY, AND BANKER POWER: 1915-1929

The rise of banker control had produced several individuals who were seen at the time as embodying the power of financial institutions. J. P. Morgan, George F. Baker, James Stillman, and Jacob Schiff built up great personal power as they presided over the rise of New York finance to a position of paramount power. Between 1910 and 1920 each of the four either retired or died.[73] The men succeeding them as heads of their respective institutions did not possess the same degree of personal power and prestige as those four. Did their passing undo the regime of banker control they had created, or did the system become institutionalized, losing its need for overwhelmingly powerful individuals to make it work?[74]

To address this question one must look at the forces that affected financial control over the succeeding decades. Between 1915 and 1929 the United States went through a world war, a sharp but brief depression, and then a prolonged period of economic prosperity that culminated in several years of widespread financial speculation. Against this background there were a number of developments that affected the structure of financial control that had been built up in the decades before World War I.

Decline in Importance of Foreign Capital

During World War I large amounts of foreign-held American securities were liquidated. The United States emerged from the war as a long-term net creditor rather than a debtor. The international power of the New York banks was greatly enhanced by the War, with New York emerging as the world's banking center. However, henceforth European capital was a

73. Carosso, p. 191.

74. Carosso believes that the apex of banker power and prestige was reached in the first decade of the twentieth century, emphasizing that thereafter no individual financiers attained the personal positions that the above four had reached (pp. 190-91). Corey contends that once the system of banker control had been established, the need for "dictatorial personalities" was ended and the passing away of those dominant personalities in itself had no effect on the structure they had created (pp. 415-16).

much less important factor in the financing of American business. Since the monopoly over European capital sources held by a few New York banks was one reason for their power, this development tended to reduce the relative power of such banks as Morgan and Company and Kuhn, Loeb and Company. However, Morgan and Company was no longer mainly a contact point between European capital and American railroads, as it had been just after the Civil War. It had long since developed domestic capital sources, and was able to adjust to the gradual decline in the importance of European capital with little relative loss of power. The Stillman-Rockefeller group, whose original source of capital was oil profits rather than European capitalists, may have gained relatively from this transformation.[75]

New Entrepreneurs

The conservatism of the great bankers led them to avoid substantial involvement in new industries. Their policy was to wait until an industry had proven itself before becoming involved. Since capitalism is a dynamic system in which new industries continually develop, this practice on the part of bankers assured that new entrepreneurs and promoters outside of their control would continually appear. In many cases the bankers would assume control after the industry had proven itself, as with railroads and steel. However, in some cases an entrepreneur might maintain independence of the banks for a long time.

Henry Ford was the leading example in this period of an entrepreneur who pioneered a new product and was able to remain free of banker influence. The automobile industry developed in the years before World War I with little help from investment bankers.[76] By the end of the war it had emerged from its infancy and was becoming an important industry. Henry Ford was able to maintain the Ford Motor Company's

75. The National City Bank took advantage of the change in the United States' world position by specializing in financing U. S. economic activity abroad. By 1926 eight leading U. S. banks had 107 foreign branches in strategic cities, of which 73 were owned by the National City Bank (Corey, p. 429).

76. The only important exception was the period of banker control of General Motors during 1910-1915, discussed above. Morgan and Company had considered raising the capital to float the General Motors Company in 1908 but withdrew when some of its advice was rejected by William C. Durant, the founder. See Seltzer, pp. 35-36.

position as the leading firm in the industry through the 1920s without raising any capital at all through bankers.[77] A total cash investment of $28,000 in 1904 created a firm with net assets worth $715 million by 1926.[78] This was possible without recourse to the banks partly because automobile assembling required relatively little fixed capital to undertake at that time, and little working capital relative to sales was required.[79] The high profits of the Ford Motor Company were also a factor, enabling the company to pay high dividends and still have ample funds for reinvestment.[80] Henry Ford's independence of bankers left him free to pursue a policy of long-term price reductions, a type of competitive behavior frowned on by the bankers.

Although kept out of the Ford Motor Company, the leading bankers were able to obtain a position of strong influence, if not control, over the second largest automobile manufacturer in this period, General Motors. Between 1915 and 1920 the du-Pont family, using the enormous fortune they were making selling munitions during the war, purchased more than one-fourth of General Motors' common stock. The wide distribution of General Motors' stock made this sufficient for control.[81] Not having banking facilities of their own sufficient to service General Motors, they established an alliance with Morgan and Company. In 1920 Morgan and Company became General Motors' investment banker, underwriting a common stock issue, and was allowed to name five representatives to the General Motors board.[82] However, Henry Ford's strong position in the industry and his hostility to bankers prevented the bankers from attaining a dominant position in this important industry.

Increasing Competition among Financial Institutions

The 1920s saw a rapid expansion of security offerings by American corporations. New securities offered by corporations rose from $2788 million in 1920 to $9377 million in 1929, the

77. Seltzer, p. 125.
78. *Ibid.*, p. 133.
79. *Ibid.*, pp. 125, 127.
80. *Ibid.*, When the postwar recession of 1920-1921 forced many other companies into closer dependence on bankers, Henry Ford was able to maintain his independence through a scheme of getting credit from his sales dealers and suppliers, in addition to effecting operating economies (Seltzer, pp. 117-18).
81. *Ibid.*, pp. 142-43.
82. *Ibid.*

rise being continuous after 1921.[83] Although no reliable data are available, there was also apparently a significant increase in the number of people investing in securities, particularly toward the end of the 1920s.[84] The sale of Liberty Bonds during World War I had acquainted many middle-income people with securities. Corporate bonds became available in smaller denominations to encourage the small investor.[85]

One consequence of these developments was increasing competition among investment banks for the growing business. The old-line firms generally refused to compete, or even to solicit business. Otto Kahn of Kuhn, Loeb and Company stated:

> It has long been our policy and our effort to get our clients, not by chasing after them, not by praising our own wares, but by an attempt to establish a reputation which would make clients feel that if they have a problem of a financial nature, Dr. Kuhn, Loeb and Company is a pretty good doctor to go to.[86]

Morgan and Company followed a similar policy. While the old-line New York banks did not lose their large corporate accounts to more aggressive newcomers, the increasing ease of selling new securities probably reduced the power of investment bankers over corporations to some extent.

The old-line investment banks remained strictly "wholesalers," selling the securities they underwrote to a few large institutional clients and distributing the remainder to other investment banks for retail distribution to smaller investors. They maintained this policy, in spite of the growing importance of retailing of securities, as the number of small investors rose.

Until 1928 bond issues raised much more new capital for corporations than stock issues. Then the rising speculative fever made sale of stock very easy. In 1928 stock issues approximately equalled bond issues in value, and in 1929 new stock issues represented over two-thirds of new security issues by value.[87] The old-line New York investment banks refused to handle much stock, preferring to concentrate on bonds. This was another reason for their losing ground relative to other

83. U. S., Bureau of the Census, *Historical Statistics of the United States, Colonial Times to 1957* (Washington, 1960), p. 658.
84. Carosso, pp. 249-50.
85. *Ibid.*
86. *Ibid.*, p. 257.
87. *Ibid.*, p. 243.

investment banks, although it applied only to the final two years of the period.

Similar developments occurred in commercial banking. Many commercial banks became more aggressive in soliciting medium-sized and small deposits. The Bank of America in California pioneered branch banking, establishing 276 branches in 199 California communities by 1927 and becoming the third largest bank in the United States.[88] The old New York banks generally maintained only one or a few offices and continued to receive deposits mainly from corporations and the wealthy.

Although the great New York banks lost relative ground as measured by size, commercial banking as a whole became substantially more concentrated during the 1920s. As a result of the spread of branch banking, mergers, and the establishment of bank holding company empires, the number of banks declined from 30,000 in 1921 to 25,000 in 1929. The share of bank assets held by the twenty largest commercial banks rose from 14 percent to 21 percent in the course of the 1920s.[89]

The booming securities markets of the 1920s led most of the large commercial banks to form security affiliates.[90] These institutions engaged in securities underwriting, holding of securities for control purposes, and various other activities.[91] By 1929 commercial banks and their security affiliates had equalled private investment banks in terms of volume of securities underwritten.[92]

The large-scale entrance of commercial banks into investment banking created competition for the private investment banks. This foreshadowed the emergence of commercial banks as the dominant financial institutions after World War II.

The economic and financial conditions of the 1920s — a prolonged economic boom and a rising volume of security issues — not only stimulated increasing competition among financial institutions in New York and other Northeastern cities.

88. Marquis James and Bessie Rowland James, *Biography of a Bank* (New York, 1954), p. 198.

89. Goldsmith, *Financial Institutions*, p. 168.

90. Carosso, p. 272.

91. There were many abuses connected with bank security affiliates such as a bank using its security affiliate as a depository or doubtful investments made by the parent bank. See Carosso, p. 276.

92. W. Nelson Peach, *The Security Affiliates of National Banks*, Johns Hopkins University Studies in Historical and Political Science, Series LVIII, no. 13 (Baltimore, 1941), p. 20.

These conditions also encouraged the development of centers of financial power in the Midwest and Far West that asserted some independence from Wall Street. The San Francisco-based Bank of America not only grew to the position of third largest commercial bank in the United States but attempted to build a nationwide banking empire. A. P. Giannini, the bank's founder, set up a holding company as a vehicle for taking over banks in other states. Through it he acquired large blocks of stock in several New York banks, which led to a long battle with the Morgan group.[93]

More important than San Francisco as a financial center, Chicago financial institutions achieved substantial independence of New York in the 1920s. The Chicago investment banking firm of Halsey, Stuart and Company pursued an aggressive policy of bidding for investment banking business. During 1927 to 1930 it actually outranked Morgan and Company in the volume of issues managed.[94] An early underwriter of utility company bonds, Halsey, Stuart and Company benefitted from the growth of utility bond issues, which became the most important segment of the bond business during the 1920s.[95] Utility promoter Samuel Insull, with backing from Halsey, Stuart and Company, was able to build a major public utility empire independent of the New York banks.[96]

Proponents of the managerial thesis argue that the growth of internal funds — retained earnings and depreciation allowances — to the point where they allegedly were sufficient to provide necessary financing without much recourse to external funds, was the key factor that weakened the hold of financial institutions over large nonfinancial corporations. During the course of the 1920s, in spite of the growing volume of security issues, one study found that there was indeed a substantial increase in the proportion of total funds coming from internal sources for large manufacturing corporations.[97] This may have

93. Victor Perlo, *Empire of High Finance* (New York, 1957), pp. 239-240. In the early 1930s the Morgan group won the battle. Giannini lost his New York bank and almost lost his holding company, the Transamerica Corporation, to Wall Street control.

94. Carosso, p. 260.

95. McDonald, p. 248.

96. *Ibid.*, p. 251.

97. Daniel Creamer, Sergei Dobrovolsky, and Israel Borenstein, *Capital in Manufacturing and Mining* (Princeton, 1960), pp. 142-43. External funds supplied 14.3 percent of total funds in 1923-1926 and 3.1 percent in 1926-1929, compared to 29.6 percent during 1900-1910, for a sample of large manufacturing corporations. However, the sample differed for the two decades. No such decline in reliance on

loosened the hold of investment bankers over large manufacturing companies to some extent.[98]

Public Utility Holding Companies

One of the most important developments of the 1920s was the extension of financial control to the electric and gas utility sector. Before the 1920s electric and gas utilities were largely local companies, outside the control of the great banks.[99] In the early 1920s utilities began to expand rapidly, experiencing declining operating costs and increasing profits. [100] Since utilities require a high ratio of fixed capital to revenue, they also began to issue a large volume of securities.

Leading investment banks moved to establish control over public utilities through the device of the holding company. Unlike the history of the railroads, competition between power utilities had ended decades ago without the need of bank involvement. It was not to enforce "community of interest" but in order to monopolize the security underwriting business of the utilities that the investment banks acted. The fact that big utilities issued bonds regularly and in large amounts made them lucrative "catches."[101]

A number of highly pyramided public utility holding company systems were created during the 1920s. With the ease of selling stock to the public, a relatively small investment in one holding company at the top of the structure could control a vast array of subholding companies and operating companies. By the close of the 1920s ten great public utility holding company systems did about three-fourths of the electric light and power business in the United States. [102] As of 1929 the Morgan group controlled the two largest, the United Corporation group and the Electric Bond and Share group. [103] The

---

external finance occurred for the category of all nonfinancial corporations. See John Lintner, "The Financing of Corporations," in *The Corporation in Modern Society*, ed. Edward S. Mason (New York, 1969), p. 180.

98. This trend turned out to be a cyclical rather than a long-term one. See below, p. 61.

99. McDonald, p. 248. An exception was the Consolidated Gas Company of New York; see above, p. 37.

100. McDonald, p. 248, and Corey, p. 443.

101. McDonald, p. 248.

102. James C. Bonbright and Gardiner C. Means, *The Holding Company* (New York, 1932), p. 91.

103. Morgan and Company, together with associated investment banks Drexel and Company and Bonbright and Company, formed the United Corporation in 1929 (Bonbright, pp. 94, 127). Electric Bond and Share was originally formed in 1905 by Morgan-affiliated General Electric. The head of Electric Bond and Share in the 1920s,

previously mentioned Insull group, controlled by Samuel Insull with backing from Halsey, Stuart and Company of Chicago, was the only one of the giant systems to remain free of New York influence. [104]   Harris, Forbes and Company of New York and Goldman, Sachs and Company, also controlled major public utility holding company systems.[105]

The holding company device was also used to achieve control over railroads. The Van Sweringen brothers of Cleveland created the Alleghany Corporation in 1929, with Morgan backing, as a holding company for a large group of railroads, including the Missouri Pacific, the Chesapeake and Ohio, and the Erie. [106]   Through a hierarchy of holding companies, the Van Sweringens held full control of railroads in which their own equity was usually less than 1 percent.[107]

Investment Trusts

Investment trusts (today called investment companies) are financial institutions that raise money through issuing stock and bonds and invest the money raised in other securities. Unimportant prior to the 1920s, they grew rapidly during that decade, exceeding $7 billion in assets by 1929. [108]   They were pioneered by individual investment managers and promoters, but investment banks soon began sponsoring them. By 1929 over 60 percent of them were sponsored by investment banks, brokers, or dealers. [109]   Some of the largest investment trusts were sponsored by Goldman, Sachs and Company, Kidder, Peabody and Company, and Dillon, Read and Company. [110]   Commercial banks and their security affiliates also sponsored investment trusts.

Sponsoring an investment trust was a way to obtain control over the capital of many small investors. An investment bank could use its investment trusts to buy stock in companies for

---

S. Z. Mitchell, had close affiliations with Morgan group investment banks. (Bonbright, p. 101, and McDonald, p. 250.)

104. McDonald, p. 251.

105. Bonbright, p. 139.

106. *Ibid.*, pp. 259-61; and Ferdinand Pecora, *Wall Street Under Oath: The Story of Our Modern Money Changers* (New York, 1968), pp. 25-28. This holding company would later be fought over by contesting financial groups.

107. Bonbright, p. 261.

108. Carosso, p. 287.

109. Hugh Bullock, *The Story of Investment Companies* (New York, 1960), p. 28.

110. Carosso, pp. 289-92.

control purposes. The investment bank profited from distribution of the trust's securities, and received management fees for operating the trust. The trust could lend money to its sponsoring bank, deposit funds in the bank, and more important, the investment trust could be used to purchase securities that the investment bank underwrote.[111] In some cases investment trusts, which bore a resemblance to holding companies, were used to obtain control over public utility holding companies.[112]

At the end of the 1920s even the old-line investment banks had given in to the speculative mania and actively supported the formation of highly pyramided holding companies and investment trusts. The financial abuses of this period would come back to haunt them in the 1930s, providing the basis for the New Deal assault on the power of financial institutions.

The Leading Groups of Financial Institutions

The developments of the 1920s reduced the degree of financial control over some companies and industries. In American Telephone and Telegraph, for example, the Morgan group played a relatively inactive role by the 1920s, according to one study.[113] However, as was shown above, financial control was extended to a new sector, the power utilities. Congressional and other governmental studies undertaken in the 1930s documented many cases of financial control over nonfinancial corporations during the 1920s.[114] The evidence suggests that through the 1920s financial control remained a major form of control, and probably the most prevalent type of control, over large manufacturing, railroad, and power utility corporations.

111. *Ibid.*, p. 285. Many of the abuses growing out of banker control of life insurance companies that were exposed in the 1905 Armstrong Committee hearings were repeated with investment trusts.

112. For example, United Founders Corporation, an investment trust controlled by Harris, Forbes and Company, obtained at least partial control over the Standard Electric and Gas System, the sixth largest public utility holding company system in 1930, and full control over a smaller system, the Central Public Service Corporation System (Bonbright, pp. 116-17, 124).

113. Gordon, pp. 207-14. Gordon emphasizes the development of strong, independent top management groups, partly due to the high profits and ease of selling equity securities in the 1920s.

114. See U. S., Congress, Senate Banking and Currency Committee, *Stock Exchange Practices*, Senate Report 1455, 73rd Congress, 2nd Session, 1934, and *Stock Exchange Practices*, Hearings, 72nd Congress, 1st Session, 1932-33, especially pts. 1, 2 (hereafter cited as *Stock Exchange Practices: Hearings* or *Report*); and Temporary National Economic Committee, *Investigation of Concentration of Economic Power*, Hearings, 1940, especially pts. 22-24.

The Morgan group remained the most powerful group of financial institutions, although it no longer exercised the clear leadership role among such groups that it had under the elder J. P. Morgan. Morgan and Company remained the center of the group; the First National Bank of New York, Bankers Trust, and Guarantee Trust remained its closest affiliates and allies.[115] J. P. Morgan, Jr., and Thomas Lamont were the chief partners in Morgan and Company and the chief spokesmen for the Morgan group during this period.[116] The Morgan group was the leading power in electric and gas utilities through its control over the two largest public utility holding companies. It controlled numerous industrial companies, adding, among others, Kennecott Copper, Radio Corporation of America, and Standard Brands to its fold.[117] It remained the dominant financial interest at United States Steel and General Electric. It had strong influence over General Motors. The Morgan group also remained powerful among railroads. In 1929 the eighteen partners of Morgan and Company held seventy-six directorships in fifty-eight nonfinancial corporations, with assets of about $15 billion.[118]

The Stillman-Rockefeller group underwent a division into two separate groups during this period. The alliance between the two families had been based on the close relationship between William Rockefeller and James Stillman. After World War I John D. Rockefeller and his associates moved away from the National City Bank, establishing their own bank, the Equitable Trust. In the 1920s they bought control of the Chase National Bank and merged it with the Equitable Trust. Chase then became the center of the developing Rockefeller group, based on the growing wealth of the Standard Oil companies. During this period the Rockefeller group obtained control of two large life insurance companies, the Metropolitan and the Equitable.[119]

Two sons of William Rockefeller had married two daughters of James Stillman, and these second generation families retained control of the National City Bank, forming the basis of a

---

115. Corey, p. 446.

116. *Ibid.*, chap 35; and S. Menshikov, *Millionaires and Managers* (Moscow, 1969), p. 237.

117. Corey, pp. 436, 441-42. Morgan and Company applied the holding company device to industrials in creating Standard Brands in 1929, combining several leading food producers under one corporate roof.

118. Corey, pp. 446-47.

119. Perlo, p. 155.

separate group. [120] The National City Bank retained control of most of the companies outside the oil industry that had been in the pre-World War I Stillman-Rockefeller group. As was mentioned above, the National City Bank specialized in international banking during this period. [121] Among other companies, it controlled the Anaconda Copper Company, with its extensive foreign copper holdings. [122] In 1929 the National City Bank apparently used its influence to maintain high copper prices in the face of declining demand, to protect the price of Anaconda stock, of which the bank held a large amount as a consequence of speculative operations by the bank in Anaconda stock. [123]

Kuhn, Loeb and Company remained a power primarily among railroads. The Mellons of Pittsburgh probably gained in relative power, as their two major holdings, Aluminum Company of America and Gulf Oil, grew rapidly.

The policy of cooperation among the leading New York groups of financial institutions that was established after 1907 was largely continued during this period. Such cooperation helped maintain their power in the face of growing competition from other financial institutions both in the Northeast and elsewhere.

DECLINE OF BANKER POWER: 1930 TO 1945

Economic depressions and crises prior to the 1930s had provided an opportunity for financial institutions to extend their power. In the first year or two of the Great Depression of the 1930s, it appeared that this historical precedent would hold true. New York bankers, led by the Morgan group, succeeded in forcing Samuel Insull out of his foundering utility empire. [124] The Mellons were able to gain a strong position in Westinghouse Electric. [125]

This depression, however, was not to follow the precedent. Its great severity and long duration would weaken financial institutions even more than nonfinancial corporations. The political response to it would weaken the financial community still further.

120. *Ibid.*, p. 174.
121. See footnote 75 above, and also Perlo, p. 175.
122. Perlo, p. 175.
123. Nourse and Drury, pp. 153-56.
124. McDonald, chap. 11.
125. O'Connor, p. 55.

Financial Institutions and the Depression

The long slide from 1929 to 1933 saw the gross national product fall from $103 billion to $55 billion. Even in real terms the gross national product declined by 30 percent over that period. [126]   Investment banks were hit very hard by the economic decline. Between 1929 and 1932 annual corporate security offerings fell from $9.4 billion to $644 million. About half of the 1932 total was for refunding. The other sources of investment banks' profits, such as call loans and letters of credit, also were drastically reduced. [127]

By 1932 an estimated 2000 investment banks and brokerage firms had gone out of business. Only one-third of the investment banks in Chicago survived the depression. Even some old-line investment banks, such as Kidder, Peabody and Company and Lee, Higginson and Company, were forced into reorganization. [128]   Morgan and Company's deposits fell from $504 million in 1929 to $319 million in 1932; Kuhn, Loeb's fell from $88.5 million in 1929 to $15.2 million in 1932. [129]

The sharp decline in security issues by nonfinancial corporations, together with the weak financial position of investment banks which was partly caused by that decline, tended to undermine investment bankers' power over nonfinancial corporations. Although security offerings increased after 1933, they never during the remainder of the 1930s attained the levels of the 1920s, except for the year 1936. [130]

Commercial banks were also hit hard. The assets of all United States commercial banks shrank by almost one-third between 1929 and 1932, and almost 40 percent of commercial banks failed. [131]   Although commercial bank holdings of bonds and stock of nonfinancial corporations rose by $2.1 billion between 1930 and 1939, commercial bank loans outstanding to nonfinancial corporations declined by $4.7 billion. [132]   The

---

126. *Economic Report of the President* (Washington, D.C., 1971), pp. 197-98.

127. Carosso, pp. 307-8.

128. *Ibid.*, pp. 319-20.

129. *Stock Exchange Practices: Report*, p. 226.

130. U. S., Temporary National Economic Committee, Monograph No. 37, *Savings, Investment and National Income*, p. 63.

131. Goldsmith, *Financial Institutions* p. 172.

132. Raymond Goldsmith, *Financial Intermediaries in the American Economy Since 1900* (Princeton, 1958), p. 222.

commercial banks were disinvesting in nonfinancial corporations, on balance.

Many investment trusts failed, and their total assets shrank by about 60 percent during 1930 to 1933.[133] Life insurance companies fared better than other financial institutions, continuing to grow even during 1930 to 1933, although experiencing large losses.[134]

By 1939 the funds supplied to nonfinancial corporations by all types of financial institutions had declined by $3.6 billion from their 1930 level. During this ten-year period funds supplied to nonfinancial corporations by all external sources were negative; thus, internal sources of funds exceeded total sources and uses of funds for nonfinancial corporations.[135] These aggregate figures do not imply that there were not many instances of nonfinancial corporations being dependent on financial institutions for funding in this period. However, they do imply that for this prolonged period of time, in the aggregate, the services of financial institutions for supplying capital to nonfinancial corporations became less important. The expected consequence would be a reduction in the power that financial institutions exercised over nonfinancial corporations. This conclusion is reinforced by the effects of New Deal legislation concerning financial institutions and corporate control.

New Deal Legislation

The Gray-Pecora investigations by the United States Senate in 1932-1934 revealed that the New York banks had participated actively in a wide range of speculative activities in the last years of the great boom. The top officers of leading financial institutions were shown to have taken advantage of small investors in many ways, such as selling questionable securities of companies they were affiliated with and operating pools to make speculative fortunes in stock trading. Some had even sold their own bank's stock short during the stock market crash.

133. Goldsmith, *Financial Institutions*, p. 173.

134. *Ibid.*

135. Goldsmith, *Financial Intermediaries*, p. 222. The sufficiency of internal sources of funds, predicted by proponents of the managerial thesis, arrived with a vengeance in the 1930s, but not due to the rising profitability of corporations. The reason was the relative stability of capital consumption allowances while practically everything else declined. Nonfinancial corporations' retained earnings were negative over the period 1930-1939.

Many abuses were uncovered involving bank sponsorship and control of investment trusts and public utility holding company systems.[136] These investigations prepared the way for legislative enactments that would greatly affect the power of financial institutions.

The Banking Act of 1933 (the Glass-Steagull Act) was probably the most important piece of legislation affecting bank power to come out of the Gray-Pecora investigations. This act prohibited commercial banks that were members of the Federal Reserve System from engaging in investment banking, either directly or through a security affiliate, except for the underwriting of government securities. Second, it forbade private banks to engage in both deposit banking and investment banking, requiring them to choose one or the other. Third, it prohibited partners and officers of investment banking firms from serving as directors or officers of commercial banks that were members of the Federal Reserve System.[137]

The Banking Act had a number of important consequences. Commercial banks lost a source of power over nonfinancial corporations — their ability to serve, through a security affiliate, as the investment banker for a nonfinancial corporation. However, the consequences for the private investment banks were much more severe. Forced to give up either investment banking or deposit banking, most chose to remain investment banks, giving up their deposits. The private investment banks' deposits had been their major source of capital, necessary for carrying an inventory of securities between purchase and sale. The result was to make investment banks dependent on commercial banks for credit.[138]

A further consequence was the disruption of many traditional investment banking relationships. Security affiliates of commercial banks either disbanded or were reformed as independent institutions. Some private investment banks gave up investment banking for deposit banking. The result was active competition among the remaining investment banks for the business of corporations whose traditional investment banking relationship had been ended by the new law. Even the staid "Dr." Kuhn, Loeb and Company began soliciting new busi-

---

136. See *Stock Exchange Practices: Report* and *Hearings*; see also Pecora, and Carosso, chap. 16.
137. Carosso, p. 371.
138. *Ibid.*, p. 372.

ness.[139] One would expect that this competition among investment banks reduced their power over nonfinancial corporations.

Before the 1930s nonfinancial corporations had occasionally sold security issues directly to one or two large institutional investors, usually life insurance companies, without going through an investment bank. However, such direct placements had been rare, accounting for less than 3 percent of all security offerings between 1900 and 1933.[140] The freeing of many corporations from their traditional investment banking relationships by the Banking Act, together with the additional expense and delays imposed on public offerings by the Securities Act of 1933,[141] encouraged the growth of direct placement after 1933. Between 1934 and 1939 direct placements accounted for about 23 percent of corporate bond and note issues.[142] This development further reduced the power of investment banks over nonfinancial corporations.

Thus, the Banking Act and Securities Act of 1933 caused a marked decline in investment banks' control over the process of providing new capital to corporations. Coming at a time when the demand for new capital had declined, the net effect was to reduce the power of investment banks over nonfinancial corporations. Commercial banks were affected to a lesser extent by these laws. Perhaps this consideration led Morgan and Company to decide in 1934 to give up investment banking in favor of commercial banking.[143]

A number of other laws passed in the 1930s tended to weaken financial control over nonfinancial corporations. The Public Utility Holding Company Act of 1935 limited public utility holding companies to a single, integrated utility system, which forced a major dismantling of the huge, nonintegrated systems that had been built up during the 1920s, largely under

139. *Ibid.*, p. 375.
140. *Ibid.*, pp. 367-68.
141. The Securities Act of 1933 imposed various requirements on the process of offering a corporation's securities for sale, including mandatory disclosure of certain types of information and a twenty-day waiting period before actual sale.
142. Carosso, p. 368.
143. However, that same year three Morgan partners, including Henry S. Morgan, together with three Morgan employees and two partners in Drexel and Company, resigned to form a new investment bank, Morgan, Stanley and Company (Carosso, p. 373). This latter company received the investment banking business of the great majority of corporations that had previously used Morgan and Company. See Temporary National Economic Committee, *Hearings*, pt. 23, pp. 12072-4.

banker control.[144]   Furthermore, the act placed the revamped public utility holding company systems under the regulation of the Securities and Exchange Commission, which was given substantial power over the relations between utility holding companies and investment bankers.[145]   This act reduced bank influence over utility holding companies.[146]

The Chandler Act of 1938 amended the Bankruptcy Act of 1898 to restrict the role of bankers in corporate reorganizations, for corporations other than railroads.[147]   This act provided for a court-appointed independent trustee to oversee corporate reorganizations.[148]   Of course, banks might be able to exercise considerable influence over the trustee; but they could no longer officially conduct a reorganization.

The Investment Company Act of 1940 established Securities and Exchange Commission oversight of investment companies. Several provisions of the act restricted the association between investment companies and investment banks.[149]

World War II

When the American economy recovered from the depression under the stimulus of war expenditures in the early 1940s, financial institutions continued to find their services in little demand for financing industry. The reason was that the Federal Government played the major role in financing expanded war production. Through the Reconstruction Finance Corporation the Federal Government had begun extending capital to railroads and manufacturing companies at the depth of the depression. From 1932 to 1940 the Reconstruction Finance Corporation's loans had increased steadily.[150]   During the war the Federal Government became the major supplier of capital to private business, directly financing approximately two-thirds of the plant expansion related to the war.[151]   Corporations raised very little capital through investment banks during the war. Most investment banks either closed or operated with reduced staffs for the duration.

144. Carosso, pp. 382-83.
145. Carosso, p. 383.
146. See Gordon, pp. 218-19.
147. *Ibid.*, p. 219; and Carosso, p. 383.
148. See William O. Douglas, *Democracy and Finance* (New Haven, 1940), pp. 180-82.
149. See Bullock, pp. 79-96.
150. Carosso, pp. 394-95.
151. *Ibid.*, p. 458.

Investment banks were weakened further during the war by the Securities and Exchange Commission Rule U-50, promulgated in 1941. It required public utility holding companies and their subsidiaries to offer securities through competitive bidding, instead of through a negotiated agreement with an investment bank. This rule was partly the result of a long campaign for competitive bidding conducted by a group of Chicago and Cleveland investment bankers, who hoped that competitive bidding would enable them to gain the business of corporations that had maintained traditional relationships with New York investment banks.[152]   Compulsory competitive bidding was extended to the railroads by the Interstate Commerce Commission in 1944. These rulings disrupted some old banker-corporate relationships and restricted investment banks' role as financial advisor to affected corporations. They also apparently contributed to the substantial drop in investment bankers' spreads that occurred in the 1940s, reducing the profits of investment banks.[153]

Commercial banks, whose assets were at a level in 1939 that barely exceeded the 1929 level, grew rapidly during the war. By 1945 their assets were approximately 2.4 times as great as in 1939.[154]   However, their growing assets did not coincide with a growing role in financing nonfinancial corporations. Bank loans to business expanded only slightly during the war years, and by 1945, 60 percent of commercial bank assets were in government securities.[155]   For all types of financial institutions, Treasury securities accounted for over half of total assets by the end of 1945, compared to only one-fifth in 1939.[156]

While commercial banks and investment banks declined as financers of private business over this fifteen-year period, one type of financial institution greatly increased in importance in this function: life insurance companies. In 1929 life insurance

152. *Ibid.*, pp. 432-33. The leaders of this group were Charles Stuart, of Halsey, Stuart and Company, Chicago; Cyrus Eaton, of Otis and Company, Cleveland; and Robert R. Young, who was fighting the Morgan group for control of the Alleghany Corporation.

153. Carosso, pp. 451-56. The "spread" is the difference between the price an investment bank pays to the issuer for a security and the price the investment bank receives for it upon sale. Both spreads and commissions for securities offerings had been declining since the 1920s, under the impact of the economic and legislative developments of the 1930s (Carosso, pp. 395-96).

154. Goldsmith, *Financial Intermediaries*, p. 73.

155. Paul B. Trescott, *Financing American Enterprise* (New York, 1963), p. 217.

156. Goldsmith, *Financial Institutions*, p. 176.

companies had held 12.0 percent of outstanding corporate bonds. This percentage rose steadily for the next fifteen years, reaching 24.7 percent in 1939 and 37.3 percent in 1945.[157] Life insurance companies had become the major providers of long-term debt capital to corporations.

Conclusion

The economic and political developments of this fifteen-year period tended to undermine the power that the leading financial institutions had accumulated over nonfinancial corporations in the preceding decades. In particular, the private investment banks were substantially weakened, as they lost their near monopolistic control over the provision of capital to nonfinancial corporations. Commercial banks were also weakened, although to a lesser degree.

During this period the managerial thesis arose and began to find acceptance among social scientists.[158]   Berle and Means showed that stockholdings in many large nonfinancial corporations had become widely dispersed, with no individual holding a sizable percentage.[159]   Many of the leading corporations had been formed in the late nineteenth century, and the descendants of the founders were no longer in control. Financial control was the form of control that had been replacing owner control since the 1890s. If financial control were now declining in importance, then management control appeared to be the only possible alternative.

It is difficult to determine, however, to what extent financial control declined during this period. One can find graphic examples of large corporations that achieved greater independence from financial institutions. For example, American Telephone and Telegraph's developing independence from the Morgan group was illustrated in 1941 when its management decided to offer a substantial bond issue through competitive bidding, instead of going through Morgan, Stanley and Company.[160]

However, it takes time for changing power relationships to work themselves out. There is some evidence that many ties

157. Goldsmith, *Financial Intermediaries*, p. 224.
158. Adolf A. Berle and Gardiner C. Means, *The Modern Corporation and Private Property* (New York, 1968), was first published in 1932. James Burnham, *The Managerial Revolution*, appeared in 1941 (London, 1941).
159. Berle and Means, pp. 47-111.
160. Carosso, p. 450.

between nonfinancial corporations and financial institutions were preserved at least through 1935. A study of "interest groups" in the American economy was undertaken for that year by the United States National Resources Committee.[161]   This study defined eight interest groups, which are groups of non-financial corporations and financial institutions that are closely allied.[162]   Leading financial institutions were associated with seven of these interest groups: Morgan-First National, Rockefeller, Kuhn Loeb, Mellon, Chicago, Cleveland, and Boston.[163] Out of a sample of the 200 largest nonfinancial corporations, ranked by assets, these seven groups were found to include 98 corporations representing 66 percent of the assets of those 200 corporations. The Morgan-First National group alone included 13 industrials, 1 retail trade company, 12 utilities, and 19 railroads, comprising about one-third of the total assets of the sample.[164]

In 1939 and 1940 the Temporary National Economic Committee investigated investment banking. The hearings uncovered evidence that the effects of the reforms of 1933 on investment banks were not as extreme as some had believed.[165]   Many traditional investment banking relationships were shown to have survived into the late 1930s.[166]   The business of investment firms that left investment banking in 1933 due to the new law was often "inherited" by successor firms.[167]

The hearings disclosed that investment banking remained highly concentrated. Between January 1934, and June 1939, six New York investment banks managed 57 percent of all registered issues sold by investment bankers; twenty New York investment banks managed 78 percent of such issues during that period. Morgan, Stanley and Company alone managed 23 percent.[168]

161. U. S., National Resources Committee, *The Structure of the American Economy*, pt. I, app. 13, Paul M. Sweezy, "Interest Groupings and the American Economy" (Washington, 1939), pp. 306-17.
162. This study made extensive, though careful, use of director interlocks, and also took account of stock ownership and capital supplier relationships.
163. The eighth interest group is the duPont group, which is an ownership group that does not include any important financial institutions. This study omitted the National City Bank group.
164. U. S., National Resources Committee, *op. cit.*
165. Temporary National Economic Committee, *Hearings*, pts. 22-24.
166. *Ibid.*
167. Carosso, pp. 415-19.
168. Temporary National Economic Committee, *Hearings*, pt. 24, pp. 12690-1.

Even the advent of competitive bidding for security issues of utilities and railroads had not affected the high concentration in investment banking very much. Between 1939 and 1948 the share of the top fifteen investment banks declined from 90 percent to 81 percent of all registered, publicly offered issues; the share of the top three investment banks rose from 41 percent to 56 percent. The composition of the top fifteen changed little over this period, although Halsey, Stuart and Company of Chicago did sharply increase its share of managements, becoming one of the three leading investment banks.[169]

Nevertheless, the power of investment banks was definitely declining, as the Temporary National Economic Committee observed in its report.[170]   The trends of the period 1930-1945 seemed to foretell the eventual end of financial control as an important phenomenon. Although financial institutions might be able to maintain a significant amount of influence for a decade or two out of the inertia of social arrangements, the undermining of their basis of power over nonfinancial corporations — control over the process of provision of capital to nonfinancial corporations — could be expected, in time, to largely eliminate that power.

In the past bankers had established their control over nonfinancial corporations under one of two circumstances: when a nonfinancial corporation was young and growing rapidly, or when a corporation was in financial difficulty. By 1929 the economy had come to be dominated by a relatively small number of large, "mature" corporations.[171] No longer growing so fast, and possessing a degree of stability coming from size, could financial institutions be expected to maintain a position of power over such corporations?

RESURGENCE: 1946-1974

The first fifteen years following the conclusion of World War II saw a fairly rapid rate of economic expansion, punctuated by relatively mild recessions every few years. The 1960s were marked by steady economic expansion, culminating in a period of speculation and mergers in the latter part of the decade. In the early 1970s the economy experienced two recessions, a mild

---

169. Carosso, p. 451.
170. Temporary National Economic Committee, Monograph 37, pp. 61-65.
171. See Berle and Means, pp. 18-46.

one in 1970 and a severe one in 1974; a rapid price inflation, which was slowed but not stopped by wage-price controls in 1971-72; and two devaluations of the dollar, in 1971 and 1973. Financial institutions have grown rapidly during this period. Their assets increased at a faster rate during 1948-1965 than in 1890-1912, although somewhat slower than in 1912-1929.[172] During 1948-1965 the assets of financial institutions continued their long-term rise relative to national wealth, reaching 47 percent of national wealth in 1965, compared to 42 percent in 1948 and 30 percent in 1929.[173]

Since the end of World War II nonfinancial corporations again have used a substantial amount of external finance. Non-financial corporations obtained between 40 percent and 45 percent of their total funds from external sources during 1946-1958 and during 1964-1974, as they did in 1900-1910 and the mid-1920s.[174] For a sample of large manufacturing corporations, 34 percent of total funds came from external sources during 1949-1954, compared to 30 percent in 1900-1910 and only 9 percent in 1924-1927.[175]

Not only did nonfinancial corporations resume substantial use of external finance after World War II, but financial institutions have been supplying a growing share of such external finance. Financial institutions supplied about one-third of the external funds used by nonfinancial corporations during 1900-1930; financial institutions' share was slightly over one-half in 1946-1955 and nearly two-thirds in 1956-1965.[176] However, this trend does not unambiguously indicate increasing importance of financial institutions in meeting the external financing needs of nonfinancial corporations. The relatively low percentage of external funds supplied by financial institutions in 1900-1930 means that wealthy individuals rather than financial institutions were the major ultimate purchasers of new bonds and stock during that period. Investment bankers were

172. Goldsmith, *Financial Institutions*, p. 157.
173. *Ibid.*
174. The sharp decline in reliance on external funds during the 1920s was for large manufacturing corporations, not for all nonfinancial corporations. Data through 1953 are from Lintner, p. 180. Those for 1954-1958 are from Goldsmith, *Financial Intermediaries*, p. 131. Those for 1964-1974 are from the *Economic Report of the President*, 1976, p. 263. The data for 1964-1974 are for nonfarm nonfinancial corporations only.
175. Creamer et al., pp. 142-43. The sample of large manufacturing corporations differed from period to period.
176. Goldsmith, *Financial Institutions*, p. 132.

the crucial intermediaries in the process, although they were not the ultimate capital suppliers. The growing share of external funds supplied by financial institutions in the post-World War II period actually indicates the growing importance of financial institutions other than investment banks, particularly life insurance companies.

Life insurance companies have become even more important in the long-term financing of corporations than they were in 1930-1945. Bond and note issues have been the major form of corporate long-term external financing in the post-World War II period. Equity financing never regained the popularity it had enjoyed in the late 1920s, accounting for less than 10 percent of external financing of nonfinancial corporations in 1956-1965 and 1966-1974. [177] During 1956-1965 life insurance companies acquired almost half of the bonds issued by nonfinancial corporations.[178]

Investment banks' control over the process of providing long-term capital to nonfinancial corporations continued to decline for the first two decades after World War II. During 1956-1965 approximately one-half of nonfinancial corporation bond issues were directly placed. [179] This compares to the previously cited figure of 23 percent of all corporate bond and note issues directly placed in 1934-1939. [180] However, this trend was reversed in the third postwar decade. During 1966-1975 only 28 percent of corporate bond issues were directly placed.[181]

Commercial banks again became important financers of nonfinancial corporations in the post-World War II period. However, it is important to observe that, during 1946-1965, bank loans supplied a relatively small proportion — about 14 percent — of the external finance used by nonfinancial corporations. Furthermore, banks account for a substantially higher proportion of liabilities for small- and medium-sized nonfinancial corporations than for large nonfinancial corporations.[182]

177. *Ibid.*, p. 137, for the years 1956–1965; *Economic Report of the President,* 1976, p. 263, for the years 1966-1974.
178. Goldsmith, *Financial Institutions* pp. 139-40.
179. *Ibid.*, p. 139.
180. See above, p. 55.
181. *Federal Reserve Bulletin* (December 1972), p. A48, and (July 1976), p. A38. The merger movement of the late 1960s may have increased the importance of investment banks. See chapter 4.
182. Goldsmith, *Financial Institutions,* pp. 134-36. Bank loans are more important to light manufacturing companies than to heavy manufacturing companies or utilities.

On the other hand, one should not underestimate the importance of bank credit to large nonfinancial corporations in the postwar period. During 1966-1974 commercial bank loans supplied 22 percent of the external funds used by nonfinancial corporations, up from the 14 percent figure cited above for 1946-1965. [183] Reliance on bank credit usually increases sharply during the late stages of a business upswing. [184] Large corporations that are in financial difficulty may become extremely dependent on commercial bank credit to avoid bankruptcy.[185] Furthermore, commercial bank trust departments buy corporate securities. One study estimated that during 1946-1960 commercial bank trust department net purchases of corporate securities equalled about three-fourths of the value of bank credit extended to business firms.[186]

Although financial institutions resumed their role as important providers of external finance to nonfinancial corporations after World War II, this does not mean such provision of external finance was as important a source of power over large nonfinancial corporations as it had been prior to 1930. As was stated above, the large, mature corporations, no longer growing so rapidly, and more stable than previously, were no longer necessarily at the mercy of financial institutions, even though they might use a substantial amount of external finance. The periodic recessions of the post-World War II period produced relatively few major bankruptcies, which had been a source of financial control in past decades. A number of large nonfinancial corporations were sufficiently dependent on external finance in this period to be controlled by a financial institutions on this basis, as will be shown in chapter 4. However, this source of financial institutions' power over nonfinancial corporations now became secondary to another source of power: the control over corporate stock.

The Stockholdings of Financial Institutions

Control over the stock of nonfinancial corporations has served as a basis of financial control in the past. The New York investment banks used voting trusts to assure full control over

183. *Economic Report of the President*, 1971, p. 286, and *Statistical Abstract of the United States*, 1975, p. 494.

184. Goldsmith, *Financial Institutions*, pp. 134-36.

185. For example, see the case of Chrysler Corporation's relationship to Manufacturers Hanover Trust, in app. B, table B-1, part B.

186. Paul B. Trescott, *Financing American Enterprise* (New York, 1963), p. 220.

railroads they were reorganizing in the 1890s. Payment for an investment bank's services in the form of stock sometimes led to the investment bank obtaining a substantial proportion of a company's stock. Before the insurance reforms of 1905, life insurance companies sometimes bought controlling interests in corporations.

However, prior to World War II, control over stock was a secondary source of financial institutions' power over non-financial corporations. The basic source of financial institutions' power was control over the process of providing capital to corporations. Financial institutions used control over stock as a supplementary source of power, usually when full control was desired to keep out rival groups. Hence, the development of stockholding into the primary source of financial institutions' power over nonfinancial corporations was something new, in spite of its historical roots.

Table 1 shows the share of all corporate stock held by financial institutions for benchmark years during this century.[187] The periods of increase have been during 1900-1922, the Great Depression, and the post-World War II period. Between 1929 and 1974 financial institutions' stockholdings grew from 9.6 percent to 33.3 percent of outstanding corporate stock.[188] Based on post-World War II trends, a study published in 1971 projected that financial institutions' holdings of corporate stock (excluding personal trust funds managed by commercial banks) would reach 36 percent of outstanding corporate stock in 1980 and 55 percent in 2000.[189]

Table 1 understates the significance of the post-World War II growth of financial institutions' stockholdings. After the middle 1950s individual investors began to leave the stock market, and during 1959-1968 the net stock purchases by financial institutions were over three times as great as the value

187. Note that the data for 1974 in the table 1 are not exactly comparable to data for years prior to 1968. However, the two sets of figures given for 1968 indicate that the differences between the two series are apparently minor. See table 1, source.

188. Note that these figures for the percentage of stock held by all financial institutions understate the actual percentage, because certain categories of bank trust department stockholdings are omitted in table 1 (see table 1, n.++). If one includes the omitted categories of bank trust department stockholdings, all financial institutions' stockholdings represented 39.1 percent of outstanding corporate stock in 1974. See U. S., Federal Deposit Insurance Corporation, *Trust Assets of Insured Commercial Banks — 1974*, p. 5. See also n. 187 above.

189. Robert M. Soldofsky, *Institutional Ownership of Common Stock: 1900-2000* (Ann Arbor, 1971), p. 209.

of new stock issued. [190]   Furthermore, the stockholdings of personal trust funds have declined as a percentage of all financial institutions' stockholdings in the post-World War II period. Before World War II personal trust funds always accounted for over 60 percent of financial institutions' stockholdings. By 1974 the share of personal trust funds had declined to 33 percent of financial institutions' stockholdings, while private noninsured pension funds' and investment companies' stockholdings combined grew to 46 percent of financial institutions' stockholdings, from only 10 percent in 1945 (Table 1). This is significant because the stock held in bank-managed personal trust funds often allows the bank no voting authority, or only

TABLE 1. The Share of Financial Institutions in Total Corporate Stock Outstanding

Year	Personal trusts*	Pension funds**	Investment companies	Life Insurance Companies	Other+	All financial institutions++
1900	4.3%	—	—	0.5%	1.9%	6.7%
1912	6.5%	—	—	0.2%	1.5%	8.1%
1922	8.3%	0.0%	0.1%	0.1%	1.1%	9.6%
1929	6.8%	0.1%	1.2%	0.2%	1.4%	9.6%
1939	12.9%	0.2%	1.2%	0.6%	2.1%	17.0%
1945	12.3%	0.2%	1.4%	0.7%	2.0%	16.5%
1952	11.4%	0.9%	3.0%	1.1%	2.5%	18.9%
1958	11.4%	3.1%	4.6%	1.1%	2.5%	22.7%
1968a	9.1%	5.6%	5.7%	1.3%	2.3%	24.0%
1968b	8.6%	6.3%	6.1%	1.4%	2.3%	24.6%
1974	11.1%	9.9%	5.4%	3.5%	3.3%	33.3%

SOURCE: For 1900-1968a, U.S., Securities and Exchange Commission, *Institutional Investor Study Report*, House Document 92-64, 1971, pt. 6, pp. 78, 144. For 1968b and 1974, U.S., Securities and Exchange Commission, *Annual Report*, 1975, table 7.

*Personal trust funds managed by commercial bank trust departments and trust companies.

**Private noninsured pension funds.

+Includes commercial banks, mutual savings banks, property insurance companies, and common trust funds.

++Excludes three categories of funds managed by commercial bank trust departments: estates, agency accounts, and employee benefit funds other than pension funds.

190. U. S. Securities and Exchange Commission, *Institutional Investor Study Report*, House Document 92-64, 1971, pt. 6, p. 150.

partial voting authority, over that stock. Private noninsured pension funds, which are largely managed by commercial bank trust departments, generally confer full voting authority over stock on the managing bank. Investment companies generally have full voting authority over stock they hold. Furthermore, in recent decades there has been a trend toward granting greater voting authority to the bank over stock held in personal trust funds. [191]   Hence, the share of all corporate stock fully controlled by financial institutions has increased more rapidly in the post-World War II period than is evident from Table 1.

Commercial banks have been the leading institutional shareholders since 1900. Commercial banks have never held a substantial amount of corporate stock for their own account, but rather hold stock in their role as trustee, or money manager. Prior to World War II commercial bank trust departments were mainly engaged in managing personal trust funds for wealthy families. The personal trust device is a method of passing on wealth to heirs that averts dissipation of the assets through taxation or the spending or investing habits of the heirs. Many founders of corporations in the late nineteenth and early twentieth centuries created trusts to pass on their holdings to their heirs.

During the 1930s bank personal trust fund stockholdings rose to over 10 percent of all corporate stock outstanding (Table 1). Such stockholdings may have formed the basis of financial control in some cases prior to World War II. One study published in 1945 states that commercial bank officers serving on corporate boards sometimes represented the bank's trust department holdings of the corporation's stock. [192]   When corporation founders retired and passed on their stockholdings to their heirs in the form of a trust, in many cases a family representative would retain voting rights over the stock. However, in some cases the heirs would have no interest in voting the shares, and that right would pass to the bank managing the trust fund. [193]   Thus, the process of dispersion of large stockholdings through inheritance did not always disperse the power associated with the stock; in some cases that power was transferred to a bank.

Since World War II commercial banks have had a second important source of trust fund assets: private noninsured pen-

---

191. *Ibid.*, p. 68.
192. Gordon, pp. 185-86.
193. For examples of this process, see chapter 4.

sion funds. The rapid postwar growth of pension funds may be seen as a consequence of the insecurity that middle and lower income groups face with regard to retirement in capitalist economic systems. In the twentieth century United States, the weakening of extended family relationships accentuated the need for an alternative old age security system. The passage of the Social Security Act during the Great Depression appeared to indicate that this problem would be handled through the government, as was generally the case in Western Europe. However, at the end of World War II, the political climate turned against such social programs, and social security payments failed to rise with inflation in the 1950s and 1960s, becoming increasingly inadequate as a means of support in old age.

In 1948 a United States Circuit Court decision in *Inland Steel v. National Labor Relations Board* held that employers must bargain with unions about pensions.[194]   There followed a rapid expansion of pension programs, as unions sought to achieve through collective bargaining what they failed to achieve through the government. From a level of less than $2 billion in 1945, the assets of private noninsured pension funds grew to $134 billion in 1974.[195]   As was mentioned above, most private noninsured pension funds are managed by commercial banks. By 1974, 38.9 percent of the trust assets managed by commercial banks consisted of pension funds and other employee benefit funds.[196]   For the ten largest commercial bank trust departments, employee benefit funds comprised 58.5 percent of trust assets in 1974.[197]

At the beginning of the post-World War II period it had been traditional to invest pension fund assets largely in bonds and preferred stock. However, partly due to competition among the leading banks for the pension fund managing business, there

194. 170 F. 2d 247 (7th Cir. 1948), cited in Daniel J. Baum and Ned B. Stiles, *The Silent Partners: Institutional Investors and Corporate Control* (New York, 1965), p. 33.

195. Goldsmith, *Financial Institutions*, p. 107; and U. S., Securities and Exchange Commission, *Annual Report*, 1975, p. 190. These figures are for book value of assets. The market value of private noninsured pension funds' assets grew to $154 billion in 1972, and then declined to $112 billion in 1974 as stock prices dropped. See U. S., Securities and Exchange Commission, *Annual Report*, 1975, p. 191.

196. U. S., Federal Deposit Insurance Corporation, *Trust Assets of Insured Commercial Banks — 1974*, p. 5. Personal trusts and estates represented 43.8 percent of bank trust department assets, and agency accounts (other than employee benefit fund agency accounts) were 17.2 percent of bank trust department assets in 1974. Banks usually have no voting authority over stock held in agency accounts.

197. *Ibid.*, p. 71.

occurred a shift toward common stock, with its promise of capital gains as well as income. By the early 1960s over 60 per-cent of new private noninsured pension fund assets were being invested in common stock. During 1956-1965 private nonin-sured pension funds' purchases of stock equalled almost three-fifths of total institutional stock purchases.[198]   By 1974 stocks represented 56.7 percent of the assets of private noninsured pension funds.[199]

The rapid growth of private noninsured pension funds in the postwar period is particularly important for financial control because, as was mentioned above, pension funds generally allow the managing bank full voting authority over stock held for the fund. A study of a sample of funds managed by the fifty largest trust banks in 1969 found that the managing bank had full voting authority over 73 percent of the common stock in the employee benefit funds in the sample.[200]

In 1974 commercial bank trust departments held a total of $171 billion in corporate stock. This represented 26.9 percent of all outstanding corporate stock, and equalled 68.8 percent of all stock held by financial institutions.[201]

Investment companies have been the second largest holders of stock among financial institutions in the post-World War II period. After suffering a setback during 1930-1945, investment companies grew rapidly through the late 1960s, as Table 1 indicates.[202]   In 1968 investment companies held one-third as much stock as bank trust departments.[203]   In the early 1970s poor investment performance led to large-scale redemption of the shares of open-end investment companies (mutual funds). As a result, investment companies' stockholdings declined as a proportion of outstanding stock between 1968 and 1974. In the latter year investment companies' stockholdings amounted to

198. Goldsmith, *Financial Institutions*, p. 108.

199. U. S., Securities and Exchange Commission, *Annual Report*, 1975, p. 191.

200. *Institutional Investor Study Report*, vol. 2, p. 438.

201. U. S., Federal Deposit Insurance Corporation, *op. cit.*, p. 5; and U. S., Securities and Exchange Commission, *Annual Report*, 1975, table 7. Note that the figure cited for the percentage of all stock held by commercial bank trust depart-ments (26.9 percent) exceeds the sum obtained from table 1 by adding personal trusts (11.1 percent) and pension funds (9.9 percent). See table 1, n.++ for an explanation.

202. Most investment companies in the post-World War II period have been open-end investment companies, which contrasts to the 1920s when most were of the more speculative, closed-end type.

203. *Institutional Investor Study Report*, pt. 6, p. 142.

only one-fifth of the value of bank trust department stock-holdings.[204]

Neither commercial bank trust departments nor investment companies face very significant government regulation over their investments. Prior to 1975 the only important legal constraint on bank trust department investment policy was the "prudent man rule." Embodied in a statute in many states, this rule places a trustee under "a duty to make such investments as a prudent man would make of his own property having primarily in view the preservation of the estate and the amount and regularity of the income to be derived." [205]   The Employee Retirement Income Security Act of 1974 (effective 1 January 1975) provides certain restrictions on the investment policy of trustees of private pension funds. The act prohibits the lending of pension fund money to "interested parties" and it also prohibits the investment of more than 10 percent of a corporate pension fund's assets in the securities of that corporation.[206]

The major legal investment constraint on investment companies is an upper limit on an investment company's holdings of a particular corporation's stock to 10 percent of the portfolio company's stock. However, this leaves a group of legally separate investment companies having a common management free to accumulate over 10 percent of a corporation's stock.

A high degree of concentration prevails among bank trust departments, investment companies, and life insurance companies. In 1974 the ten largest bank trust departments held 32.2 percent of total bank trust department assets. Employee benefit fund assets were particularly concentrated, with the ten largest bank trust departments holding 48.4 percent of such fund assets.[207]   Open-end investment companies (mutual funds) are even more highly concentrated. In 1975 the ten largest open-end investment company complexes held 58.2 percent of the total assets held by open-end investment companies.[208]

204. Table 1 and U. S., Federal Deposit Insurance Corporation, *op. cit.*, p. 5.

205. Austin W. Scott, *Law of Trusts*, 3rd ed., 1967, pp. 1805-06 – cited in *Institutional Investor Study Report*, vol. 2, p. 440; see also pp. 439-50.

206. Employee Retirement Income Security Act of 1974 (Pub. Law 93-406), Sections 1106 and 1107. There are exceptions to both prohibitions.

207. U. S., Federal Deposit Insurance Corporation, *op. cit.*, pp. 71, 5. By comparison, the ten largest commercial banks held 20.2 percent of all commercial bank deposits in 1974 – *Statistical Abstract of the United States*, 1975, p. 469.

208. *Vickers Directory of Investment Companies*, March 1976, pp. 128-139 (reproduced in U. S., Congress, Senate Government Operations Committee, Subcommittee on Reports, Accounting, and Management, *Institutional Investors' Common*

The ten largest life insurance companies held 55.6 percent of all life insurance company assets in 1974.[209]

Table 2 lists the ten largest bank trust departments in 1974. The four largest belonged to New York banks. The leading trust banks are the descendents of the most powerful financial institutions of the pre-World War II period. The Morgan group banks, Morgan Guarantee Trust and Bankers Trust, rank first and third. The Rockefeller group bank, Chase Manhattan, is

TABLE 2. The Ten Largest Commercial Bank Trust Departments, 1974

Bank	Trust assets (millions of dollars)	Percent of all bank trust assets
1. Morgan Guarantee Trust, New York	17,437	5.4
2. First National City Bank, New York	15,645	4.8
3. Bankers Trust Company, New York	14,503	4.5
4. Chase Manhattan Bank, New York	12,135	3.7
5. Mellon National Bank, Pittsburgh	9,336	2.9
6. United States Trust Company, New York	8,735	2.7
7. Manufacturers Hanover Trust, New York	8,042	2.5
8. Bank of America, San Francisco	6,466	2.0
9. Harris Trust, Chicago	6,417	2.0
10. First National Bank of Chicago	6,066	1.9

SOURCE: U.S., Federal Deposit Insurance Corporation, *Trust Assets of Insured Commercial Banks — 1974*, pp. 5, 71.

Stock: Holdings and Voting Rights, 94th Congress, 2nd Session, 1976); and *Federal Reserve Bulletin*, July 1976, p. A39. An investment company complex is a group of investment companies having the same investment advisory firm making the investment decisions.

209. *Statistical Abstract of the United States*, 1975, table 792, p. 484.

fourth. First National City Bank, the descendent of National City Bank, is second. The Mellon group bank is fifth. For a discussion of the evolution of the ties among financial institutions in the leading financial groups during the post-World War II period, see chapter 4.

The growth of financial institutions' holdings of stock during recent decades may be viewed as an aspect of the growing institutionalization of social savings. Financial institutions have become the managers of savings belonging to all income groups. Personal trust funds represent the savings of the upper income group, particularly the economically inactive sections of that group. Investment companies gather in the savings of small investors from the upper-middle income groups. Employee benefit funds mainly represent assets that "belong" to middle and lower income groups. This process of institutionalization of savings has given a great deal of potential power to the leading financial institutions. As the power of financial institutions over nonfinancial corporations based on the capital supplier relationship has declined due to the historical trends discussed above, the process of institutionalization of savings has placed a growing share of the ownership claims over large corporations under the control of financial institutions, particularly the leading commercial banks. To what extent has this latter trend provided a significant basis for continuing financial control over the large corporations that dominate the American economy? I shall attempt to answer this and other related questions in the succeeding chapters.

The Extent of Financial Control Over the 200 Largest Nonfinancial Corporations, 1967-1969

The preceding chapter discussed the rapid growth of financial institutions, particularly commercial bank trust departments, in the period since World War II. Have financial institutions come to play an important role again as controllers of large nonfinancial corporations, as a consequence of this recent growth? This chapter presents the results of a study of the 200 largest nonfinancial corporations during 1967 through 1969 which attempts to answer that question. It also provides information on the characteristics of financial control and owner control in the present period.

THE SAMPLE OF 200 CORPORATIONS

There are several indices of the size of a corporation. The most commonly used in studies of this type are total assets or total sales. An asset index was used here for constructing the sample of the 200 largest nonfinancial corporations, ranking corporations according to the value of their total assets on 31 December 1969.[1] However, there were two departures from strict asset rankings in the construction of the sample, one involving the treatment of electric, gas, and communications utilities, the second involving corporations that are unconsolidated subsidiaries of other corporations.

A sample chosen on the basis of asset ranking will have a relatively larger representation of utilities and transportation companies, and a relatively smaller representation of industrial

---

1. In a few cases the value of assets of a company was for a different date in 1969. The source for corporate assets was *Fortune*, May 1970.

(manufacturing and mining) and retail trade companies, than a sample chosen on the basis of sales ranking. The difference between the two types of samples is by far the greatest for utilities. For the year 1969 the 200 largest nonfinancial corporations ranked by sales (or operating revenue) included 6 utilities; ranked by assets, it included 47 utilities — 3 percent versus 23.5 percent of the total. This occurs because utilities' assets are extremely large relative to their operating revenue, as well as being very large relative to their value added or number of employees. To include the full component of 47 utilities in this sample would make the composition of the sample too dependent on the particular size criterion chosen, and too different from a sample chosen on the basis of sales or value added. Hence, only the ten largest utilities have been included.

The second departure from strict asset ranking involves the problem of subsidiary corporations. A corporation was considered a subsidiary if another corporation owned more than half of its outstanding voting stock. Seven corporations that were large enough to be included in the sample were removed because they were subsidiaries of other corporations. Two of the excluded companies were subsidiaries of foreign corporations: Shell Oil, a subsidiary of the British-Dutch Royal Dutch/ Shell Group, and Seagram and Sons, a subsidiary of Distillers Corporation-Seagrams Ltd. of Canada. Three more companies were excluded that were subsidiaries of other corporations among the 200 largest: Western Electric, a subsidiary of American Telephone and Telegraph; Armour, a subsidiary of Greyhound; and the Chicago, Burlington and Quincy Railroad, a joint subsidiary of the Great Northern Railway and the Northern Pacific Railway.[2]

Two companies were subsidiaries of corporations that were not large enough to rank in the top 200: Kaiser Steel, a subsidiary of Kaiser Industries; and the Missouri Pacific System, a subsidiary of the Mississippi River Corporation. So as not to lose those two corporations completely, the parent companies, Kaiser Industries and the Mississippi River Corporation, were added to the sample in place of their subsidiaries. This procedure was not followed for the two subsidiaries of foreign corporations in order to restrict the sample to United States

2. The Northern Pacific Railway and the Great Northern Railway jointly owned 97.2 percent of the stock of the Chicago, Burlington, and Quincy Railroad since 1901 (Moody's *Transportation Manual*, 1970, p. 742). In 1970 the three railroads merged to form the Burlington Northern.

corporations. Adding the parent company to the sample was unnecessary for the three corporations whose parents ranked among the top 200.

Another problem involving the treatment of subsidiaries affects the accuracy of the official value of assets of each corporation. On the consolidated balance sheet of a corporation, the total assets of all consolidated subsidiaries are included. However, for unconsolidated subsidiaries only the value (market or book) of the parent's investment in the subsidiary is included. Hence, the recorded assets of a corporation may understate the actual assets that are fully controlled by the corporation. In studies of industrial concentration it is advisable to make corrections for this inaccuracy. Such corrections were not made here, since strict accuracy of asset ranking is not of great importance for this study.

The final sample of 200 nonfinancial corporations included the 188 largest nonfinancial, nonutility, nonsubsidiary corporations; the 10 largest utilities; and 2 more corporations that owned subsidiaries ranking among the 190 largest nonfinancial, nonutility corporations.[3] The companies ranged in size from American Telephone and Telegraph, with assets of $43,903 million, to the Mississippi River Corporation, with assets of $226 million. Except for the special treatment accorded utilities and the two parent corporations added to the sample, the minimum value of assets necessary for inclusion was $588 million. The 200 companies had combined assets of $432,800 million at year-end 1969.[4]

Broken down by sector, the sample includes 152 industrial companies, 21 transportation companies, 15 retail trade companies, 10 electric, gas, and communications utilities, and 2 "others." The last category includes Columbia Broadcasting System, a television and radio broadcasting company, and Kaiser Industries, a construction company. Each company was placed in the sector from which a majority of its sales revenue was derived in 1969. As a result of the conglomerate merger movement of the 1960s, a number of large railroads became subsidiaries of conglomerates that fall into the industrial sector. Thus, the Illinois Central Railroad and the Chicago and Northwestern Railway are not found in the sample, but Illinois

3. See app. A for a list of the 200 corporations in the sample ranked by assets. An alphabetical list of the 200 corporations is found in table B-3 of app. B.

4. This total involves some double-counting, due to intercorporate stockholdings and trade debt.

Central Industries and Northwest Industries, their respective parent corporations, are among the industrials. Similarly, Tenneco Inc. appears as an industrial, although it is also a major public utility corporation, because a majority of its revenue was derived from manufacturing and mining.

CONTROL CATEGORIES

This study employs four basic control categories: financial control, owner control, a miscellaneous category, and no identified center of control. The miscellaneous category includes control by foreign corporations and control by self-administered funds. A self-administered employee benefit fund, not managed by a commercial bank or life insurance company, was not regarded as a financial institution. Hence, when such a fund was found to hold a sufficiently large percent of the voting stock of a corporation in the sample, the corporation was placed in the miscellaneous control category rather than the financial control category. Only 5 of the 200 companies were placed in the miscellaneous category, although two, United States Steel Corporation and Sears Roebuck, were among the largest companies in the sample.

The term "no identified center of control" was used for the residual category, instead of the more common "management control."[5] The reason is that although the residual category may be expected to include all cases of management control, it is likely to also include a number of undiscovered cases of owner or financial control, due to the incompleteness of the available data.

Explicit sets of criteria were used to determine the control classification of each corporation. These sets of criteria, or "working definitions," allow some scope for taking account of the unique features of each case, but they mainly rely on uniform standards for recurring relationships. The working definitions of full and partial financial control combine the two main sources of power that financial institutions may have over nonfinancial corporations, the control over stock and the provision of debt capital. They also take account of the presence of

---

5. T.N.E.C., Monograph No. 29, used a similar term. See U. S., Temporary National Economic Committee, *Investigation of Concentration of Economic Power*, Monograph No. 29, "The Distribution of Ownership in the 200 Largest Nonfinancial Corporations," 1940.

representatives of financial institutions on the boards of directors of nonfinancial corporations, which are regarded as an indication, although not a source, of financial control.[6] The working definitions of full and partial owner control and the miscellaneous category are based on stockholdings, also taking account of director representation.

In the following working definitions, the term "stockholder" refers to institutional holders of record as well as individual beneficial stockholders. Phrases appearing with quotation marks are explained following the presentation of each working definition.

Full Financial Control

A corporation is classified in this category if any one of the following three conditions is met:

1. A financial institution holds 10 percent or more of the corporation's voting stock, with sole or partial voting authority over the stock. No other stockholder has 10 percent or more of the stock.

2. A financial institution meets *both* conditions a *and* b as follows:

a) the financial institution holds 5 percent or more of the corporation's voting stock, with sole or partial voting rights over the stock. No other stockholder has 5 percent or more of the stock;

b) the financial institution either:

1) is a "leading supplier of capital" to the corporation, or

2) has "strong representation" on the corporation's board of directors.

3. There are "unique circumstances" which provide reliable and compelling evidence of full control by a financial institution.

A "leading supplier of capital" is a major long-term or short-term creditor; or a major indirect supplier of capital through an investment banking or lead commercial bank relationship.[7] "Strong representation" on the corporation's board

6. See chapter 2.
7. See chapter 2 for a discussion of "indirect" capital suppliers. For a more detailed discussion of the application of the concept of capital supplier to particular cases, see below, pp. 80-81.

of directors means that the financial institution has two representatives on the corporation's board, or one representative serving as a high-level officer of the corporation or serving on the executive or finance committee of the corporation's board. A "representative" of the financial institution is someone who is judged to be representing the financial institution's interests on the corporation's board. For a discussion of "unique circumstances," see below.

Partial Financial Control

A corporation is classified in this category if it is not under full financial or owner control and if one of the following three conditions is met:

1. A financial institution holds 10 percent or more of the corporation's voting stock, with sole or partial voting rights over the stock. However, another stockholder also has 10 percent or more of the stock.

2. A financial institution holds 5 percent or more of the corporation's voting stock, with sole or partial voting rights over the stock. No stockholder has 10 percent or more of the stock.

3. A financial institution that is a leading supplier of capital to the corporation also has strong representation on the corporation's board of directors. No stockholder has 10 percent or more of the stock.

The working definitions of full and partial financial control have been stated for control by a single financial institution. To apply them to a case of control by a group of financial institutions, merely substitute the phrase "group of financial institutions" for "financial institution" in each place that the latter term appears in the working definitions.[8] Two separate classifications of the 200 largest nonfinancial corporations are presented, one that excludes control by groups of financial institutions, and a second that includes such group control. (However, when several investment companies were affiliated with a single investment advisor, they were treated as a single financial institution.)[9]

---

8. For the definition of groups of financial institutions, see below, pp. 84-89.

9. The *Institutional Investor Study Report* followed the same practice. U. S., Securities and Exchange Commission, *Institutional Investor Study Report,* House Document 92-64, 1971.

Full Owner Control

A corporation is classified in this category if an individual or a "group of related individuals" satisfies one of two conditions:

1. The individual or group holds 10 percent or more of the company's voting stock, and is the only stockholder with 10 percent or more.

2. The individual or group holds 5 percent or more of the company's voting stock and has strong representation on the company's board of directors. No other stockholder has 5 percent or more of the stock.

A "group of related individuals" means a group of relatives by blood or marriage, or a small group of business associates. The relationship between business associates had to go beyond their joint presence on the board of the company in question, in order to consider them a group for purposes of owner control.

Partial Owner Control

A corporation is classified in this category if it is not under full financial or owner control and if one of the following two conditions is met:

1. An individual or group holds 10 percent or more of the company's voting stock, but another stockholder also has 10 percent or more.

2. An individual or group holds 5 percent or more of the company's voting stock, and no other stockholder has 10 percent or more.

Miscellaneous Control

A corporation is classified in this category if it satisfies the working definition of full or partial owner control with the phrase "foreign corporation" or "self-administered fund" substituted for "individual or group" in the working definition.

No Identified Center of Control

Corporations that do not satisfy the working definition for any of the preceding control categories are placed here. For a number of corporations in this category, there was substantial evidence of financial or owner control but not enough to meet the criteria for those categories. Such cases of "suspected" financial or owner control were indicated as such in the presentation of the results. For example, in 1968 the First National

City Bank was apparently the leading subscriber to a $100 million revolving credit agreement with Consolidated Edison, a heavy user of long-term debt financing.[10] In addition, the bank held $37.6 million of Consolidated Edison's preferred stock in 1967. Two representatives of First National City Bank sat on the utility's board. However, since the bank held only about 4 percent of Consolidated Edison's long-term debt, the company was not classified under financial control, but was regarded as a case of suspected financial control.

The Singer Corporation provides an example of suspected owner control. According to Singer's 1969 proxy statement, S. C. Clark was the largest stockholder, with 1.2 percent of the voting stock. He also sat on the executive committee of the board. However, the 1964 proxy statement reported that Clark and his associates owned 25 percent of the outstanding stock. While Clark and his associates may have sold this huge block of stock in the five-year period, it is more likely that the departure of family members from the board or a reallocation of the holdings among family members eliminated the need to report most of the stock they held.

The working definitions of full control by any source were constructed in such a way as to make full control an exclusive possession. If one financial institution or individual meets the criteria for full control over a particular corporation, then no other institution or individual could simultaneously fit the working definition of either full or partial control for that corporation. Since partial control is not an exclusive form of control, the working definitions permit more than one institution and/or individual to have partial control over the same corporation.

RATIONALE FOR THE WORKING DEFINITIONS

All students of corporate control seem to agree that holdings of large blocks of stock are the single most significant source of control for any controlling group. The Patman Report, which plays down the sole importance of stock, nevertheless states,

10. Data sources on the Consolidated Edison-First National City Bank relationship included Con Ed.'s 1969 Annual Report, Proxy Statement, and report to the Federal Power Commission, and U.S. Congress, House Banking and Currency Committee, Subcommittee on Domestic Finance, *Commercial Banks and Their Trust Activities*, 90th Congress, 2nd Session, 1968.

"the percentage of stock, held by an entity, is still an extremely important factor — and perhaps the single most important factor — in determining control." [11] A sufficiently large block of stock can virtually assure control; whereas, being a supplier of capital to a corporation, while it may provide the basis for influence or even control, is not as secure a basis as is holding stock.

What percentage of the outstanding stock constitutes a controlling block? [12] Ten percent is the figure used most often in the literature on owner control, for a large corporation whose remaining stock is widely held. [13] Since financial institutions have more potential sources of power over nonfinancial corporations than do most noninstitutional stockholders, and are usually well-informed about corporate policies and have good connections with other institutional stockholders, it seems reasonable to use the 10 percent figure for identifying full financial control.

Only that portion of the stock held by a financial institution was counted over which the institution had sole or partial voting authority, for two reasons. [14] First, as was argued above, the right to vote the stock is the most important source of stockholder power. Second, stock which a financial institution holds but has no voting authority over is likely to be actively voted by the beneficial owners (or their representative). In such cases it seems more reasonable to attribute the power associated with the stock to the beneficial owners rather than the financial institution.

The power associated with a capital supplier relationship is more dependent on circumstances than the power associated with stockholdings. Therefore, no percentage figure was speci-

11. *Commercial Banks and Their Trust Activities,* vol. 1, p. 23.

12. Of course, to select any fixed percentage involves an element of arbitrariness.

13. This percentage is used by Larner, Sheehan, and the T.N.E.C. Monograph No. 29. In addition, the Public Utility Holding Company Act of 1935 provides for presumption of control if one person owns 10 percent or more of the stock of a public utility. (Some other laws specify different percentages for presumption of control, however.)

14. The Federal Communications Commission conducted an investigation into full and partial voting rights held by banks over stock of communications companies in 1969-1972. At the end of the investigation, the FCC decided that full and partial voting rights should be treated in the same way. See U. S., Congress, Senate Government Operations Committee, Subcommittee on Intergovernmental Relations, and on Budgeting, Management, and Expenditure, *Disclosure of Corporate Ownership,* 93rd Congress, 1st Session, 1973, pt. II (by R. Soldofsky), p. 155.

fied as indicating control for the capital supplier relationship; and it was used only in combination with other sources or indications of power over the corporation. In deciding whether a financial institution is a "leading supplier of capital" to a corporation, account is taken not only of whether the financial institution is one of the two or three biggest creditors, the traditional investment banker, or the lead commercial bank, but also of the corporation's degree of reliance on external funds.

The ratio of long-term debt to total assets was used as the measure of reliance on external finance in most cases.[15] No corporation having a long-term debt-to-asset ratio of less than two-thirds of the average ratio for manufacturing corporations was classified as under financial control based on a capital supplier relationship. Almost all corporations so classified had well above the average ratio. Furthermore, account was taken of the type of external capital used by a corporation. An investment bank would not be considered a leading capital supplier to a firm that raised some capital through the investment bank but obtained most of its long-term debt capital in the form of term loans from banks or life insurance companies, which do not require the services of an investment bank.

Representation of a financial institution on the board of a nonfinancial corporation was also used only in combination with other factors. Although strong representation on the board is probably by itself an indication of significant influence by the financial institution, it does not seem proper, as a general rule, to regard this as establishing such influence, in the absence of any evidence that there also exists a potential source of such influence.

A 5 to 10 percent stockholding by a financial institution in a nonfinancial corporation, for which no stockholder has 10 percent or more, is regarded as conferring on the holder the power to determine basic corporate policies, at least within limits set by other powerful groups — that is, as conferring partial control. In recent decades a 5 percent or larger stockholding has increasingly come to be regarded as significant for control. The Patman Report states, "The Subcommittee . . . determined that in general a stockholding of five percent or more of any class of stock in a single corporation was a

---

15. In a few cases short-term financial pressure on a corporation was considered in determining its degree of reliance on external finance. An example was Chrysler Corporation — see app. B, table B-1, part B.

significant factor in judging the extent to which a bank might have substantial influence or control over a corporation."[16] The Bank Holding Company Act of 1956 requires a bank holding company to obtain Federal Reserve Board approval before acquiring more than 5 percent of the voting stock of any bank. Recently the Securities and Exchange Commission lowered the minimum percentage stockholding that must be reported in a corporate proxy statement from 10 percent to 5 percent of the outstanding stock.

When a 5 to 10 percent stockholding is combined with a leading capital supplier relationship, this is regarded as establishing full control. When a financial institution has strong representation on the board of a corporation in which it also holds 5 to 10 percent of the voting stock, the strong board representation is interpreted to indicate that the 5 to 10 percent holding is sufficient for full control.

When a financial institution is a leading capital supplier to a corporation and also has strong representation on the corporation's board, it seems reasonable to conclude that the board representation indicates that the capital supplier relationship does constitute a source of power over the corporation. This is regarded as establishing partial control. Criterion 1 for partial financial control is intended to cover cases in which a financial institution would appear, on the basis of its relationship to a nonfinancial corporation, to be in the position of controller, except that there is another financial institution or individual that is approximately as strong.

Criterion 3 for full financial control is included because one cannot ignore the cases that sometimes come to light of undeniable financial control, where the basis for such control rests on unique or hidden circumstances. This criterion was used only once, for the Union Pacific Railroad. Three partners of Brown Brothers Harriman, a private commercial bank, sat on the executive committee of the Union Pacific in 1969. One of those partners was chairman of the board and another was chairman of the executive committee, both positions being higher in the official corporate hierarchy than the president of that company.[17] The railroad had been associated with the bank and its controlling family, the Harrimans, since about 1900, when E. H.

16. *Commercial Banks and Their Trust Activities*, p. 30.

17. Sources for the relationship between Brown Brothers Harriman and Union Pacific included the railroad's 1968 report to the Interstate Commerce Commission, its 1969 Annual Report, and Moody's *Transportation Manual*, 1970.

Harriman acquired control of the railroad. However, since the bank held no more than 2.1 percent of the voting stock and was apparently not a leading capital supplier, it did not meet the regular criteria for full or partial control. The railroad was classified under full financial control by virtue of criterion 3.

The working definitions of full and partial owner control are similar to those for full and partial financial control, with the omission of the capital supplier relationship. The major difference between the definition of owner control used here and that used by Larner and most other students of corporate control is the inclusion of a partial control category. The somewhat weaker partial control category introduces a greater measure of realism. Although Larner states that a 10 percent holding is the minimum percentage for "minority control," he actually classifies some companies as minority controlled when a family has more than 5 percent plus strong board representation.[18] This is similar to criterion 2 above for full owner control.[19]

One of the criticisms made of the Temporary National Economic Committee study was that it emphasized "immediate control" rather than "ultimate control." A classification of a sample of nonfinancial corporations by immediate control regards a nonfinancial corporation as owner controlled if another nonfinancial corporation holds a big block of stock in it. To classify one nonfinancial corporation as "owner controlled" by another is appropriate for showing the direct ties between nonfinancial corporations. However, the purpose here is to examine the nature of control over large nonfinancial corporations, and it gets one nowhere to say that they control one another. The relevant controlling agents must be something other than the entities being studied.

Thus, ultimate control is emphasized in this study. This means that, if nonfinancial corporation A is found to be immediately controlled by nonfinancial corporation B, then whoever controls corporation B is held to control A as well. This process is carried back as far as necessary to eliminate nonfinancial corporations from controller status. The only exception is the miscellaneous category of control by a foreign corporation, which involved only two corporations in the sample. Cases of immediate control of one nonfinancial corporation by

18. An example is Mead Corporation.
19. T.N.E.C. Monograph No. 29 followed the same practice, with its category of "small minority control" (T.N.E.C. Monograph No. 29, p. 109).

another are noted, however, in Appendix B, which presents the detailed results of this study.

GROUPS OF FINANCIAL INSTITUTIONS

It is possible to study financial control over nonfinancial corporations by treating the single financial institution as the only source of financial control. The Patman Report follows that approach. However, most students of financial control have concluded that individual financial institutions often work together to exert influence. Chapter 3 discussed the close alliance between J. P. Morgan and Company and the First National Bank of New York in the two decades preceding World War I. This alliance was the basis of J. P. Morgan's enormous power. Also discussed in the previous chapter was the struggle waged by leading bankers for control over life insurance companies, which were important assets to a banker that wanted to be able to meet all of the financial needs of a group of corporations.

There are a number of ways to attempt to take account of alliances among financial institutions. One is to assume that all financial institutions that hold large amounts of stock in a particular corporation have common interests as trustees for the beneficial owners, and would act together on many matters. The Securities and Exchange Commission's *Institutional Investor Study Report* suggests that that is the case.[20] However, while the financial institutions that happen to hold stock in the same corporation would have some common interests, they may also have important competing interests. In the case of commercial banks, there is potential competition over obtaining the corporation's deposits, over management of company pension funds, and over the company's loan business.

The Senate subcommittee study *Disclosure of Corporate Ownership* focuses on the combined stockholdings that the seven New York banks with the greatest value of trust assets have in a sample of large corporations.[21] The top New York banks no doubt do have some common interests, including the desire to maintain the primacy of New York as the financial center of the United States. However, New York finance has

---

20. *Institutional Investor Study Report*, pt. 5, p. 2551.
21. *Disclosure of Corporate Ownership*, pt. I.

always been characterized by a certain amount of competition between various groups, sometimes sharp, sometimes muted.

In this study groups of financial institutions are defined primarily based on historical alliances. Four such groups have been identified here: the Chase group, the Morgan group, the Mellon group, and the Lehman-Goldman, Sachs group. These include the following financial institutions:

Chase Group
Chase Manhattan Bank, New York
Chemical Bank, New York
Metropolitan Life Insurance Company, New York
Equitable Life Assurance Society, New York

Morgan Group
Morgan Guarantee Trust, New York
Bankers Trust Company, New York
Prudential Life Insurance Company, Newark
Morgan, Stanley and Company, New York
Smith, Barney and Company, New York

Mellon Group
Mellon National Bank and Trust, Pittsburgh
First Boston Corporation, New York

Lehman-Goldman, Sachs Group
Lehman Brothers, New York
Goldman, Sachs and Company, New York

The definition of groups of financial institutions presents many problems. One wants to place in a group those financial institutions that have "close ties" and "work closely together." These are elusive concepts, ones that are more difficult to establish by clear evidence than is the concept of control. For control, concrete evidence can be produced of the power that an institution or individual has over a corporation, as in the form of stockholdings. The basis for believing that a group of financial institutions works closely together is usually much weaker, often dependent on opinions of knowledgeable observers. For these reasons the control classification of the sample that includes control by groups of financial institutions has been segregated from the classification excluding control by groups of financial institutions.

Two of the groups defined above do not present very serious problems. The Mellon group includes only two financial institutions. The First Boston Corporation, an investment bank, was formed by the merger of T. F. Mellon and Sons, the Mellon family's investment bank, with First Boston and Company.[22] In 1970 the Sarah Mellon Scaife Foundation, a Mellon family foundation, owned 10.8 percent of First Boston Corporation's voting stock.[23] A newspaper report in 1973 claimed that the Mellons owned a total of 20 percent of First Boston's stock.[24] The Mellons also owned at least 29 percent of the stock of Mellon National Bank and Trust in 1962.[25]

Lehman Brothers and Goldman, Sachs and Company have a close relationship that goes back to the first decade of this century. In about 1905 the two investment banks, then relatively small, began handling the securities of light industrial and retail trade companies, which had previously been shunned by investment banks. Co-managing numerous issues, they became leading investment banks within a few decades.[26] Among the corporations in the sample, there were many more instances of co-management of security issues by these two investment banks than issues managed either singly by one of them or by one of the two together with a third investment bank during the late 1960's.

The two larger groups present more serious difficulties. Aside from old historical ties, there is such evidence as family ties between the top officers of financial institutions, director interlocks, and the opinions of the few social scientists who have done extensive studies of the groupings among financial institutions. One whose work is very useful in this regard is S. Menshikov, a Soviet social scientist whose study *Millionaires and Managers* was described briefly in chapter 1.[27] A second is James C. Knowles of the University of Southern California, who did a study of financial institutions and nonfinancial corporations associated with the Rockefeller family in the late 1960s, based on documentary sources.[28]

The Chase group includes two commercial banks and two

22. James C. Knowles, "The Rockefeller Financial Group," in *Superconcentration/Supercorporation*, ed. R. L. Andreano, Warner Modular Publications, Book 1 (1973), Module 343, pp. 3-4.

23. Sarah Mellon Scaife Foundation *Annual Report* for 1970.

24. Milton Moscowitz in the San Francisco *Chronicle*, 8 March 1973, p. 41.

25. U. S., Congress, House Select Committee on Small Business, *Chain Banking*, 87th Congress, 1963, p. 175.

26. Carosso, pp. 82-83.

27. See p. 9 above.

28. Knowles, *op. cit.*

life insurance companies. Chase Manhattan Bank, and its prede-cessor Chase National Bank, have been associated with the Rockefeller family since the 1920s.[29]   David Rockefeller has been president or chairman since 1962.[30]   Both Menshikov and Knowles place the Chemical Bank in close association with Chase Manhattan, relying mainly on ties of top officials of the Chemical Bank to the Rockefellers.[31]   Because director inter-locks between banks in the same geographic region are illegal, one cannot look at this source for information about ties between commercial banks.

Menshikov and Knowles both place Metropolitan and Equi-table Life in close association with Chase and Chemical.[32] Although director interlocks have limited reliability as indica-tors of control,[33]   they may indicate a close alliance between institutions. In 1967 Equitable Life had five director interlocks with Chase and four with Chemical; it had none with Morgan Guarantee Trust, Bankers Trust, First National City Bank, or Manufacturers Hanover Trust, the other four leading New York banks.[34]   Metropolitan Life had three interlocks with Chase and none with Chemical; it had two with First National City Bank, and one each with Morgan Guarantee Trust, Bankers Trust, and Manufacturers Hanover Trust.[35]   A study in the early 1950s found that Equitable and Metropolitan both kept much larger deposits in Chase National Bank than in other leading New York banks.[36]

The Morgan group is not family-based as is the Chase group, but it is descended from the old Morgan interests. In 1933 the Glass-Steagull Act separated commercial and investment bank-ing. J. P. Morgan and Company elected to give up investment banking and become solely a commercial bank. Several Morgan partners, including Henry S. Morgan, the grandson of J. P. Morgan, Sr., left to form Morgan, Stanley and Company, a new

---

29. S. Menshikov, *Millionaires and Managers* (Moscow, 1969), pp. 260-61.

30. Chase Manhattan Bank *Annual Reports,* 1962-1970.

31. Knowles, p. 8; and Menshikov, pp. 264-66. See also *Who's Who in America,* 1970-71, under Hulbert S. and Malcolm P. Aldrich.

32. Knowles places the New York Life Insurance Company in the "Rockefeller financial group" but Menshikov does not.

33. See chapter 2.

34. U. S., Congress, House Banking and Currency committee, *Control of Com-mercial Banks and Interlocks Among Financial Institutions,* 90th Congress, 1st Session, 1967; reprinted in *Commercial Banks and their Trust Activities,* v. 1, p. 970.

35. *Ibid.*

36. Victor Perlo, *Empire of High Finance* (New York, 1957), p. 319.

investment bank.[37]   H. S. Morgan was a partner in the bank until his retirement in 1969,[38] and according to Menshikov, he controlled it through owning 30 to 50 percent of the capital.[39]

J. P. Morgan and Company, the commercial bank, merged with Guarantee Trust in 1959 to form Morgan Guarantee Trust. The old Guarantee Trust had been allied with the Morgan group, according to Menshikov.[40] Bankers Trust was formed by J. P. Morgan and his partners in 1903, to be a sort of reserve bank for New York bankers.[41] Up to 1935, it had three Morgan partners on its board, when bank director interlocks were still legal. Menshikov studied a sample of 150 large nonfinancial corporations; of the 13 having director interlocks with Bankers Trust, 9 were either interlocked with Morgan Guarantee Trust or Morgan, Stanley, and Company or used Morgan, Stanley as their leading investment bank.[42]

In 1934 when the investment banking affiliate of Guarantee Trust was forced to dissolve by the Glass-Steagull Act, several of its executives and more than half of its employees went to the investment bank Smith, Barney and Company. As of the early 1960s most of the large nonfinancial corporations that Smith, Barney serviced were, according to Menshikov, also tied to Morgan Guarantee Trust.[43]

Prudential Life Insurance Company, the largest life insurance company in the United States, has been associated with the Morgan interests since the turn of the century, according to Perlo. At that time a Morgan lawyer designed its mutualization to prevent New Jersey bankers from gaining control.[44] In the early 1950s Perlo found that Prudential had larger deposits in Morgan-associated banks than in Chase or in First National City Bank's predecessor, National City Bank, although National City Bank was a close second.[45] Menshikov also placed Prudential in the Morgan group. In 1967 Prudential had one director inter-

37. Vincent P. Carosso, *Investment Banking in America: A History* (Cambridge, Mass., 1970), pp. 372-73.
38. *Who's Who in America,* 1970-71.
39. Menshikov, p. 236.
40. *Ibid.,* p. 235.
41. *Ibid.,* pp. 240, 231.
42. *Ibid.,* pp. 240-41. The date of the study was apparently about 1960.
43. *Ibid.,* pp. 242-43.
44. Perlo, p. 82.
45. *Ibid.,* p. 319.

lock with Morgan Guarantee Trust and none with any of the other five leading New York banks.[46]

One could include a few more financial institutions in each of the four groups. However, the evidence for making such inclusions is weaker than that for the financial institutions that were included. One could also define additional groups of financial institutions, some based in New York and some elsewhere. For example, Menshikov defined eight financial groups based in New York.[47] However, other possible groups that were considered were not found to be important for financial control over the corporations in the sample.

It must be re-emphasized that the evidence for the groups of financial institutions defined here is of varying reliability. The results that include control by groups of financial institutions must be read with that in mind. Fortunately, as Appendix B, Table B-2 shows, slightly over half of the corporations having their control classification affected by the inclusion of control by groups of financial institutions involved the financial institutions for which the evidence of close ties was relatively strong: Mellon National Bank and First Boston Corporation; Lehman Brothers and Goldman, Sachs; Morgan Guarantee Trust and Morgan, Stanley; and Chase Manhattan Bank and Equitable Life.

DATA SOURCES

Many data sources were used to provide information on stockholdings, capital supplier relationships, and director representation for the 200 corporations in the sample. The most comprehensive sources of data on financial institutions' holdings of stock in nonfinancial corporations for the late 1960s are the Patman Report and the *Institutional Investor Study Report.* Such special government studies are important because, with the exception of airlines, railroads, and utilities, nonfinancial corporations are nowhere required to report the amount of their stock, no matter how large, that is held by a bank trust department. Securities and Exchange Commission reporting requirements concentrate on beneficial stockholders rather than holders of record such as bank trust departments.

46. House Banking and Currency Committee, 1967, v. 1, p. 971.
47. Menshikov, chap. 6.

The Patman Report gives information on bank trust department stockholdings in the top 500 industrial corporations, the top 50 transportation companies, the top 50 retail trade companies, and the top 50 utilities in 1967 (ranked by sales). This includes all but 5 of the 200 corporations in my sample. For each corporation, the report lists banks that hold 5 percent or more of the outstanding stock — the name of the bank, the percent of shares held, the type of share (common or preferred), and the percentage of shares held for which the bank has sole voting authority, partial voting authority, and no voting authority. The banks for which these data are supplied are 49 leading trust banks. These banks controlled 54 percent of the trust assets of all commercial banks in 1967.[48] However, the 49 omit a few of the largest banks in terms of trust assets, such as the fifth largest (U. S. Trust) and the eighth largest (Wilmington Trust) in 1967.

The Securities and Exchange Commission's *Institutional Investor Study Report* provides information on institutional investors' stockholdings in a sample of 800 corporations in 1969. The institutional investors covered by the relevant section of the study include the 50 largest bank trust departments, investment advisors for the 71 largest investment company complexes, and the 26 largest life insurance companies. These 50 banks held 72.2 percent by value of the corporate stock held by all bank trust departments in the United States in 1969; the investment company complexes held 84.6 percent and the life insurance companies 82.4 percent of the total stock held by their respective groups.[49] The 800 corporations in the *Institutional Investor Study Report's* sample include 103 of the 200 corporations in my sample.

For each of the 800 corporations, the *Report* tells the number of financial institutions of each type whose stockholdings must be combined to equal 1 percent, 2.5 percent, 5 percent, and 10 percent of the corporation's outstanding common stock. In one set of tables the information is restricted to stockholdings over which the financial institutions have sole or partial voting authority. However, the identities of the financial institutions involved are not divulged.

The problem of unidentified financial institutions was partly remedied by the publication of the Senate subcommittee

48. *Commercial Banks and their Trust Activities*, vol. 1, p. 88.
49. *Institutional Investor Study Report*, vol. 5, p. 2553.

study *Disclosure of Corporate Ownership.* A section of this study was prepared by Robert Soldofsky based on the original data collected by the Securities and Exchange Commission for its *Institutional Investor Study Report.* Soldofsky reported the percentage of common stock in particular large corporations held by particular bank trust departments. The banks were listed by code number rather than name, in an attempt to preserve confidentiality; however, this attempt was not wholly successful. By cross-checking the Soldofsky data against other sources, it was possible to discover the identity of the bank in almost every case that mattered for this study.[50]

The main part of *Disclosure of Corporate Ownership* was based on voluntary replies from 163 large corporations to a questionnaire sent by Senator Lee Metcalf to 324 large corporations. This part of the study contains much information on bank stockholdings in large corporations, but the data have two shortcomings. One is that the questionnaire data on the top twenty stockholders of record were for 1972, which falls outside the period of this study by three years. The second problem is that the questionnaire data do not break down bank trust department stockholdings into sole, partial, and no voting rights. Nevertheless, it was possible to make use of the data in a few cases, particularly for owner control.

The main source of information on the stockholdings of individuals was corporation proxy statements, which were examined for all the corporations in the sample for the year 1969.[51] Securities and Exchange Commission rules require corporations to disclose in their proxy statements the stockholdings of officers and directors as well as those of anyone holding 10 percent or more of any issue of the company's stock.[52] A person required to report his holdings must include stock owned by members of his immediate family. However, the holdings of relatives not living with the person are not reported. As a result, the recorded stockholdings of an officer or director may understate the actual holding of the person and his relatives.

Two examples of this were turned up by the study *Disclosure of Corporate Ownership.* The 1969 proxy for Dow

---

50. The above statement was true only for the classification excluding groups of financial institutions.

51. In some cases the year was 1968 or 1970.

52. As mentioned above, the 10 percent requirement was recently reduced to 5 percent.

Chemical showed Dow family members and relatives holding a total of 3 percent of the voting shares. *Disclosure of Corporate Ownership* listed the holdings of four additional family members, bringing the total up to 5.7 percent of the stock. This was sufficient for full owner control, given the Dow family occupancy of the top management positions. A second example was the McDonnell Douglas Corporation. Its 1969 proxy showed the McDonnells with 8.6 percent of the voting shares. *Disclosure of Corporate Ownership* added two more McDonnells and the family foundation, raising the stock controlled to 19.3 percent of the total. Unfortunately, the Senate subcommittee study had full information for only a small percentage of the sample of 200 corporations.

Another source for the stockholdings of financial institutions and individuals was annual reports that railroads, airlines, and utilities file annually with their regulatory commissions. Reports to the Interstate Commerce Commission list the stockholdings of the twenty top stockholders of record in railroads. Civil Aeronautics Board reports list any record holder of 5 percent or more of an airline's stock. Federal Power Commission reports disclose the holdings of the top ten stockholders of record in electric and gas utilities. Bank trust department stockholdings in regulated companies appear in the reports under nominee names used by the banks, not under the bank's name. The identity of the bank behind the nominee was usually very difficult or impossible to discover before Senator Metcalf entered the publicly unavailable nominee list, published by the American Society of Corporate Secretaries in the Congressional Record on 24 June 1971.

Other sources for stockholdings included annual reports of key foundations; Moody's *Industrial, Transportation,* and *Public Utility Manuals;* Standard and Poors Corporation Records; annual schedules of investments published by life insurance companies; and occasional articles in business periodicals such as the *Wall Street Journal* and *Fortune.* Business periodicals were used sparingly as a source of data for this section.

The above sources of data on stockholdings were far from ideal, but they did provide a large quantity of information on both financial institutions' and individuals' stockholdings in the 200 corporations in the sample. The data available on creditor relationships were inferior by comparison. The main source on creditor relationships between nonfinancial corporations and commercial banks was corporate proxy statements, and, for the airlines, Civil Aeronautics Board reports. Although not required by law to do so, many corporations report in their proxy statements their business relationships with any firm having a representative on its board of directors. Hence, the amount of money owed specific banks was often listed for those banks represented on the board. Civil Aeronautics Board reports list the major creditors of airlines and the value of debt held by each creditor.

Life insurance companies' holdings of the bonds of particular corporations are listed in their schedules of investments. Moody's manuals and Standard and Poors *Corporation Records* report bond issues of corporations going back for decades, specifying the investment bank or investment banks that offered each issue for sale. Occasionally business periodicals provided information on capital supplier relationships.

The directors of all of the corporations in the sample were analyzed for 1969, and in some cases for 1965 through 1969, to discover their primary affiliations. The data sources used for this were annual reports of corporations, proxy statements, *Who's Who in America*,[53] and Dun and Bradstreet's *Million Dollar Directory*.[54]

PROBLEMS IN APPLYING THE WORKING DEFINITIONS

A number of problems were encountered in applying the working definitions of control. One set of problems involved the time period that this study covered. The type of control over a corporation may change over time. Thus, a study of control should apply to a short time interval. However, the available information relevant to the control over even a single corporation usually does not all apply to the same date, and the situation is worse for a large sample of corporations.

A period of three years was selected, 1967 through 1969, to increase the quantity of scarce control information that could be found. The price that was paid for selecting a three-year-long period was that the type of control changed over the course of

---

53. *Who's Who in America* (Chicago), published semi-annually.
54. Dun and Bradstreet's *Million Dollar Directory*, published annually.

the period for a number of companies in the sample. In such cases the corporation was classified according to its control situation in 1969. In a few cases this rule did not resolve the matter, and judgment had to be used.

The case of General Dynamics Corporation illustrates this problem. Henry Crown was the largest stockholder in General Dynamics in the early 1960s, but in 1966 the directors voted to call his preferred (voting) stock.[55] A few years later Crown put together a buying group to purchase General Dynamics shares. According to a feature article in *Fortune,* in late December 1969, the Crown group's holding rose to just over 10 percent.[56] The company proxy statement for 1970 stated that the Crown group had 18 percent of the voting stock on 10 April 1970. In May of 1970 Crown and four associates joined the board of directors, with Crown as chairman of the newly formed executive policy committee. We also know that as of September 1969, an unknown investment company complex had between 7.5 percent and 10 percent of the voting stock of General Dynamics.[57]

How should this corporation be classified? Clearly, by May 1970 Crown had control. I decided that, for 1969, it was partially controlled by Crown and partially by the investment company complex, since Crown probably had between 5 and 10 percent during most of the latter part of 1969.

The great merger movement going on during 1967 to 1969 compounded the difficulties of timing. In some cases there was evidence for 1967 of financial control over a company which merged with another later in the period. In such cases the terms of the merger were studied to determine whether the new merged company would satisfy the requirements for financial control.

In general 1969 was considered the primary year for collection of data. Where there was a choice, data were always gathered for that year. In a few cases some 1970 data were used, usually when the 1969 proxy for a company was unavailable.[58]

Another problem in applying the working definitions involved voting rights for securities other than common stock. A substantial minority of the corporations in the sample had one

---

55. Carol J. Loomis, "Who Wants General Dynamics?," *Fortune* (June 1970), pp. 76-79, 185-93.

56. *Ibid.,* p. 193.

57. *Disclosure of Corporate Ownership*, pt. II.

58. Proxy statements for 1968 and earlier were very difficult to obtain.

or more issues of preferred stock with voting rights attached to those shares, in some cases more than one vote per share. References to a holding of 5 percent or 10 percent of the voting stock of a company in the working definitions actually mean 5 or 10 percent of the total votes eligible to be cast, including votes by common and preferred shares. However, preferred stock which carried voting rights only under special conditions or only on certain restricted matters was not counted.[59] In a few cases a financial institution was known to have more than 5 percent of the common stock of a corporation but no information was available about its holdings of the company's voting preferred, resulting in the company not meeting the requirements for financial control.

The working definitions of financial control counted stock held by financial institutions only if the financial institution had sole or partial voting rights over the stock. In two cases stockholdings were counted in spite of uncertainty about the voting rights. One was Columbia Broadcasting System, which the Metcalf Report found to have 14.1 percent of its voting shares held by Chase Manhattan Bank in 1972. The late date was overlooked because CBS was not covered by either the Patman Report or the *Institutional Investor Study Report*, the two main sources of information on financial institution's stockholdings for 1967 through 1969. Chase Manhattan usually has sole or partial voting rights over a high proportion of the stock it holds.[60] Hence, CBS was classified as under partial financial control, assuming Chase had voting authority over 5 to 10 percent of the outstanding shares.

The second case in which a financial institution's stockholding was counted, in spite of uncertainty about voting rights, was for Safeway Stores. Merrill, Lynch, Pierce, Fenner and Smith held 8 percent of the voting stock in 1969, according to the 1969 proxy for Safeway. In the 1930s the Merrill and Lynch families owned 14.6 percent of the stock of Safeway.[61] The chairman and chief executive officer of Safeway in 1969, R. A. Magowan, was a principal partner in Merrill, Lynch from

59. In some cases the preferred stock carries voting power only if several consecutive preferred dividends are missed.

60. That was not found to be true for all large banks. For example, First National Bank of Boston often had no voting authority over large blocks of shares it held in companies in the sample. This probably indicates it was favored as a place to keep trust accounts by active capitalists, or as a custodian for investment company shares.

61. T.N.E.C. Monograph No. 29, p. 1495.

1938 to 1955, at which time he left Merrill, Lynch to head Safeway. His son, Merrill Magowan, was an executive of Merrill, Lynch and a director of Safeway in 1969.[62] These factors, together with the unlikelihood that Merrill, Lynch would hold such a large block of Safeway stock as part of its normal brokerage business, suggest that Merrill, Lynch had voting power over the stock. Safeway was classified under partial financial control.

In one case, that of Diamond Shamrock Corporation, the criteria for partial financial control were bent to take in a company that just missed satisfying the working definition in two different ways. It was possible to deduce from several sources[63] that the Mellon National Bank and Trust held between 4.8 percent and 5 percent of the voting stock (with voting authority) in 1969, down from the 14.4 percent the bank held in Diamond Alkali in mid-1967, prior to the merger with Shamrock Oil and Gas that formed Diamond Shamrock in December 1967. Mellon was also the lead bank for Diamond Shamrock, which was a heavy user of external finance; and Mellon had a representative on Diamond Shamrock's board. Since this just missed satisfying both criteria 2 and 3 for partial financial control, the company was classified under partial financial control.

There were four cases of partial financial control in which the identity of the financial institution involved could not be determined. Two involved commercial banks and two involved investment company complexes. For these four nonfinancial corporations (Colt Industries, AMK, General Dynamics, and International Harvester), the *Institutional Investor Study Report* found that one financial institution had 5 to 10 percent of the voting shares, specifying only the type of financial institution, and the identities of the financial institutions could not be discovered from any other source.

OVERALL RESULTS

The complete results of this control study can be found in Appendix B. In Table B-1 of Appendix B is found the control

62. Safeway Stores Proxy statement, 1969.

63. The sources include *Commercial Banks and their Trust Activities,* the *Institutional Investor Study Report,* Diamond Shamrock's Proxy Statement and Annual Report for 1969 and Moody's *Industrial Manual,* 1972.

classification of each of the 200 corporations in the sample, excluding control by groups of financial institutions. Table B-2 sets out the changes in classification that result from the inclusion of control by groups of financial institutions.

Table 3 summarizes these results. Excluding control by groups of financial institutions, 69 corporations, or 34.5 percent of the sample, were found to be under financial control. A

TABLE 3. Summary of Control over the Top 200 Nonfinancial Corporations

Control category	Excluding control by groups of financial institutions		Including control by groups of financial institutions	
	Number of companies	Percent of companies	Number of companies	Percent of companies
1. Full financial control	13	6.5	16	8.0
2. Partial financial control only	46	23.0	51	25.5
3. Both partial financial control and partial owner control	10	5.0	11	5.5
4. Full owner control	31	15.5	30	15.0
5. Partial owner control only	2	1.0	2	1.0
6. Miscellaneous	5	2.5	5	2.5
7. No identified center of control	93	46.5	85	42.5
All categories	200	100.0	200	100.0
Financial control (1+2+3)	69	34.5	78	39.0
Owner control (3+4+5)	43	21.5	43	21.5
Financial or owner control (1+2+3+4+5)	102	51.0	110	55.0
Suspected financial control only	8	4.0	7	3.5
Both suspected financial and owner control	3	1.5	1	0.5
Suspected owner control only	18	9.0	16	8.0
No confirmed or suspected center of control	64	32.0	61	30.5

total of 43 corporations, or 21.5 percent of the sample, were under owner control. Combining those two categories, a total of 102 companies, or 51 percent of the sample, were under financial control, owner control, or both.[64]

The miscellaneous category covers 5 companies, or 2.5 percent of the sample. That leaves 93 companies, or 46.5 percent, with no identified center of control. Deducting the cases of suspected financial and owner control, 64 companies, or 32 percent of the sample, are left having no confirmed or suspected center of control.

The finding that just over a third of the corporations in the sample were under financial control indicates that financial control was a very important form of control over large nonfinancial corporations in the late 1960s. Financial control was more than one and a half times as common as owner control in the sample. The financial control category was more numerous than the group of companies having no confirmed or suspected center of control.

Of the 34.5 percent of the sample under financial control, only 13 companies, or 6.5 percent, were under full financial control. This suggests that in the typical case of financial control, the controlling financial institution must contend with other powerful institutions and/or individuals, and is not able to determine all policies of the corporation exactly as it might wish. On the other hand, most of the cases of partial financial control involved only one identified center of control. Of the 56 companies under partial financial control, 10 were partially controlled by both financial institutions and individuals, 8 were partially controlled by two or more financial institutions, and the remaining 38 were partially controlled by only one financial institution. Therefore, 51 companies, or 25.5 percent of the sample, were under financial control by only one financial institution, with no other control center identified; and 59 companies (including the 51 companies), or 29.5 percent, were controlled by one or several financial institutions, with no other type of control center identified.

Within the owner-control category, full control was much more common than partial control. Thirty-one companies were under full owner control and 12 under partial owner control.

---

64. The combined category is less than the sum of the financial control and owner control categories, since ten companies were under both partial financial control and partial owner control.

This is the reverse of the situation that was found for financial control. Part of the reason for the low incidence of partial owner control relative to full owner control is probably the lack of information on the stockholdings of individuals with less than 10 percent of the outstanding stock. Holders of more than 10 percent must report their holdings in the corporation's proxy statement, while those with less than 10 percent need not, except for officers and directors. However, even if the 21 cases of suspected owner control were added to the cases of confirmed partial owner control, full owner control would still be approximately as numerous (31 companies under full owner control compared to 33 companies under partial owner control or suspected owner control).

These contrasting results are not surprising. An individual owner-controller today usually has control over only one major corporation.[65]   In most cases he is the founder or a descendant of the founder. He is likely to have a strong psychological identification with the firm and to want unchallenged authority over it. Unlike a financial institution with its loanable funds and its connections with other institutions, the individual owner-controller may have his block of stock as his only source of power over the corporation, and his only protection against rival big stockholders, and particularly, against a possible take-over raid by another corporation. The individual owner-controllers most famous for their crusty independence and autocratic methods generally try to keep a very large percentage of the stock in their hands. Examples are J. Paul Getty (62.4 percent of Getty Oil) and J. Howard Pew (41.7 percent of Sun Oil).

On the other hand, a major financial institution is likely to want influence over numerous nonfinancial corporations. Although a position of unchallenged authority has some advantages, the financial institution can probably obtain what it wants from the corporation without such a strong position being necessary.[66]   Both considerations suggest a strategy of obtaining partial control rather than full control over corporations in most cases.

A further reason for expecting partial financial control to be

65. The two exceptions found in this study were E. F. Kaiser (Kaiser Industries and Kaiser Aluminum and Chemical) and H. T. Mandeville (White Consolidated Industries and Allis Chalmers).

66. See chapter 5 for a discussion of the question of what a financial institution might want from a nonfinancial corporation.

more common than full financial control is that financial institutions are very wary of charges that they control nonfinancial corporations. This provides an additional motivation to keep their stockholding in a company at the minimum level necessary for the degree of influence they may wish to exert. Furthermore, a financial institution, which is not usually tied to a particular corporation for psychological reasons as an individual capitalist is, may be expected to keep its holdings in each corporation sufficiently small. Then if the long-run prospects of the company or its industry should worsen, the financial institution would be able to get out with minimum capital loss.

When control by groups of financial institutions is included, the results are not very different from those excluding group control. As Table 3 shows, full financial control is raised from 13 to 16 companies, and partial financial control from 56 to 62. Nine companies are moved into the financial control category by the inclusion of control by groups, raising the total to 78, or 39 percent of the sample. The number of companies with no identified center of control is lowered from 93, or 46.5 percent, to 85, or 42.5 percent. The number of companies with no confirmed or suspected control center is lowered from 64, or 32 percent, to 61, or 30.5 percent.

Although the inclusion of control by groups of financial institutions does not change the above overall results very greatly, it does place three quite large companies in the financial control category. General Electric, Southern California Edison, and Ling-Temco-Vought, which are the 14th, 26th, and 29th largest companies in the sample, are found to be controlled by groups of financial institutions. Standard Oil of New Jersey, the second largest company in the sample, although remaining in the category of no identified control center, is under suspected financial control by the Chase group.

It is likely that better data availability would make the inclusion of control by groups of financial institutions have a greater effect on the number of companies found to be under financial control. The two main data sources on the stockholdings of financial institutions in nonfinancial corporations, the Patman Report and the *Institutional Investor Study Report,* present their data in such a way as to make it very difficult to discover the combined stockholdings of a specific group of financial institutions in a particular corporation. This is an additional reason, besides the problems associated with the definition of groups of financial institutions, for regarding the results for control including groups of financial institutions as of inferior reliability compared to the results that exclude groups of financial institutions.

RESULTS BY ASSETS AND SIZE GROUP

Financial control appears somewhat less significant if one looks at the percentage of corporate assets under financial control rather than the percentage of corporations. Table 4 shows that companies under financial control (excluding control by groups of financial institutions) represent 25.4 percent of the assets of the 200 companies. This compares to the 34.5 percent of the 200 companies by number that are under financial control. A similar result is obtained for owner-controlled companies, which represent 14.1 percent of the assets of the top 200 compared to 21.5 percent of the top 200 by number. Companies with no identified center of control represent 59.3 percent of total assets, compared to 46.5 percent by number; and companies with no confirmed or suspected center of control represent 48.2 percent of total assets, compared to 32 percent by number.

Much of the difference between the results by number of companies and by assets can be explained by the control results for the 10 largest companies in the sample. The distribution of assets among the sample is very skewed at the top. The 10 largest companies comprise only 5 percent of the sample by number, but they represent 30.4 percent of the sample by assets. Among the top 10 were found one case of financial control (Gulf Oil), one case of owner control (Ford Motor Company), and one case of miscellaneous control (Sears Roebuck). The remaining 7 had no identified center of control, either excluding or including control by groups of financial institutions, although one (Standard Oil of New Jersey) was under suspected financial control.

Table 5 presents the control results for the 190 "smallest" companies in the sample. With the top 10 companies of the sample excluded, financial control is almost as large a percentage of the sample by assets as by number of companies, particularly when group control is included. A significant difference between the two measures remains for owner control,

TABLE 4. Summary of Control over the Top 200 Nonfinancial
Corporations by Assets

Control category	Excluding control by groups of financial institutions		Including control by groups of financial institutions	
	Assets*	Percent of Assets	Assets*	Percent of Assets
1. Full financial control	24,362	5.6	27,434	6.3
2. Partial financial control only	72,656	16.8	84,585	19.5
3. Both partial financial control and partial owner control	12,741	2.9	15,685	3.6
4. Full owner control	46,330	10.7	43,386	10.0
5. Partial owner control only	2,088	0.5	2,088	0.5
6. Miscellaneous	17,796	4.1	17,796	4.1
7. No identified center of control	256,844	59.3	241,843	55.9
All categories	432,817	100.0	432,817	100.0
Financial control (1+2+3)	109,759	25.4	127,704	29.5
Owner control (3+4+5)	61,159	14.1	61,159	14.1
Financial or owner control (1+2+3+4+5)	158,177	36.5	173,178	40.0
Suspected financial control only	18,259	4.2	28,026	6.5
Both suspected financial and owner control	8,546	2.0	6,851	1.6
Suspected owner control only	21,223	4.9	19,300	4.5
No confirmed or suspected center of control	208,816	48.2	187,666	43.4

*Assets are in millions of dollars.

TABLE 5. Summary of Control over Nonfinancial Corporations with Asset
Rank 11 through 200

Category	Excluding control by groups of financial institutions		Including control by groups of financial institutions	
	Percent of companies	Percent of assets	Percent of companies	Percent of assets
Financial control	35.8	33.7	40.5	39.7
Owner control	22.1	17.2	22.1	17.2
No identified center of control	45.3	49.7	41.1	44.7
No confirmed or suspected center of control	30.0	33.8	28.9	32.6

which suggests that owner control is more common among the
smaller companies in the sample.[67]   Companies with no identified center of control are still a larger percentage by assets
than by number, but the difference is greatly reduced from the
difference found for the entire sample. The difference in the
percentage by assets and by number is also greatly reduced for
companies with no suspected or confirmed center of control.

One can get a clearer picture of what size companies are
under financial control and owner control by looking at the
distribution of those control categories by size groups. In Table
6 the sample of 200 companies is divided into fifths, according
to asset rank. Table 6 shows the distribution of financial and
owner control over the sample by these size groups. The results
are similar whether control by groups of financial institutions is
included or excluded; hence, the results that include control by
groups of financial institutions are not shown in Table 6.

Financial control is less frequent than average among companies in the top and bottom fifths of the sample. It has slightly
above average frequency in the second and fourth quintiles, and
well above average frequency in the middle fifth. Companies in
the top 40 are so large that it is difficult for any single financial
institution, or small group of financial institutions, to attain a
position of control. Some of the top 40, such as American
Telephone and Telegraph and Standard Oil of New Jersey, were
once under financial control but today are so large that no

67. See table 6.

TABLE 6. Financial and Owner Control over the Top 200 Nonfinancial
Corporations, by Size Group

	Financial control*		Owner control	
Asset rank	Companies under financial control	Percent of size group	Companies under owner control	Percent of size group
1 – 40	7	17.5	4	10.0
41 – 80	15	37.5	8	20.0
81 – 120	23	57.5	8	20.0
121 – 160	15	37.5	8	20.0
161 – 200	9	22.5	15	37.5
All size groups	69	34.5	43	21.5

*Excluding control by groups of financial institutions.

single financial institution can hold enough stock, or provide enough debt capital, to achieve control by itself.

Financial control is also relatively infrequent at the bottom end of the sample. The leading financial institutions may find these smaller corporations less desirable to control. Their stock and debt instruments are riskier, and they do not have as much business to offer a major financial institution. Smaller financial institutions would presumably find the smaller corporations highly desirable; however, the data sources used provide better coverage for the holdings of the largest financial institutions — the top 50 banks and top 71 investment companies — than for smaller ones.

Owner control is distributed by size group quite differently than is financial control. Referring again to Table 6, owner control is much more frequent than average among the bottom fifth, of approximately average frequency among the middle three-fifths, and much less frequent than average among the top fifth. Owner control is thus concentrated toward the bottom of the sample, while financial control is concentrated toward the middle. The distribution of owner control accords with the common view that owner control is widespread among smaller corporations, but becomes less common among larger corporations. This is true of the distribution in Table 6, except that owner control maintains a constant frequency across the middle three quintiles. Owner control is found to be a more frequent form of control than financial control among the bottom fifth of the sample; financial control is more frequent than owner control over the upper four-fifths.

RESULTS BY SECTOR

Table 7 breaks down the results for financial and owner control by industrial sector. Financial control is found to be relatively most frequent among transportation companies.[68]   Financial control is about equally frequent among the two major types of transportation companies in the sample, railroads and airlines. Seven of the 13 railroads and 4 of the 7 airlines are under financial control.

Both railroads and airlines are heavy users of long-term debt financing, compared to industrial or retail trade companies. This provides a good reason for financial institutions to attain a position of influence. In the case of airlines, banks have established the practice of buying new airplanes directly and leasing them to the airlines, which has reportedly been very profitable for the banks, partly due to special tax treatment of depreciation on such assets.

Two special factors arise in the case of railroads. One is the long history of financial control that dates back to the late 19th century. The second factor involves certain Interstate Commerce Commission procedures. When one railroad owns a big block of stock in another railroad, either in preparation for a merger or as a long-term tie between two separate railroads, a competing railroad's protest often leads the Interstate Commerce Commission to order the block of stock to be held by one or more bank trust departments as voting trustees. In such cases the bank or banks may hold the stock for many years. Of the seven railroads under financial control in the sample, two — the Chicago, Milwaukee, St. Paul and Pacific Railway and the Norfolk and Western Railway — involved such cases.

Financial control was found to be relatively least frequent among utilities; not a single case of financial control (by a single financial institution) was found among the 10 utilities in the sample. This seems surprising in view of their heavy use of long-term debt financing and the history of widespread financial control over public utilities prior to World War II. However, the collapse of the banker-backed public utility holding company empires during the Great Depression produced strong opposition to financial control over utilities. As was mentioned above, a 1941 Securities and Exchange Commission rule requiring competitive bidding on public utility holding company security

---

68. The high frequency for the "other" category can be ignored, since it includes only two companies.

TABLE 7. Financial and Owner Control over the Top 200 Nonfinancial Corporations, by Sector

Sector	Number of companies in sample	Financial control excluding control by groups of financial institutions		Owner control		Financial control including control by groups of financial institutions	
		Number of companies	Percent of sector	Number of companies	Percent of sector	Number of companies	Percent of sector
Industrials	152	53	34.9	35	23.0	59	38.8
Retail trade	15	4	26.7	6	40.0	6	40.0
Transportation	21	11	52.4	0	0.0	11	52.4
Utilities	10	0	0.0	0	0.0	1	10.0
Other	2	1	50.0	2	100.0	1	50.0
All sectors	200	69	34.5	43	21.5	78	39.0

issues reduced the influence of investment banks over utilities.[69]

Another factor working against financial control over utilities is the slow rate at which utility stocks appreciate in value. Bank trust departments in the post-World War II period have experienced competitive pressure to invest in stocks that show reasonably rapid capital appreciation. This may explain the relatively small bank trust department holdings of utility stocks. The above explanations are not completely satisfying, however. There would seem to be strong motivations for financial institutions to obtain control over utilities, in view of their enormous borrowings.

When control by groups of financial institutions is included, there is a significant increase in the percentage of retail trade companies under financial control, from 26.7 percent to 40 percent of the retail trade companies in the sample. Also, one utility, Southern California Edison, is under financial control by the Chase group.

Owner control was relatively most frequent among retail trade companies. One might be tempted to explain this by the small size of the retail trade companies in the sample. Ten of the 15 retail trade companies are found in the bottom 40 percent of the sample. However, this fact, together with the greater frequency of owner control among the smaller companies, does not account for the high incidence of owner control among retail trade companies. If owner control were distributed by size group among the retail trade companies in the sample in the same manner that it is distributed among all companies in the sample (the distribution shown in Table 6), then only 3.6 retail trade companies, or 24 percent of the 15 in the sample, should be under owner control. That is, the concentration of retail trade companies at the bottom of the size distribution would explain only a small part of the actually observed high relative frequency of owner control among retail trade companies.

The correct explanation is probably an historical one. It is widely assumed that owner control is the rule among small firms, and that when a small firm grows very large, in time owner control is likely to come to an end. Large corporations did not emerge in retail trade until the first few decades of the

69. Of the nine electric and gas utilities in the sample, three were public utility holding companies.

twentieth century. The high relative frequency of owner control among these firms is probably a result of their more recent attainment of the status of giant corporations.

Owner control is relatively least frequent among transportation companies and utilities. Railroads were the first companies to attain the status of large corporations, and the absence of owner control among them makes sense on that score. Airlines, however, are of quite recent origin. Aircraft manufacturing companies, with which the airlines were connected prior to World War II, show a relatively high frequency of owner control. The absence of owner control among airlines may be related to the particularly strong position of financial institutions in the airline industry. All 7 airlines in the sample met the criteria for financial control at some date during 1967 through 1969. When Howard Hughes, the late billionaire industrialist, tried to gain control of a major airline (Trans World Airlines), he was repulsed by the banks after a widely reported battle in the early 1960s.[70] It may be that the banks have acted to prevent owner control from arising in the airline industry. However, a more certain answer would require an investigation of the origins of the airline industry. Similarly, the absence of owner control among utilities is probably related to the particular history of that sector.[71]

For a breakdown of financial control and owner control by industry (among the industrials in the sample), see Appendix C.

TYPES OF FINANCIAL INSTITUTIONS

Four types of financial institutions were found to have control over at least one company in the sample: commercial banks, investment banks, investment company complexes, and a life insurance company. Table 8 shows the number of companies controlled by each type of financial institution.[72] Commercial banks were found to be the most important by far. Of the 69

70. See Robert Fitch and Mary Oppenheimer, "Who Rules the Corporations?" pt. 2, *Socialist Revolution*, vol. 1, no. 5, 1970, pp. 86-89.

71. It is interesting to note that financial control was most frequent in a regulated sector, while owner control was completely absent in the two regulated sectors.

72. Table 8 refers to the classification excluding control by groups of financial institutions. Since some of the groups of financial institutions include two or more different types of financial institutions, it is ambiguous as to what would be meant by a breakdown of the classification including group control by type of controlling financial institution.

TABLE 8. Financial Control over the Top 200 Nonfinancial Corporations, by Type of Controlling Financial Institution

Type of controlling financial institution	Number of companies controlled*
Commercial banks only	52
Investment banks only	10
Investment companies only	3
Life insurance companies only	1
Commercial banks and investment banks	1
Commercial banks and investment companies	2
All types	69

*Excluding control by groups of financial institutions.

companies under financial control, 55 were controlled by commercial banks. This result confirms the view presented in chapter 3 that commercial banks have replaced investment banks as the most powerful financial institutions.

Investment banks were the second most powerful financial institutions, controlling 11 companies, one-fifth as many as did commercial banks. Investment company complexes and life insurance companies together controlled 6 companies in the sample.

Although investment banks are no longer as important as commercial banks, they are important for one particular group of companies: the "high-flying" conglomerates of the 1960s. Five such companies that were active participants in the 1960s merger movement were found to be under financial control. The 5 were International Telephone and Telegraph, Ling-Temco-Vought, Avco Corporation, FMC, and Ogden.

It is not difficult to see why investment banks would gain influence over these conglomerates. Their program of one merger after another required the issuance of many kinds of securities: common and preferred stock, debentures, notes, warrants, and so forth. Heavy dependence on the capital market can lead to dependence on an investment bank. Investment banks would be likely to want a position of influence over such companies, since it would bring them a lot of business. The investment bank receives fees not just for planning and floating new security issues, but for finding merger partners as well.

The working definitions of financial control recognized two sources of power over nonfinancial corporations, stockholding and a capital supplier relationship. Table 9 shows the frequency of those two sources of power among the cases of financial control in the sample. Stockholding was found to be a much more common source of financial control than was the capital supplier relationship. This result probably partly reflects the greater caution with which the capital supplier relationship was treated in setting up the working definitions of financial control. However, these results do suggest an historical change in the basis of financial control. Prior to World War II and the rapid growth of bank trust departments, the capital supplier relationship was the most important basis of financial control. In the current results the capital supplier relationship assumes greater importance when control by groups of financial institutions is included, but it is still much less important than stockholdings.

THE MOST POWERFUL FINANCIAL INSTITUTIONS

Which particular financial institutions were found to be most important in this study? Table 10 lists the financial institutions that controlled two or more companies in the sample. The Chase Manhattan Bank stands out, controlling 16 companies, more than twice as many as Morgan Guarantee Trust, which controls the second largest number of companies. In terms of the value of assets of companies controlled, however, Mellon National Bank is the second most important.

As has been the case since the late nineteenth century, New York City stands out as the center of financial control. Of the 13 commercial and investment banks that controlled two or

TABLE 9. Financial Control Over the Top 200 Nonfinancial Corporations, by Source of Control

	Number of companies under financial control	
Source of financial control	Excluding control by groups of financial institutions	Including control by groups of financial institutions
Stockholding only	49	48
Capital supplier only	15	22
Both of above	4	7
Other	1	1
All sources	69	78

TABLE 10. Financial Institutions Controlling More Than One Company
among the Top 200

Financial institution	Number of controlled companies	Assets of companies controlled (millions of dollars)
Chase Manhattan Bank, New York	16	21,691
Morgan Guarantee Trust, New York	7	9,212
First National Bank, Chicago	6	10,953
Bankers Trust Company, New York	5	5,764
Mellon National Bank, Pittsburgh	3	11,190
Kuhn, Loeb and Company, New York	3	8,930
First National City Bank, New York	3	6,198
Lehman Brothers, New York	3	3,435
Cleveland Trust Company, Cleveland	3	3,383
Lazard, Freres and Company, New York	2	6,443
U.S. Trust, New York	2	3,830
Wachovia Bank and Trust, Winston-Salem	2	2,990
Mercantile-Safe Deposit and Trust, Baltimore	2	2,387

more companies, 8 are based in New York. Of the 69 companies
under financial control, 46, or just over two-thirds, were controlled by a New York financial institution. The other important cities for financial control were Chicago, Pittsburgh, and
Cleveland. Chicago financial institutions, which came in second
to New York, controlled 7 companies.

The New York financial institutions that were found to be most powerful in 1967 through 1969 are directly descended from the most powerful financial groups of the early part of this century. As was discussed above, Chase Manhattan Bank is associated with the Rockefeller family, and Morgan Guarantee Trust and Bankers Trust are descended from the old Morgan interests. The First National City Bank is descended from the old Stillman-Rockefeller National City Bank. Kuhn, Loeb and Company was a leading New York investment bank and controller of railroads beginning in the late nineteenth century. Lehman Brothers has its origins as a powerful financial institution in the first decades of this century.

Table 11 shows the number and total assets of companies controlled by the four groups of financial institutions. The Chicago and Cleveland financial institutions have been added to this table as groups. They have not been defined as groups for control purposes, and adding them to Table 11 merely combines the companies controlled by the individual financial institutions in each of those cities.

The Chase group is found to be the largest in terms of number and assets of companies controlled. The Morgan group is approximately three-fourths as large in terms of either number or assets of companies controlled.

Appendix D presents information on the companies controlled by each of the 6 groups of financial institutions covered by Table 11. The Chase group controls more than 10 percent of the top 200 nonfinancial corporations, representing 6.9 percent of the assets of the top 200. This group of financial institutions controls 5 transportation companies, including 3 airlines and 2

TABLE 11. Number and Assets of Companies among the Top 200 Controlled by the Four Groups of Financial Institutions and by Cleveland and Chicago Financial Institutions

Group	Number of companies controlled	Assets of companies controlled (millions of dollars)
Chase group	21	29,966
Morgan group	15	22,417
Chicago financial institutions	7	12,150
Mellon group	5	14,278
Lehman-Goldman, Sachs group	5	7,262
Cleveland financial institutions	4	4,937

railroads (Table D-1). It also controls 2 aircraft companies, 2 chemical companies, 2 diversified manufacturing companies, and 2 retail trade companies.[73] All of the companies in transportation, aircraft manufacturing, chemicals, and diversified manufacturing that are controlled by the Chase group are also controlled by Chase Manhattan Bank as a single institution.

The Morgan group shows even greater specialization by industry than the Chase group. Five of the 15 companies controlled by this group are office machinery and professional and scientific equipment firms (including computers). The Morgan group has a strong position in a sixth, International Business Machines.[74] The Morgan group also controls 3 paper companies and 2 nonferrous metal producers.

Firms controlled by the Chicago financial institutions include 3 railroads or railroad holding companies. The Chicago financial institutions, like the Mellon group, rarely share control with outside financial institutions or individual stockholders. The Mellon group shows a marked preference for heavy industrial producer goods. This no doubt reflects its base in Pittsburgh where such industries are concentrated.

The importance of investment banks in the control of conglomerates was discussed above. The Lehman-Goldman, Sachs group controls 2 conglomerates, Avco Corporation and Ling-Temco-Vought. Both the Lehman-Goldman, Sachs group and the Cleveland financial institutions show a greater frequency of shared control with individual stockholders than do the other groups.

FINANCIAL CONTROL AND OWNER CONTROL

Many corporations begin their life as owner-controlled corporations and later come under financial control. Chapter 3 described a case of such a transition, J. P. Morgan's successful effort to force Andrew Carnegie to allow his steel company to

73. For a discussion of the industry groupings referred to here and below, see app. C.

74. Banker's Trust had a representative on I. B. M.'s executive committee, and Prudential Life held $273 million of I. B. M.'s long-term debt, equal to 49 percent of the company's long-term debt. However, I. B. M. used very little long-term debt financing, its long-term debt equalling only 7 percent of assets in 1969, which was less than half the average for manufacturing corporations. Therefore, I. B. M. did not meet the requirements for control by the Morgan group. (Sources: I. B. M. *Annual Report*, 1969; Prudential Life *Schedule of Securities*, 1969; Moody's *Industrial Manual*, 1971.)

become part of Morgan's United States Steel Company in 1901. By analyzing the control situation of 3 companies in the sample during 1967-1969, one can get a suggestive cross-sectional picture of the development of owner control into financial control.

The first of the 3, H. J. Heinz Corporation, was controlled by H. J. Heinz, II, son of the company's founder. He held 26 percent of the company's stock and was chairman of the board. Another family member, V. I. Heinz, also served on the board.[75]

Also serving on the board of Heinz was J. A. Mayer, the chairman of Mellon National Bank. The bulk of H. J. Heinz, II's holdings of Heinz Corporation stock was kept in the trust department of the Mellon National Bank. However, the bank merely acts as holder of the stock and does not have authority to vote the shares.[76] At this point the bank may be said to be an ally of the Heinz family, helping them to perpetuate their control over the corporation and providing loan funds and probably financial advice for the company.[77]

The agreement under which the bank holds the stock specifies that H. J. Heinz, II, has the right to vote the shares as long as he is a director of the Heinz Corporation.[78] When Mr. Heinz retires, if he has a son, daughter, or other relative who wishes to run the business, control may remain in the family. If not, one may speculate that the right to vote the stock, and with it control over the company, may, over time, pass to the bank.

The relationship between Firestone Tire and Rubber Company and Cleveland Trust Company exemplifies a more advanced stage of transition to financial control. The Firestone family owned beneficially 21.1 percent of the company's stock.[79] Four family members served as directors; one of them was chairman and chief executive officer, and two were presidents of divisions.[80]

At least one-fourth of the reported family holding of the company's stock was kept in the trust department of Cleveland Trust.[81] Whether the family has voting rights over that portion

75. H. J. Heinz Corporation Proxy statement, 1970; *Commercial Banks and their Trust Activities*, vol. 1, table 16.

76. *Ibid.*

77. The Mellon National Bank had a maximum of $18 million in short-term loans to the company during April 1969 through April 1970 (H. J. Heinz Corporation Proxy statement, 1970).

78. H. J. Heinz Corporation Proxy statement, 1970.

79. Firestone Tire and Rubber Proxy statement, 1970.

80. Firestone Tire and Rubber *Annual Report*, 1969.

81. Firestone Proxy statement, 1970.

of the stock is uncertain. It is known that Cleveland Trust has sole or partial voting authority over 13.2 percent of Firestone Tire and Rubber's stock.[82] The president of the bank sits on the board of Firestone. Unlike the case of Mellon National Bank and the H. J. Heinz Corporation, Cleveland Trust has an important source of power over the Firestone company. This latter case appears to represent shared owner and financial control.

The relationship between Seaboard Coast Line Industries, a major railroad, and Mercantile-Safe Deposit and Trust of Baltimore, presents a graphic example of full transition from owner control to financial control. The bank held 54.4 percent of the stock of Atlantic Coast Line Company in 1967, having full voting rights over 51.7 percent and partial voting rights over 2.4 percent.[83] The Atlantic Coast Line Company was a holding company which owned 16.5 percent of the stock of Seaboard Coast Line Industries in 1969.[84] The chairman of Mercantile-Safe Deposit and Trust, William E. McGuirk, Jr., was also chairman of the executive committee of Atlantic Coast Line Company and of Seaboard Coast Line Industries. This represents as clear a case of bank control as one could find.

According to the 1969 report to the Interstate Commerce Commission filed by Atlantic Coast Line Company, the huge block of its stock held by the bank was held under a large number of trusts and wills, with fifty-one beneficiaries. The bulk of the stock was in trusts for the descendents of a Henry Walters.[85] According to John Moody, Henry Walters put together the Atlantic Coast Line Railroad around 1900.[86] In 1967 the Atlantic Coast Line Railroad merged with the Seaboard Air Line Railroad to form the Seaboard Coast Line Railroad. Seaboard Coast Line Industries is the parent holding company of Seaboard Coast Line Railroad.[87]

One can surmise that in the seventy years since 1900, Henry Walters' controlling block of stock in Atlantic Coast Line Railroad was divided among a particularly numerous group of heirs. Continuing the surmise, the block apparently stayed intact, and perhaps supplemented by additional shares, found its way into Mercantile-Safe Deposit and Trust's trust department. Over time

82. *Commercial Banks and their Trust Activities,* vol. 1, table 16.
83. *Ibid.*
84. Seaboard Coast Line Industries Proxy statement, 1969.
85. *Disclosure of Corporate Ownership,* table 10.
86. John Moody, *The Masters of Capital* (New Haven, 1919), p. 107.
87. Moody's *Transportation Manual,* 1970, pp. 440-42, and 1967, pp. 69-70,
88.

the bank obtained full voting authority over almost all of the shares.

Not all cases of financial control are based on a bank's obtaining a big block of stock from a founding family. By 1969 a greater share of the trust assets of the 50 largest commercial banks (ranked by trust assets) came from employee benefit plans than from personal trusts.[88] In many cases a bank simply buys a large block of stock in a company, using its employee benefit plan funds. Whether this route to financial control is more typical than the route of transfer from a founding family cannot be ascertained from the available data. One would expect the former to be the more rapidly growing phenomenon of the two. When a bank trust department uses employee benefit fund assets to buy a controlling block of a company's stock, this may also represent a transition from owner to financial control, although an indirect one.

COMPARISON OF LARNER'S RESULTS
TO THESE RESULTS

It is instructive to compare these results for control over the 200 largest nonfinancial corporations for 1967-1969 to the widely cited study of corporate control by Robert Larner for 1963.[89] Larner also classified the 200 largest nonfinancial corporations, ranked by assets, according to type of control. He employed five control categories: private ownership, majority control, minority control, control through a legal device, and management control. The first four categories are different subcases of what is classified in this study as owner control; Larner did not have a category of financial control.[90] He found 16.5 percent of his sample to be under owner control, classifying the remaining 83.5 percent under management control.[91]

Before comparing Larner's results to mine, one must take account of the difference in the treatment of utilities. Larner's sample was based on strict asset ranking; as a result, it had 59 utilities, compared to my 10. A better comparison looks at

88. *Institutional Investor Study Report*, vol. 2, p. 430.

89. Robert J. Larner, "Ownership and Control of the 200 Largest Nonfinancial Corporations, 1929 and 1963," *American Economic Review* (September 1966); also Larner, *Management Control and The Large Corporation* (Cambridge, Mass., 1970).

90. Larner's definition of owner control is close to ours but not identical. See above, p. 83.

91. Larner, *Management Control*, p. 12.

Larner's 141 industrial, retail trade, and transportation companies, and my 141 top nonfinancial corporations excluding utilities.

Tables 12 and 13 compare Larner's classification of his top 141 non-utility companies with my classification of my top 141 non-utility companies (excluding control by groups of financial institutions). His results show 22.7 percent under owner control and 77.3 percent under management control. I found owner control slightly less common, amounting to 19.1 percent of the reduced sample. However, 40.4 percent are under financial control. Only 42.6 percent of my 141 companies have no identified center of control.

TABLE 12.   Larner's Control Results for the 141
Largest Nonfinancial Corporations Excluding
Utilities, 1963*

Control category	Number of companies	Percent of companies
Owner control**	32	22.7
Management control	109	77.3
All categories	141	100.0

*From Robert J. Larner, *Management Control and the Large Corporation* (Cambridge, Mass., 1970), p. 12.
**I have combined Larner's categories of private ownership, majority ownership, minority control, and control through a legal device under the title "owner control."

TABLE 13.   My Control Results for the 141 Largest Nonfinancial
Corporations Excluding Utilities, 1967-69*

Control category	Number of companies	Percent of companies
1. Financial control only	49	34.8
2. Both financial and owner control	8	5.7
3. Owner control only	19	13.5
4. Miscellaneous	5	3.5
5. No identified center of control	60	42.6
All categories	141	100.0
All financial control (1+2)	57	40.4
All owner control (2+3)	27	19.1

*Excluding control by groups of financial institutions.

The widely held belief that the managerial revolution of corporate control was almost complete by the 1960s is based on evidence that overlooks one of the most important forms of corporate control. Financial control, which was so widely recognized in the early part of this century, remains an important form of control over large nonfinancial corporations in the present. In the post-World War II period, bank trust department assets, the main basis of the power of financial institutions today, have been growing rapidly. A comparison of Berle and Means' results, Larner's results, and my results suggests that owner control has been declining in importance. If both of these trends continue, and unless some counteracting trends develop, one would expect financial control to become still more widespread among large nonfinancial corporations in the future.

CHAPTER FIVE

The Exercise of Financial Control and Its Significance

In the study of the 200 largest nonfinancial corporations during 1967 to 1969, a substantial proportion were found to be controlled by financial institutions. The definition of control being used, however, is a passive one. A financial institution controlling a nonfinancial corporation has the *power* to determine the broad policies guiding that corporation. This suggests the question: how actively do financial institutions exercise their power? Spokesmen for financial institutions generally deny that they exercise significant influence over nonfinancial corporations that they hold stock in or supply capital to. However, historical experience indicates that such assurances cannot be taken at face value. J. P. Morgan at the height of his power denied that he exercised any influence over American business.[1]

In cases of financial control, the evidence suggests that a range of relationships exists between the controlling institution and the controlled corporation. In some extreme cases representatives of the financial institution actively supervise the nonfinancial corporation on a continuing basis. An example involves the Union Pacific Railroad. In 1969 two partners in Brown Brothers Harriman, a private bank located in New York, served as board chairman and chairman of the executive committee of the Union Pacific; a third partner in the bank was a member of the executive committee.[2] This relationship goes back to the early part of this century, when E. H. Harriman obtained control over the Union Pacific with Stillman-Rockefeller backing.[3]

1. See chapter 3.
2. See app. B, table B-1, section A.
3. See chapter 3.

In other cases a financial institution may play a relatively passive role for some time and then intervene actively as a result of special problems that arise for the nonfinancial corporation. For example, Anaconda Copper was found to be controlled by the Chase group in 1969. Chase Manhattan and Metropolitan Life together held 23 percent of the company's long-term debt, and each had a representative on Anaconda's board.[4] During 1971 the Chilean Government expropriated Anaconda's facilities in that country, which represented two-thirds of the company's copper production.[5] This placed Anaconda in a precarious financial position. Large injections of capital would be required to enable the company to develop new copper sources.

In May of 1971 Anaconda announced that its chairman, C. Jay Parkinson, was stepping down. The former Salt Lake City lawyer was replaced by John M. B. Place, the vice chairman of Chase Manhattan Bank. Place took over the presidency as well as the chairmanship of Anaconda. Apparently Chase wanted to be able to exercise control over Anaconda directly, while raising the capital to steer the company through a difficult period.[6]

In yet other cases a financial institution may exercise its power over a nonfinancial corporation occasionally by giving advice to management or by voting its stock against management proposals that are submitted to the stockholders. If the management's performance generally satisfies a controlling financial institution, the latter may not intervene at all for a long period of time.

This chapter will first consider the extent to which financial institutions use the several means available to them for exercising their control over nonfinancial corporations. Second, the implications that present-day financial control has for the market behavior of nonfinancial corporations will be analyzed. Finally, this chapter will discuss the broader social and economic significance of financial control.

THE MEANS OF EXERCISING FINANCIAL CONTROL

A financial institution can actively exercise its control over a nonfinancial corporation in two main ways: by placing a repre-

---

4. See app. B, table B-2.
5. Anaconda Copper *Annual Report*, 1971, p. 3.
6. *Fortune*, June 1971, p. 33. See also Anaconda Copper *Annual Report*, 1970, 1971.

sentative in the management of the nonfinancial corporation, or by exerting informal pressure on the nonfinancial corporation's management from the outside.[7] Another more limited method of exercising control, which is available to a financial institution holding stock in a nonfinancial corporation, is actively voting the stock on proposals that are submitted to the stockholders. Each of these means of exercising financial control will be considered in turn.

Representation in Management

The results of the above study of control over the 200 largest nonfinancial corporations provide evidence on the extent to which financial institutions place representatives on the boards of nonfinancial corporations that they control. Ideally, one would want to ask, for all the nonfinancial corporations found to be under financial control: in how many cases did the controlling financial institution have representatives on the nonfinancial corporation's board? However, such a figure would be misleading as an indicator of how frequently financial institutions use this means of exercising control. The reason is that director representation was one of the *criteria* for determining whether a nonfinancial corporation was under financial control. Specifically, if a financial institution that was a leading capital supplier to a nonfinancial corporation also had strong representation on the nonfinancial corporation's board, the corporation was classified under financial control.[8] This difficulty arises from regarding director representation to be both an indication of the existence of financial control and a means of exercising financial control. This problem can be avoided by restricting attention to those cases of financial control not involving director representation as part of the basis of the control classification. Thus, one can inquire about the frequency of director representation as a means of exercising financial control for those instances in which a stockholder relationship, or a stockholder plus a capital supplier relationship, were the sole basis of classifying the nonfinancial corporation as under financial control.

An *instance* of financial control will be defined to be a financial institution — nonfinancial corporation pairing in which

---

7. The reader should be reminded that the term "management" refers to the directors and senior officers of a corporation.

8. See chapter 4.

the financial institution has control over the nonfinancial corporation. Since a number of the corporations found to be under financial control were controlled by two or more financial institutions, the number of instances of financial control exceeds the number of corporations under financial control. For example, Sperry Rand was under financial control by both Chase Manhattan Bank and Bankers Trust, which gives two instances of financial control. Excluding control by groups of financial institutions, there were 81 instances of financial control, involving 69 nonfinancial corporations, among the sample of 200 nonfinancial corporations. Director representation was part of the basis of classification in 20 of those instances. In 4 additional instances, the identity of the controlling financial institution was unknown. That leaves 57 instances of financial control (involving 47 nonfinancial corporations) which we can examine for frequency of director representation as a means of exercising financial control.

In only 14 of these 57 instances did the controlling financial institution have a representative on the board of the corporation it controlled. Of the 14 cases of director representation, 8 involved "strong representation" (two representatives or one "key" representative — see chapter 4).

Stockholding was the basis of financial control in all of the 57 instances under consideration. The frequency of director representation was significantly related to the percent of the nonfinancial corporation's stock held by the controlling financial institution. Of the 10 instances of financial control for which the controlling financial institution held 10 percent or more of the corporation's outstanding stock, 6 involved director representation of the financial institution on the corporation's board. Of the 42 instances of financial control for which the controlling financial institution had between 5 percent and 10 percent of the corporation's stock, only 6, or 14 percent of the instances, involved director representation of the financial institution on the corporation's board.[9]

These results suggest that, in instances of financial control in which the controlling financial institution holds 10 percent or more of the corporation's stock, the controlling financial

9. The total number of instances for the two categories does not add up to fifty-seven because five of the instances of financial control involved indirect financial control through an intermediary nonfinancial corporation, which made it impossible to place the relationship unambiguously into the percentage categories used.

institution usually does use board representation as a means of exercising control.[10] However, in the far more numerous instances of financial control based on a 5 percent to 10 percent stockholding, the results indicate that exercise of financial control by means of board representation is the exception rather than the rule.

A possible source of error in these results is that some cases of representatives of financial institutions sitting on corporate boards may have gone undetected. A financial institution may be represented on the board of a nonfinancial corporation not only by an officer of the financial institution but also by a member of a corporate law firm associated with the financial institution, by a retired officer of the financial institution, by an officer of an affiliated financial institution or nonfinancial corporation, or by a personal or business associate of a top officer of the controlling financial institution. Although it was easier to discover board representation when the representative was an officer of the financial institution, attempts were made to uncover the less obvious cases of board representation as well. It is unlikely that a sufficiently large number of financial institution representatives were overlooked to basically alter the results. Even if only half of the actual cases of board representation by financial institutions holding 5 percent to 10 percent of a corporation's stock were detected, this would increase the number of such instances of board representation to only 12 out of the 42 instances of financial control involving a 5 percent to 10 percent stockholding. Including control by groups of financial institutions does not appreciably alter the results. Only two additional instances of board representation by the controlling group are found when control by groups of financial institutions is included.

There are several possible explanations for the low incidence of board representation as a means of exercising financial control. One reason, applying only to a subset of the sample, is regulatory barriers to director interlocks. A bank that is a major equipment lessor to airlines is considered to be "engaged in a phase of aeronautics"; hence, any director interlocks between such a bank and an airline would be subject to investigation by

10. Of course, the presence of representatives of a financial institution on a corporate board does not prove that these representatives use their position to actively exercise control over that corporation. Only case studies can provide conclusive proof for individual cases.

the Civil Aeronautics Board.[11]   This may well explain the absence of any representatives of Chase Manhattan Bank, a major equipment lessor to airlines, on the boards of the three airlines it controls.

A second reason is that financial institutions are anxious to avoid the appearance of actively intervening in the affairs of corporations that they hold stock in. Since J. P. Morgan, Jr., and his partners stepped down from the boards of twenty-seven corporations in the wake of the Pujo Committee Hearings in 1914, bankers have been wary of charges that director representation forms the basis of "financial empires."[12]   It may be that when a financial institution's stockholding in a nonfinancial corporation exceeds 10 percent, the financial institution's possession of control becomes sufficiently obvious that little is lost by placing a representative on the corporate board. With holdings of 5 percent to 10 percent, however, control is less obvious, and the public relations payoff of avoiding director representation is greater.[13]

A third reason for the low incidence of director representation is the passive role that boards of directors play in some nonfinancial corporations. The activeness of corporate boards varies from company to company, and in cases where the board is largely ceremonial, director representation would be an ineffective way of exercising control.[14]

Whether a board is active or passive, a controlling financial institution may prefer to exercise its control by other means than director representation. Even in the heyday of interlocking directorates, the powerful investment banker Jacob Schiff had a policy of not sitting on corporate boards.[15]   Control may be exercised more effectively in some cases in one-to-one discussions between a financial institution's representative and the

11. U. S., Congress, Senate Government Operations Committee, Subcommittee on Intergovernmental Relations, and on Budgeting, Management, and Expenditure, *Corporate Disclosure*, Hearings, 93rd Congress, 2nd Session, 1974, vol. I, p. 206, testimony of Reuben H. Robertson III (hereafter cited as *Corporate Disclosure*, Hearings).

12. See chapter 3.

13. One may also interpret this as evidence that when a financial institution holds 5 percent to 10 percent of a corporation's stock, such a holding is usually too little to provide the basis for financial control, whereas a 10 percent or greater stockholding is sufficient for control. However, such a conclusion overlooks the other methods of exercising financial control apart from director representation.

14. For example, see Stanley C. Vance, *The Corporate Director* (Homewood, Ill., 1968); and Myles L. Mace, *Directors: Myth and Reality* (Boston, 1971).

15. See chapter 3, n. 5.

chief executive officer of a nonfinancial corporation than in the context of a meeting of twelve or sixteen directors with differing interests in the corporation. Although membership on the corporation's board, particularly membership on the finance committee or executive committee, may increase the effectiveness with which a financial institution's representative can pressure the chief executive officer in a one-to-one discussion, the lack of such membership may not be much of a handicap for a financial institution possessing a stockholding of 5 percent or more of the nonfinancial corporation's stock.

The Voting of Stock

The legal form of the corporation is that of a "representative democracy" of shareholders rather than a "direct democracy."[16] While some issues are put directly to the shareholders for a vote, such as executive stock option plans or changes in shareholder rights, basic corporate policies are set by the management and are not usually voted on directly by shareholders. However, occasionally shareholders vote on issues that have an important impact on the corporation. When a proxy fight is initiated by dissident shareholders to replace the existing management, the right to vote stock becomes a very powerful right. Do financial institutions exercise their voting rights over stock in nonfinancial corporations in such a way as to influence the direction of the corporation? Or do they automatically vote with management?

Spokesmen for commercial banks generally say that they vote the stock they hold in trust according to their evaluation of the interests of the beneficiaries. A report of the Trust and Investment Division of Morgan Guarantee Trust made the following statement about its voting policy:

> Just as with investment decisions, officers of the [Trust and Investment] Division consider proposals in term of the best interests of the party or parties for whom the shares are held. Not surprisingly, since the holding of a company's shares as an investment reflects confidence in the management, most of our votes on proposals have coincided with the recommendation of company managements.[17]

16. Of course, this type of "democracy" does not go by the rule "one person, one vote," since a shareholder's voting power depends on the number and type of shares held.

17. *Report of the Trust and Investment Division of Morgan Guarantee Trust Company,* May 1972, p. 13.

The above report goes on to state that sometimes the bank does vote against management recommendations, having done so eight times in 1971 and four times in 1970.[18]   Thus, in some cases the bank did exercise its voting power in opposition to management, although it is not known whether the instances referred to involved large or small portfolio companies.[19]

The Securities and Exchange Commission's *Institutional Investor Study Report* obtained some systematic evidence on the frequency with which various types of institutional investors vote against management.[20]   The sample of institutional investors included forty-nine major bank trust departments, seventy-six major investment advisors (most of which manage investment company complexes), and twenty-six major life insurance companies. Only 18 percent of the banks and 20 percent of the investment advisors had policies of automatically voting with management or turning in blank ballots. Thirty-one percent of the life insurance companies had such a policy.[21]

Among the forty-nine banks in the sample, twenty-eight, or 57 percent, had voted against management at least once during 1967-1969. These twenty-eight banks opposed management in 351 instances. Opposition to management was much less common among investment advisors and life insurance companies. Only 20 percent of the investment advisors had opposed management at least once, involving 143 instances; 38 percent of the life insurance companies had voted against management at least once, involving 62 instances.[22]

The results of this study indicate that, although financial institutions, commercial banks included, usually vote to support management's recommendations, most large commercial banks do sometimes vote negatively. A few financial institutions told the Securities and Exchange Commission that, in the words of the study's authors, "even if negative voting did not result in the defeat of a mangement proposal, it might have a broader impact in terms of confining managerial discretion."[23]   Finan-

18. *Ibid.*

19. The *Institutional Investor Study Report* uses the term "portfolio company" to refer to a corporation, the stock of which is held by an institutional investor. U. S., Securities and Exchange Commission, *Institutional Investor Study Report*, House Document 92-64, 1971.

20. The data applied to the period 1 January 1967 to 30 September 1969.

21. *Institutional Investor Study Report*, vol. 5, p. 2764.

22. *Ibid.*, p. 2766.

23. *Ibid.*, p. 2754.

cial institutions voted negatively most often on the following matters: proposals to abolish or limit pre-emptive rights of shareholders; proposals to increase the percentage of shareholder votes needed to approve a proposal (having the effect of insulating management against take-overs); issuance of additional stock; and plans to grant stock options, warrants or rights.[24] Thus, financial institutions opposed management attempts to increase management power and privileges and reduce shareholder power and privileges. This apparent conflict between stockholding financial institutions and portfolio company managements will be discussed below, in evaluating the implications of the growth of financial control for the managerial thesis.

Informal Pressure

Financial institutions do not rely very frequently on director representation as a means of exercising their control over nonfinancial corporations, at least where a 5 percent to 10 percent stockholding is the source of the financial institution's control. Voting on proposals submitted to shareholders is normally not an important means of influencing corporate policy. If financial institutions do often actively exercise their control over nonfinancial corporations, one must conclude that they do so mainly by exerting informal pressure on the nonfinancial corporation's management.[25]

The Securities and Exchange Commission's *Institutional Investor Study Report* asked a sample of leading financial institutions how often the institution expressed its views about corporate policy to a portfolio company's management. The financial institutions reported a low frequency of such "participation," as the Securities and Exchange Commission called it. Less than one-fifth of the financial institutions, and less than one-fourth of the commerical banks, admitted to participating in general corporate matters at least once between 1 January 1968 and 30 September 1969.[26] Cases of participation most commonly involved financing or acquisitions matters, and also, although

---

24. *Ibid.*
25. As discussed in chapter 2, a financial institution's control over a corporation may be translated into policy making passively, if the management of the corporation attempts to follow the financial institution's wishes on major matters in order to forestall intervention by the financial institution. See chapter 2.
26. *Institutional Investor Study Report*, vol. 5, pp. 2768-9.

somewhat less frequently, selection of directors and officers, accounting policy, operations, and dividends and distributions.[27]

The *Institutional Investor Study Report* stated, however, that its quantitative results on this subject "appear inconsistent with narrative responses . . . and with interviews conducted by the Study staff."[28] Specifically, the report said that the quantitative data appeared to understate the extent of institutional participation, particularly regarding corporate acquisitions, and that "the extent of their informal participation in corporate affairs remains largely unknown."[29] Explaining the inaccuracy of these results, the report concluded:

> At a time when institutional growth and its implications are under Congressional as well as general governmental scrutiny, it must be anticipated that many institutions may attempt to project a rather low profile of involvement in corporate affairs. The Study recognized that its inquiries into these matters might generate defensive responses reflecting sensitivity to the underlying policy implications.[30]

Under these circumstances, aggregate questionnaire data on financial institutions' participation in portfolio companies' affairs are of limited reliability. Detailed case studies, which are outside the scope of this study, must be undertaken to determine the extent of informal pressure that financial institutions exert on the management of corporations that they have control over.

In their public statements, spokesmen for financial institutions generally deny that they exert informal pressure on corporations they hold stock in, although they acknowledge that they may do so in certain cases with corporations that are debtors of the financial institution. George M. Lingua, a Senior Vice-President of First National City Bank, was asked by Senator Charles Percy, during a Senate Subcommittee hearing, whether First National City Bank would be more likely "to get pretty deep into the management and into supervising the decisions which are made . . ." for a company in debt to the bank or for a company in which the bank held a large block of stock. Mr. Lingua replied, "It is much more likely to happen in the

27. *Ibid.*, p. 2770.
28. *Ibid.*, p. 2762.
29. *Ibid.*, pp. 2762-3.
30. *Ibid.*

commercial side of the bank. It would not happen on the trust side of the bank."[31]

Mr. Lingua stated that in cases where the bank held a significant percentage of a corporation's stock, "If they were to take a course which we believe (sic) was detrimental in the long run to the interests of the corporation and stockholders, we would sell the shares."[32] However, Mr. Lingua said that his bank might have "influence" over a portfolio corporation, although not "control."[33] He stated, "It is not quite passive for them to know if we disagree strongly for good reason that we would sell their stock. That is a more effective vote than executing a proxy and sending it in."[34]

There are reasons for doubting the banker claims that a disagreement with management always leads to sale of the stock rather than pressure on the management to change its course. If a financial institution holds 5 percent or more of the stock of a large corporation, selling the stock in a short period of time may harm the financial institution as much as the nonfinancial corporation, if the large sales drive down the price. The *Institutional Investor Study Report* said that one bank reported "that it might prefer to exert its influence over a portfolio company in which it had a substantial holding rather than engage in a costly sale of shares and a purchase of a comparable alternative investment."[35] There are also reported cases of other types of financial institutions exerting informal pressure on managements. A study of investment advisors found such instances involving an investment company manager named Fred Alger: "Twice in 1968, when stocks Alger owned showed signs of going sour, he refused to unload them. Instead he spent much time discussing the companies' problems with management, and eventually he helped arrange mergers for both companies."[36]

It is hoped that case studies to be undertaken in the future by this author and other researchers will shed more light on the question of financial institutions' use of informal pressure on the managements of corporations they control, particularly in

31. *Corporate Disclosure*, Hearings, pt. I, p. 78.
32. *Ibid.*, p. 64.
33. *Ibid.*, p. 63.
34. *Ibid.*, p. 64.
35. *Institutional Investor Study Report*, vol. 5, p. 2761.
36. Gilbert E. Kaplan and Chris Wells, *The Money Managers* (New York, 1969), pp. 31-32.

cases of control based on stockholdings. Control based on stockholdings has become the most widespread form of financial control and is becoming still more widespread; and it is in cases of control based on stockholdings that the question of exercise of financial control is most heavily disputed by the financial institutions.

THE IMPLICATIONS OF FINANCIAL CONTROL FOR MARKET BEHAVIOR

The finding that financial institutions, particularly commercial banks, have control over a substantial number of large nonfinancial corporations has implications for the expected market behavior of large nonfinancial corporations. This section will explore these implications of financial control. Wherever possible, examples and statistical studies will be cited to illustrate and support the behavioral hypotheses developed.

Financial Markets

Proponents of the managerial thesis disagree among themselves about many of the implications of the alleged ascendance of corporate managements to a position of ultimate controller. However, all of them agree that management-controlled corporations would avoid the use of external debt financing, in order to preserve management's freedom of action.[37] Management-controlled corporations are expected to follow a policy of retaining a high proportion of after-tax profits and relying mainly on retained earnings, along with depreciation allowances, to meet the firm's capital needs. A management-controlled corporation may use some external debt capital, but when it does so, the corporate borrower is seen as the dominant figure in the transaction. According to this view, banks and other financial institutions compete vigorously to obtain the business of providing capital to large, management-controlled corporations. Thus, when it does seek external debt financing, the management-controlled corporation is assumed to be usually able to get what it needs on terms that are quite favorable to the borrower.

---

37. For example, see Adolf A. Berle, *The Twentieth Century Capitalist Revolution* (New York, 1954), pp. 39-42; Robin Marris, *The Economic Theory of 'Managerial' Capitalism* (Glencoe, Ill., 1964), p. 107; Carl Kaysen, "Another View of Corporate Capitalism," *Quarterly Journal of Economics* (February 1965), pp. 41-51.

The financial control thesis leads to different expectations about the financing of large corporations. A corporation controlled by a commercial bank would not be expected to avoid use of external debt financing. Whether the source of the bank's control is stockholding or a capital supplier relationship, the bank, as a potential supplier of loans, would have an interest in the corporation utilizing a substantial amount of external debt capital. Similarly, a corporation controlled by an investment bank or life insurance company can also be expected to use a substantial amount of external debt capital. Thus, one would not expect a nonfinancial corporation that is under financial control to avoid external debt financing, as a management-controlled corporation would; rather, a corporation under financial control would use external debt capital at least to the extent dictated by profit maximization, and possibly to a greater extent.[38] Of course, the controlling financial institution, as a creditor of the corporation, would not be likely to favor such excessive reliance on external debt that the safety of the financial institution's loans to the company would be put in question.

The managerial thesis would lead one to expect that, as management control progressively replaced owner control and financial control among large corporations, the relative reliance on external finance would decrease. Chapter 3 cited data which showed that no such long-run trend has occurred between the first decade of this century and the early 1970s.[39] These data may be explained by the continuing importance of financial control, which has limited the growth of power of corporate managements.

The managerial thesis view that the borrowing corporation is normally dominant in loan markets would also be disputed by the financial control thesis. A corporation under financial control by a bank, rather than being in a position to choose freely among many lenders, may be under pressure to borrow from the controlling bank and its allied financial institutions, on terms that are relatively favorable to the financial institutions. The *Institutional Investor Study Report* included some statistical analyses that tend to support the hypothesis that banks which control corporations use their power to obtain a sizable

38. A nonfinancial corporation controlled by an investment company would be expected to use external debt capital to the extent dictated by profit maximization.
39. See chapter 3.

proportion of the corporation's loan business. The report's data applied to 49 of the largest commercial banks and their relationships to a large number of portfolio companies (including corporations not large enough to be in the top 200). Multiple regression analysis found the percentage of a portfolio company's outstanding stock held by a bank trust department to be a signficant explanatory variable for the percentage of the portfolio company's loans held by the bank.[40] This relationship was not statistically significant for life insurance companies or investment advisors. This suggests that banks may use the power associated with holding a large share of a company's stock to influence the share of the company's loan business going to the bank.

Market Competition

The rise of financial control in the late nineteenth century was closely associated with declining market competition. New York investment bankers originally intervened in the railroad industry in an effort to persuade the vigorously competing entrepreneurs to cooperate with one another. The rise of thorough banker control over the leading railroads in the 1890s led to the replacement of vigorous competition by the "community of interest" principle advocated by J. P. Morgan.[41]

In the steel industry the period before bankers achieved dominance was marked by vigorous, often cutthroat competition. Recurring attempts to form pools did not succeed in bridling the short-run competitive behavior of Carnegie, Gates, and other steel entrepreneurs. Once Morgan became the dominant figure in the industry through the creation of United States Steel, cooperation based on price leadership became the rule. Judge Gary, whom Morgan placed in charge of U.S. Steel, held famous "Gary dinners" at which representatives of the leading steel companies formulated common policies.

This suggests the question: does financial control today tend to modify competitive market behavior and encourage

40. *Institutional Investor Study Report*, vol. 5, p. 2747. Other significant independent variables were director interlocks and bank management of portfolio company employee benefit funds, as well as regional proximity, portfolio company size, and bank size. One independent variable, the stock of the portfolio company held by the bank as a percentage of the bank's total stock portfolio value, was not significant.

41. See chapter 3.

more cooperative behavior? The high degree of market concentration found in many industries encourages various forms of tacit collusion in price matters, regardless of the nature of control over the leading companies. However, market structure is not a complete determinant of market conduct. Even in a highly concentrated industry there may be powerful factors tending to undermine cooperative behavior. For example, in an industry with fixed costs that are high relative to total costs, the temptations to violate price agreements are great, particularly when industry demand is depressed. An industry whose sales occur mainly in the form of large, infrequent orders at irregular intervals may have difficulty establishing cooperative pricing behavior.[42] For price cooperation to be effective under such circumstances, each major firm must put the long-run interests of the industry above its own short-run interests. The presence of financial control over the leading firms in an industry may strengthen price cooperation by reinforcing long-run, industry-oriented behavior.

The clearest case occurs when a single financial institution has control over two or more competing firms. For the firm, price cuts may improve its position, but at the expense of its competitors. A controlling financial institution having a large stock interest in and/or creditor relationship to several firms in the industry would have a compelling reason to encourage joint profit-maximizing behavior among the firms — that is, monopolistic price setting.

The United States Department of Justice took the position that financial control may reduce competition, when it filed a civil antitrust suit against Cleveland Trust Company in 1970. This case involves one of the 200 largest nonfinancial corporations, White Consolidated Industries. The complaint focused on Cleveland Trust Company's relationship to four manufacturers of automatic screw machinery. Cleveland Trust held 25 percent of the common stock of Acme-Cleveland Corporation, 14 percent of the common stock of Pneumo-Dynamics Corporation, 5 percent of the common stock of Warner and Swasey Corporation, and a "substantial part(s)" of the common stock of White Consolidated Industries, though less than 5 percent. In each case Cleveland Trust had full or partial voting power over the

---

42. For a detailed discussion of the problems of price coordination in a concentrated industry, see F. M. Scherer, *Industrial Market Structure and Economic Performance* (Chicago, 1971), pp. 183-212.

shares.[43]   Cleveland Trust had a representative on the board of each company, and did "substantial banking business" with all four.[44]   In 1967 Warner and Swasey was the largest seller of automatic screw machinery in the United States, Acme-Cleveland was the third largest, Pneumo-Dynamics the fourth largest, and White Consolidated the seventh.[45]

The complaint charged that Cleveland Trust did not hold stock in the four companies solely for investment: "Cleveland Trust consistently exercises the voting rights to these shares of stock to elect directors, and to influence important management and policy decisions."[46]   The complaint charged that the relationship between the bank and the four companies may tend to lessen actual and potential competition among the four. This case, if the government claims were valid, presents a good example of financial control significantly affecting the degree of competition in an industry. The largest of the four manufacturers involved in the suit accounted for 22.3 percent of total automatic screw machine sales in 1967, but together the four represented 50.6 percent of such sales.[47]

Appendix D records a number of cases of a bank, or group of financial institutions, controlling two or more competing companies. For example, Chase Manhattan Bank was found to control three airlines: Eastern, Northwest, and Trans World Airlines. The Morgan group was found to control three paper manufacturing companies: Crown-Zellerbach, International

43. U. S. vs. Cleveland Trust Company, Civil No. C-70,301, Northern District of Ohio, complaint filed 3/26/70.

44. *Ibid.* White Consolidated Industries was classified under financial control by Cleveland Trust, since Cleveland Trust was a leading capital supplier to White, a heavy user of external finance, and had a representative on the executive committee of White.

45. *Ibid.*

46. *Ibid.*

47. *Ibid.* The case was settled on 14 November 1975 by a consent decree that did not resolve the key issues that the case raised. The consent decree prohibited officers of Cleveland Trust from sitting on the boards of Warner and Swasey and White Consolidated Industries as long as both were engaged in the specified machine tool business. The part of the case dealing specifically with Cleveland Trust's stockholdings in the four companies was dropped in two stages. On 4 October 1972 the Justice Department amended its complaint, limiting the stockholding-related claim to two of the companies, Acme-Cleveland and Pneumo-Dynamics. Then Pneumo-Dynamics sold its machine tool operations, and as a result the court dismissed the section of the complaint dealing with Cleveland Trust's stockholdings in the companies, on 31 July 1974. See *Antitrust and Trade Regulation Report,* 9 September 1975, No. 729, pp. A19-A20.

Paper, and Scott Paper. If the frequency of financial control continues to grow, such cases can be expected to multiply.

Although a case of one financial institution or a close group of financial institutions controlling two or more competing companies carries the clearest implication of reduced competition, there might also be a reduction in competition when two or more competing companies are controlled by unrelated financial institutions. If major financial institutions advocate a policy of "community of interest," as they did in the early part of this century, then their influence may tend to reduce competition even in this weaker case. For example, in the copper industry the Chase group is in control of Anaconda Copper and Morgan Guarantee Trust in control of Kennecott Copper. The Chase and Morgan groups of financial institutions are certainly in a position to exert influence toward cooperative behavior in that industry. On the other hand, if different financial institutions act in a rivalrous manner, such cases of financial control could support competitive practices. The historical evidence suggests to this author, however, that cooperative behavior is the more likely outcome in such situations.

Vertical Relationships

Financial control may affect the behavior of firms not only toward competitors but also toward potential customers or suppliers. In the idealized picture of a market, it is assumed that sellers and buyers — the two sides of the market — are independent of each other. A buyer seeks the best possible purchase in terms of price, quality, and service, and a seller looks for the best possible sale, from his (opposite) point of view. In practice various types of vertical relationships external to the market are found which violate this idealized picture. The most extreme departure occurs within a vertically integrated firm, when one subsidiary "purchases" a product from another subsidiary. A less extreme departure involves a market exchange between two firms, one of which owns a minority stock interest in the other. Informal vertical relationships are commonly found in which a firm establishes a practice of obtaining all of its supplies, or a certain portion of its supplies, of an input product from a particular supplier firm. Such informal vertical relationships may be encouraged by director interlocks, friendships between executives, or the inertia of established practice.

A further possible basis of informal vertical relationships is control by a common source. This suggests the hypothesis that a financial institution may encourage firms under its control to establish regular vertical relationships with one another. The financial institution's aim might be to provide greater stability for the firms involved, through assured markets for the seller and assured sources of supply for the buyer.

In some cases such an arrangement might be set up, not for the mutual benefit of buyer and seller, but for the aid of the seller at the expense of the buyer. For example, if a bank had made large loans to a corporation which was experiencing financial difficulty, it might be in the bank's interest to pressure another corporation under its control to increase purchases of the first corporation's product. If the buyer corporation is a firm possessing a high degree of monopoly power and selling a product with relatively inelastic demand, it may be possible to pass on the cost of helping out the supplier company to the customers of the buyer company by means of price increases.

I have not come across any recent clear-cut examples of banks using their control over large nonfinancial corporations to establish informal vertical relationships. The possibilities are present, however, and this is an important subject for investigation. For example, Chase Manhattan Bank is in control of two aircraft manufacturing companies as well as three airlines. Some writers have suggested that Chase and other New York banks use their control over airlines to influence their buying of airplanes.[48]

If banks do use their power to establish informal vertical relationships, this would have two important economic implications. Since vertical integration, whether formal or informal, involves replacing the market mechanism by a form of planning, bank encouragement of informal vertical integration would further restrict the scope of the market as a resource allocator and expand the role of planning. Writers such as J. K. Galbraith have commented on the expansion of planning that accompanies the rise of the large, vertically integrated corporation.[49] Bank-encouraged informal vertical relationships would represent a further step in that direction.

48. Robert Fitch and Mary Oppenheimer, "Who Rules the Corporations?" pt. 2, Socialist Revolution, vol. 1, no. 5, 1970, pp. 89-91.
49. See John Kenneth Galbraith, New Industrial State (Boston, 1967).

A second implication involves the consequences for competition. Regular vertical relationships between firms may constitute a barrier to entry into a market, if input supplies or sales outlets are "tied up." If banks do encourage regular vertical relationships, this would reduce the degree of market competition over time.

Mergers

In the merger wave of 1898-1903, investment banks played the leading role in encouraging, planning, and carrying out the great industrial combinations. This suggests the question: did financial institutions use their position of control over many nonfinancial corporations to play a role in the great merger wave of the 1960s?

Chapter 3 discussed the dual aims that investment bankers had in fostering mergers during 1898-1903: to reduce competition in manufacturing industries, and to profit from the process of merger.[50] The 1960s merger movement largely involved conglomerate mergers; thus, a desire to reduce competition would not have been such an important motivating force as it was in the 1898-1903 merger wave. However, that still leaves the second aim: the opportunity to profit from the merger process. An investment bank can earn money in various ways by sponsoring a program of mergers and acquisitions on the part of a corporation that the investment bank controls. The investment bank may receive fees for finding merger partners, for providing financial advice regarding mergers and arranging financing for them, and for managing tender offers. The investment bank may also benefit by obtaining the business of new subsidiaries acquired by the corporation.

Investment banks are no longer the most powerful financial institutions, but there were investment banks in control of several active participants in the 1960s merger movement: International Telephone and Telegraph, controlled by Lazard Freres and Company and by Kuhn, Loeb and Company; Ling-Temco-Vought, controlled by the Lehman-Goldman, Sachs group (and by James Ling); Avco Corporation, controlled by Lehman Brothers (and by the Harringtons); FMC, controlled by Lehman Brothers; and Ogden, controlled by Allen and Company. A House Committee investigation of conglomerates in 1969-1971

50. See chapter 3.

found that major investment banks played an active and important role in many of the conglomerate mergers of the 1960s.[51] For example, Lazard Freres was found to have been "intimately associated with ITT's merger program." During 1964-1969 Lazard Freres' income from merger and acquisition services rose 584 percent while its gross income rose only 256 percent.[52]

The rapid series of mergers undertaken by conglomerates in the 1960s usually conferred financial benefits on the stockholders of those companies, at least until the merger movement collapsed in 1969. However, a group of stockholders in one conglomerate, Ogden, charged that Allen and Company, the investment bank which was found to be in control of Ogden (see Appendix B, Table B-1, Section A), had manipulated Ogden's merger program in ways detrimental to Ogden shareholders. One 1968 lawsuit against Ogden's directors and Allen and Company charged that Ogden had purchased one company, Western California Canners, at an inflated price from another corporation, American Transportation Enterprises. Allen and Company, its partners, and their relatives owned 80 percent of the stock of American Transportation Enterprises; it was charged that American Transportation Enterprises, and ultimately Allen and Company, benefitted at Ogden's expense from the transaction.[53] A second stockholder suit in 1967 charged that a $500,000 fee paid by Ogden to Allen and Company for services in connection with another Ogden acquisition was a "waste and spoliation of Ogden's assets for the benefit of Allen and Company, Inc."[54]

Commercial banks have become far more important than investment banks as sources of control over nonfinancial corporations; have commercial banks been involved in stimulating mergers? The House investigation cited above also found examples of commercial bank involvement in the merger movement. The relationship between Gulf and Western Industries and the bank found to have control over Gulf and Western, Chase Manhattan Bank (see Appendix B, Table B-1, Section C), illustrates such involvement.

51. U. S., Congress, House Judiciary Committee, *Investigation of Conglomerate Corporations* (Staff Report of the Antitrust Subcommittee), 92nd Congress, 1st Session, 1971 (hereafter cited as *Investigation of Conglomerate Corporations*).

52. *Ibid.*, pp. 150-51.

53. Ogden Corporation Proxy statement, 1969.

54. *Ibid.*

In January 1964, Chase Manhattan Bank convinced Gulf and Western to open a line of credit with Chase.[55] Gulf and Western was already a conglomerate, having grown by a series of mergers. However, in the next six years Gulf and Western's mergers became increasingly ambitious, transforming it into one of the major U.S. industrial corporations. By 1969 Gulf and Western was the thirty-third largest industrial corporation (by assets) in the United States.

The House study cited above remarked that "G&W's acquisition program was outstanding in the extent of participation and influence by Chase Manhattan."[56] Chase provided short-term loans to Gulf and Western specifically to enable Gulf and Western to purchase the stock of take-over target companies. Chase served as lead bank in large credit agreements with Gulf and Western. According to the study, "One phase of the relationship included a flow of information from Chase about companies in which G&W had an interest, including suggestions for acquisition."[57]

What benefits accrued to Chase Manhattan for aiding and encouraging Gulf and Western's acquisition program? Apart from receiving a large share of Gulf and Western's growing loan business, Gulf and Western had new subsidiaries transfer their checking accounts to Chase, deposit payroll and withholding taxes with Chase, and transfer pension and savings plans to Chase Manhattan's trust department. In addition, Chase received inside information on Gulf and Western's acquisition plans, which was valuable information for Chase Manhattan's trust department.[58]

The key individual in the relationship between Chase and Gulf and Western was Roy T. Abbot. In 1964 Mr. Abbot was the Assistant Vice-President of Chase who secured and then managed the Gulf and Western account. In 1966 Abbot gave up his position at Chase and became a vice-president and director of Gulf and Western. In that role he steered new business to Chase whenever possible, as indicated in the flow of memoranda between Abbot and Chase executives made public by the House investigation. Abbot, while nominally in the employ of Gulf and Western, once even checked with Chase to make sure that

55. *Investigation of Conglomerate Corporations*, p. 168.
56. *Ibid.*
57. *Ibid.*, p. 171.
58. *Ibid.*, pp. 169-70.

the terms of one arrangement were sufficiently profitable for Chase. The internal Chase memorandum stated: "During a discussion with Roy Abbot yesterday, Roy asked me whether or not the transfer agency relationships we have from G&W are profitable to us. Roy felt that because of the high volume, these may not be showing the profit that we would like." [59]

The relationship between Chase Manhattan and Gulf and Western shows that commercial banks as well as investment banks sometimes use their position of control over nonfinancial corporations to encourage a program of mergers and acquisitions. This suggests that the extent of financial control may affect the rate of merger activity and, as a consequence, it would affect the degree of aggregate concentration in the economy. [60] Some economists believe that growing aggregate concentration, and the presence of large conglomerate firms, have negative effects on the degree of market competition. [61] Growing aggregate concentration is also of concern for its implications with respect to the concentration of economic and political power.

THE ECONOMIC AND SOCIAL SIGNIFICANCE OF FINANCIAL CONTROL

The Goals of the Corporation

An important assumption of neoclassical economic theory is that business firms seek maximum profits as their goal. Marxian economics also assumes that the capitalist will pursue maximum profits, in order to expand his capital as rapidly as possible. [62] The managerial thesis presents a challenge to both neoclassical and Marxian economics by questioning the assumption that a

59. *Ibid.*, p. 183.

60. Of course, the rate of merger activity depends heavily on various economic and stock market conditions, apart from the motivations of whoever controls corporations. A period that is favorable for mergers may cause nonfinancial corporations to seek aid from financial institutions in their acquisition plans, offering a measure of influence or control to the financial institution. Thus, a period favorable to mergers may cause a growth in financial control which, in turn, intensifies the merger wave.

61. For example, see John Blair, *Economic Concentration* (New York, 1972), pp. 41-50.

62. The assumptions have somewhat different rationales. In the neoclassical model, the owner of a firm wants profits in order to increase his future consumption of goods and leisure. Marx's capitalist seeks neither leisure nor consumption goods as his primary aims, but abstract wealth as an end in itself.

maximum of profits is the only, or primary, goal of the modern corporation. Managerialist writers have suggested such alternative corporate goals as maximization of the level or growth rate of sales, the exercise of technological expertise, or service to society.[63]

The managerial thesis claims about changes in corporate goals seemed particularly important in view of what had appeared to be overwhelming evidence that the great majority of large corporations had come under management control. Many large corporations previously assumed to be management controlled are actually under financial control. The frequency of financial control among large corporations appears to be growing. In view of this, it is important to consider the implications of financial control for corporate goals.

In most cases of financial control today, a commercial bank is the controlling institution. In most cases of financial control by a commercial bank, the basis of the bank's power is the possession by the bank's trust department of a large block of the corporation's stock.[64] When an individual is the beneficial owner of a large block of stock in a corporation, that individual, as a claimant on the corporation's profits, has an interest in the corporation pursuing the goal of maximum profits.[65] However, when a bank holds stock in a corporation through its trust department, the bank itself does not receive the income from the stock. That income belongs to the trust fund and, ultimately, to its beneficiaries. Hence, a commercial bank's interest in a portfolio company would appear, at first glance, to be substantially different from a beneficial stockholder's interest in the company.

However, a commercial bank's interest in a portfolio company's profitability, abstracting from other relationships that the bank may have to the portfolio company apart from holding its stock, is normally quite similar to the interest of a beneficial stockholder, for two reasons. First, banks are generally paid for managing trust funds in the form of a fee that is a given percentage of the market value of the assets of the

63. See chapter 1.
64. See chapter 4, tables 8, 9.
65. Possible differences among stockholders with regard to their time perspective are ignored here. One stockholder may want maximum dividends this year, while another may prefer growing income over time. A large stockholder is usually closer to the latter outlook.

fund.[66]   Dividends and capital gains on stock held by a fund increase the bank's fee for managing it. Second, the banks compete with each other for the money-managing business that wealthy families and large corporations have to offer. This puts pressure on the bank to act as it is legally supposed to act when it is a trustee — that is, as the representative of the beneficiaries. In the case of corporate pension funds, the future pensioners who are the ultimate beneficiaries have no control over which bank manages the fund; that decision is made by the corporate officers. However, the latter have an interest in the fund earning as high an income as is consistent with reasonable safety, since the corporation's periodic contributions to the pension fund can usually be reduced if the fund's investments earn a higher income than had been forecast.

Thus, a bank that holds stock in a nonfinancial corporation through the bank's trust department would have an interest in the corporation maximizing its profits. But a commercial bank usually has a second major relationship to a nonfinancial corporation under its control: a creditor relationship. A bank's interest in a corporation is somewhat different as a creditor than as a stockholder. While a stockholder is interested primarily in profitability, a creditor is interested primarily in solvency. The creditor wants the corporation to follow policies that will ensure that it can repay the debt on schedule. Therefore, a creditor would want the corporation's management to follow more cautious, conservative policies than might be dictated by long-run profit maximization. The difference between a creditor's and a stockholder's interest in a corporation is less sharp for a long-term or medium-term creditor than for a short-term creditor. The long-run profitability of a corporation is a major determinant of its ability to meet its debt obligations over a long period of time; liquidity is more important than profitability in determining a corporation's ability to make its short-term debt payments.

Taking account of a commercial bank's typically dual role as stockholder and creditor, one would expect a corporation controlled by a commercial bank to pursue maximum profits, but with caution. A maximum of profits would be the primary aim but risks would be conservatively evaluated in making policy decisions. The degree of caution might vary among indi-

66. *Institutional Investor Study Report*, vol. 2, p. 476. The marginal percentage usually declines as the value of the fund increases.

vidual cases, being greater if the bank holds a large amount of the corporations's short-term debt, and being less if the bank holds mainly medium-term debt in addition to stock.

In cases of control by investment banks, the investment bank's most important relationship to the corporation is as an intermediary in the supply of long-term debt capital. Investment banks usually act as representatives of the long-term creditors.[67] The investment bank is not normally a significant stockholder in large corporations, although there were two cases of control by an investment bank based on stockholdings, among the top 200 nonfinancial corporations.[68] One would expect that a corporation controlled by an investment bank would pursue a goal of cautious profit maximization, in accord with the interests of long-term creditors. Similarly, one would expect a corporation controlled by a life insurance company to also follow cautious profit maximization.

Investment companies hold stock in nonfinancial corporations as the beneficial holder, not just the holder of record. The large investment companies that are in a position to control large nonfinancial corporations do not usually hold substantial amounts of the debt of nonfinancial corporations. Therefore, an investment company's interest in a corporation is in the role of stockholder, pure and simple. One would expect a corporation controlled by an investment company to pursue profit maximization, without the caution proviso.

Summing up, one would expect nonfinancial corporations under financial control, whatever the type of financial institution involved, to pursue maximum profits, with more or less caution, as the primary corporate goal. Thus, the goal of the financially-controlled corporation is similar to that of the owner-controlled corporation. Viewed historically, as the power of individual stockholders has declined, the power of financial institutions has increased, preventing a new class of corporate managers from rising to the position of ultimate controller over

67. See chapter 3. This is not to deny that an investment bank may occasionally take advantage of a corporation to the detriment of both shareholders and bondholders. The suit against Allen and Company cited above presents an example of such behavior, if the charges contained in the suit are accurate. However, in my view the major financial institutions do not usually engage in such behavior. (Note that Allen and Company is a relatively small investment bank.) For further discussion of this matter, see below, pp. 146-47.

68. The two were Safeway Stores, controlled by Merrill, Lynch, Pierce, Fenner, and Smith; and Ogden Corporation, controlled by Allen and Company. See app. B, table B-1.

most large corporations, and preventing the managers from imprinting the modern corporation with their own personal goals. In corporations under financial control, the managers' desire for security, prestige, and income can be satisfied only by contributing to the maximizing of corporate profits, not by maximizing the corporation's sales or growth rate of sales. A manager of a corporation under financial control who decided to balance the interests of stockholders, employees, consumers, and the general public — Kaysen's "soulful corporation" — would be likely to soon be looking for a new job, in some line of work where "soulfulness" is more highly regarded.

There have been a number of empirical studies of differences in profit rates between owner-controlled corporations and management-controlled corporations. One such study found management-controlled corporations to have substantially lower profit rates than owner-controlled corporations.[69]   Others have found little or no statistically significant difference in profit rates between the two groups of corporations.[70]   All of these studies overlooked the category of financial control, which renders their results of questionable value, and might explain the conflicting results of the different studies. Although there are serious drawbacks to using econometric techniques to test hypotheses on the relationship between type of control and corporate goals, it does seem that more meaningful results could be obtained by including three control categories in such studies.

The above conclusion about corporate goals provides support to theorists both of the neoclassical and Marxist schools. Both schools assume profit maximization to be the primary corporate goal. However, the social significance of concluding that corporations still maximize profits is different within these two different perspectives. To the neoclassical economist, profit maximization is the basis of the rationality of capitalism; it is the driving force compelling the firm to optimally satisfy the wants of consumers. To the Marxist, the profit motive has a

69. R. J. Monson, J. Chin, and D. Cooley, "The Effect of Separation of Ownership and Control on the Performance of the Large Firm," *Quarterly Journal of Economics,* August, 1968, pp. 435-51.

70. For a study that found a slightly lower profit rate for management controlled corporations, see Robert Larner, *Management Control and the Large Corporation* (Cambridge, Mass., 1970), pp. 25-32. For a study that found no effect of control on profit rates, see David Kamerschen, "The Influence of Ownership and Control on Profit Rates," *American Economic Review,* June, 1968, pp. 432-47.

progressive aspect, in that the pursuit of profits underlies the capitalist's drive to accumulate capital and apply scientific methods to the production process, which together ensure a growing productiveness of labor. However, in the Marxist view profit maximization is also the basis of the irrationality of capitalism and of the capitalists' exploitation of the working class.

Concentration of Economic and Political Power

The degree of concentration of economic and political power is important apart from its effect on competition in particular markets. Supporters of capitalism rely heavily on the claim that, through the working of competitive markets, capitalism assures a wide sharing of power among the populace. The rise of the giant corporation in the late nineteenth century challenged the alleged link between capitalism and decentralization of power. In 1972 the 200 largest manufacturing corporations held 60 percent of the assets of all manufacturing corporations.[71] Few doubt that the leading corporations exercise significant political power on both the state and federal level.

Two hundred corporations, although a tiny percentage of all the business firms in the United States, are certainly more than a handful. An important implication of this study is that concentration data on the top 200 nonfinancial corporations, impressive as they are, may greatly understate the actual degree of concentration of economic and political power. I found just over 10 percent of the 200 largest nonfinancial corporations to be controlled by a single group of financial institutions, the Chase group. The three leading groups of financial institutions based in New York City — the Chase group, the Morgan group, and the Lehman-Goldman, Sachs group — together controlled 20 percent of the top 200 corporations. By adding to the latter three groups the Mellon group and the two leading banks in Cleveland and in Chicago, there results an ensemble of financial institutions controlling 28 percent of the top 200 corporations.

The phenomenon of financial control has created a much higher degree of concentration of power than would exist in its absence. As noted in chapter 4, financial control appears to be on the increase; this suggests a further increase in concentration

71. *Statistical Abstract of the United States*, 1975, p. 502.

of power in the future. Even today enormous power is held by the Chase group, by the Morgan group, and by the Mellon group.

What is the nature of this power? Its economic dimension involves the power to determine the major policies of the corporations that a financial institution or group of financial institutions controls. A group of financial institutions such as the Chase or Morgan group has the power to determine or influence the allocation of capital over a significant portion of the economy. It can affect many cities and towns by influencing plant shutdown and new location decisions. It can affect consumers by influencing the amount of resources devoted to the production and promotion of various consumer products. It can affect the balance of payments by influencing the buying and investing decisions of companies it controls. It can affect workers by influencing labor policies and policies with respect to the introduction of new machinery and changes in the organization of work.

While the potential for such centralized exercise of economic power is present in the Chase or Morgan group, the extent to which it is used is not known. If the term "financial group" is used to refer to a financial institution, or group of financial institutions, together with the nonfinancial corporations controlled by it, then what is being discussed here is the cohesiveness of financial groups.[72]   In a very cohesive financial group, each constituent nonfinancial corporation would act, not to maximize its own profits, but to maximize the long-run profits of the group. If such strongly group-oriented behavior does occur within financial groups, it would represent a qualification of the earlier assertion that financial control makes profit maximization the primary goal of the corporation. It would imply that the individual corporation should not be treated as the basic, independent decision-making unit for economic analysis but rather the financial group should be treated as the basic unit. An important subject for further investigation is the cohesiveness of financial groups — that is, to what extent the constituent companies act together as a group.

Some writers have suggested that banks use their power over

_____

72. The reader should bear in mind the distinction between the term just defined — "financial group" — and the related term, "group of financial institutions." The latter term was defined in chapter 4, pp. 84-85.

nonfinancial corporations to profit at the expense of the nonfinancial corporation — to "milk" the corporation of its income and assets.[73] This view does not seem very plausible. The big banks' own profits are tied to the long-run success of the corporations they control. A bank holding a large amount of stock in a nonfinancial corporation and/or being a leading creditor would have little motivation to steal from the corporation, unless the bank took a very short-run view. The historical evidence indicates that the leading banks, while not averse to taking a quick profit when it does not harm long-run interests, are primarily concerned with long-run profits.

Another important question for further study is the nature of the relationships between financial groups. One study has argued that the major financial groups are heavily intermeshed with one another, through director interlocks and joint interests in many major corporations.[74] Do such interrelationships lead financial groups to act in a largely cooperative manner toward each other? Or do the leading financial groups have important conflicting economic interests that lead them to behave in a rivalrous manner in certain instances?

The degree of cohesiveness of financial groups and the nature of the relations among financial groups have important implications for our understanding of American politics. For example, does the Chase group have distinct political interests that it pursues? Do the different financial groups contend with one another politically? Can some political divisions in the United States be traced to such contention between financial groups? For example, the conservative wing of the Republican Party has long been associated with midwestern financial and industrial interests. The moderate wing of the Republican Party has been associated with the Rockefeller interests. Some New York Jewish investment banks and retailing companies have been associated with the liberal wing of the Democratic Party. Are such associations connected to the predominant economic interests of the various financial groups? It is hoped that this study will be helpful in the effort to answer these questions about the relations between the concentration of economic power and politics.

73. See Fitch and Oppenheimer, pt. 2, pp. 109-11.
74. S. Menshikov, *Millionaires and Managers* (Moscow, 1969), chap. 6.

The Basis of Economic Power under Modern
American Capitalism

In the nineteenth century few would have questioned the proposition that the ultimate power of decision making over business firms was held by those who invested capital in them. Many take that to be a defining characteristic of a capitalist economic system. As business firms grew larger and became more complex, the capitalist had to enlist a growing army of experts to help him run the firm. Business and engineering schools trained this new social stratum of managers, who provided specialized knowledge of production, sales, finance, labor relations, and so forth.

The managerial thesis implies that a basic change in capitalism has taken place. The new managerial social stratum, born for the purpose of serving the capitalists, is held to have effectively expropriated them. This alleged transformation has been widely applauded. The managers' basis of power is their expertise, their specialized knowledge and experience. The capitalists' basis of power is wealth. It is widely held that a meritocracy is superior to a plutocracy. Why should the offspring of millionaires — whether genius or slow-witted, hardworking or lazy, socially concerned or purely selfish — hold sway over business enterprises and thus over the lives of the rest of us? It is said to be far better to have proficiency at running things be the ticket to the top. It seems more democratic and more efficient. Since the managerial stratum is selected from a broader section of the population than the offspring of big capitalists, the managerial revolution is held to promise an improvement, not only in the efficiency and rationality with which corporations are run, but in the social conscience and social responsibility of business. The John D. Rockefellers and Henry Fords may have played a useful historical role, but their supposed replacement by nameless graduates of the Harvard Business School has been welcomed.

The financial control thesis runs counter to this view. According to the financial control thesis, the managerial stratum remains what it was created to be: servants of the capitalists, although well-paid and influential servants. The basis of economic power is not expertise but ownership and control over abstract capital — that is, ultimate power resides with the bankers who are the major stockholders in and creditors of the modern large corporation. It is still a plutocracy.

Who are these bankers? The leading banks seem to be controlled primarily by the descendents of the great capitalists who earlier presided over the creation of the large corporation. For example, David Rockefeller, grandson of John D., stands at the helm of Chase Manhattan Bank. James Stillman Rockefeller, descendant of William Rockefeller and James Stillman, headed First National City Bank in the early 1960s. The Mellon family owns at least 29 percent of the stock of the Mellon National Bank, and R.K. Mellon was its Chairman in the middle 1960s.[75]

It is not surprising that the wealthiest and most powerful capitalists operate through banks. Any particular industrial corporation may decline in the long run, under the impact of changing technologies and new products. A bank, on the other hand, is tied to no particular industry in the long run. The future of banking will become clouded only when that of capitalism itself does. Through a bank, a capitalist can shift his main sphere of investment over time.

A further reason why banks tend to become the centers of control under capitalism is that a capitalist who operates through a bank obtains access to other people's capital. J. P. Morgan rose to a position of power by combining the capital belonging to himself and his partners with that of the richer capitalists of England, who funneled their investments in United States railroads through Morgan's bank. Almost a century later the great commercial banks tap the capital not only of much of the capitalist class but also a portion of the wealth of independent professionals and the working class, in the form of small checking accounts and pension funds. The Rockefellers and Mellons can thus control corporate empires of far greater worth than their own personal fortunes. Berle and Means were indeed correct when they forecast a growing separation of ownership and control. However, it has taken a form different from what they had expected. The managerial stratum has not expropriated the capitalists. Rather, a few of the capitalists have expropriated much of the remainder of their class and other classes as well.

75. U. S., Congress, House Select Committee on Small Business, *Chain Banking*, 87th Congress, 1963, p. 175. However, some of the major banks do not appear to have close connections with descendents of the families that founded the financial group of which the bank is a part. For example, although descendants of J. P. Morgan played a leading role in Morgan, Stanley and Company during the 1960s, they did not appear to play a similar role in Morgan Guarantee Trust or Bankers Trust. For a discussion of this issue, see Menshikov, pp. 236-42.

The Sample of 200 Corporations

The following table presents the list of the 200 largest nonfinancial corporations in the United States. For a discussion of the method by which this list was prepared, see chapter 4, pp. 72-75.

TABLE A-1. The 200 Largest Nonfinancial Corporations Ranked by Assets at Year-end 1969

Company	Assets (millions of dollars)	Sector*
1. American Telephone and Telegraph	43,903	U
2. Standard Oil (New Jersey)	17,538	I
3. General Motors	14,820	I
4. Texaco	9,282	I
5. Ford Motor Company	9,199	I
6. Gulf Oil	8,105	I
7. International Business Machines	7,390	I
8. Mobil Oil	7,163	I
9. Sears, Roebuck	7,079	R
10. General Telephone and Electronics	6,910	I
11. Penn Central Company	6,851	T
12. United States Steel	6,560	I
13. Standard Oil of California	6,146	I
14. General Electric	6,007	I
15. International Telephone and Telegraph	5,193	I
16. Standard Oil (Indiana)	5,157	I
17. Chrysler	4,688	I
18. Atlantic Richfield	4,235	I
19. Consolidated Edison	4,070	U
20. Tenneco	4,054	I
21. Pacific Gas and Electric	4,015	U
22. DuPont (E. I.) de Nemours	3,453	I
23. Union Carbide	3,356	I
24. Bethlehem Steel	3,224	I
25. Phillips Petroleum	3,102	I

TABLE A-1. The 200 Largest Nonfinancial Corporations Ranked by
Assets at Year-end 1969 (Continued)

Company	Assets (millions of dollars)	Sector*
26. Southern California Edison	3,002	U
27. Southern Pacific	2,979	T
28. Commonwealth Edison	2,948	U
29. Ling-Temco-Vought	2,944	I
30. Continental Oil	2,897	I
31. Eastman Kodak	2,830	I
32. American Electric Power	2,787	U
33. Marcor	2,779	R
34. Goodyear	2,763	I
35. Southern Company	2,738	U
36. Chesapeake and Ohio Railway	2,671	T
37. RCA	2,634	I
38. Norfolk and Western Railway	2,633	T
39. Dow Chemical	2,620	I
40. Boeing Aircraft	2,602	I
41. Sun Oil	2,528	I
42. Westinghouse Electric	2,478	I
43. Union Oil	2,476	I
44. Aluminum Company of America	2,428	I
45. Public Service Electric and Gas	2,331	U
46. Union Pacific	2,322	T
47. Occidental Petroleum	2,214	I
48. Santa Fe Industries	2,194	T
49. Gulf and Western	2,172	I
50. Cities Service	2,066	I
51. International Harvester	2,026	I
52. Firestone Tire	2,019	I
53. Monsanto	2,012	I
54. Boise Cascade	1,984	I
55. United Air Lines	1,946	T
56. El Paso Natural Gas	1,908	U
57. Columbia Gas System	1,894	U
58. International Paper	1,887	I
59. Getty Oil	1,859	I
60. Armco Steel	1,846	I
61. Republic Steel	1,782	I
62. Anaconda Copper	1,764	I

TABLE A-1. The 200 Largest Nonfinancial Corporations Ranked by
Assets at Year-end 1969 (Continued)

Company	Assets (millions of dollars)	Sector*
63. Reynolds Metals	1,761	I
64. Rapid American	1,701	I
65. Reynolds Tobacco	1,693	I
66. Proctor and Gamble	1,692	I
67. Caterpillar	1,662	I
68. Celanese	1,654	I
69. Kennecott Copper	1,652	I
70. Weyerhaeuser	1,644	I
71. Pan American World Airways	1,626	T
72. North American Rockwell	1,591	I
73. Litton Industries	1,580	I
74. Georgia Pacific	1,558	I
75. Xerox	1,555	I
76. Standard Oil (Ohio)	1,554	I
77. Grace, W. R.	1,541	I
78. Allied Chemical	1,524	I
79. Southern Railway	1,511	T
80. McDonnell Douglas	1,508	I
81. American Brands	1,508	I
82. American Airlines	1,491	T
83. United Aircraft	1,488	I
84. Kaiser Aluminum and Chemical	1,457	I
85. National Steel	1,454	I
86. National Cash Register	1,445	I
87. Singer	1,439	I
88. Signal Companies	1,435	I
89. Trans World Airlines	1,422	T
90. Northwest Industries	1,407	I
91. Deere	1,405	I
92. Lykes-Youngstown	1,402	I
93. American Can	1,372	I
94. Penney, J. C.	1,361	R
95. Minnesota Mining and Manufacturing	1,344	I
96. Inland Steel	1,326	I
97. Woolworth, F. W.	1,301	R
98. Marathon Oil	1,300	I
99. Burlington Industries	1,297	I

TABLE A-1. The 200 Largest Nonfinancial Corporations Ranked by
Assets at Year-end 1969 (Continued)

Company	Assets (millions of dollars)	Sector*
100. Seaboard Coast Line Industries	1,292	T
101. Sperry Rand	1,284	I
102. Lockheed Aircraft	1,271	I
103. Uniroyal	1,259	I
104. Goodrich, B. F.	1,256	I
105. Owens-Illinois	1,250	I
106. Honeywell	1,222	I
107. Avco	1,214	I
108. American Standard	1,205	I
109. Continental Can	1,200	I
110. Illinois Central Industries	1,197	I
111. International Utilities	1,196	I
112. U. S. Plywood-Champion Papers	1,179	I
113. General Foods	1,176	I
114. Control Data	1,169	I
115. PPG	1,164	I
116. Burroughs	1,116	I
117. Federated Department Stores	1,102	R
118. Louisville and Nashville Railroad	1,095	T
119. Olin Mathieson	1,078	I
120. Borden	1,069	I
121. General Dynamics	1,066	I
122. AMK	1,051	I
123. Eastern Airlines	1,030	T
124. TRW	1,028	I
125. FMC	1,021	I
126. City Investing	1,016	I
127. Loews Theaters	1,011	I
128. Crown Zellerbach	1,009	I
129. American Cyanimid	1,001	I
130. Great Northern Railway	993	T
131. Amerada Hess	982	I
132. Bendix	980	I
133. Kraftco	978	I
134. Philip Morris	976	I
135. Northern Pacific Railway	967	T
136. St. Regis Paper	949	I

TABLE A-1. The 200 Largest Nonfinancial Corporations Ranked by Assets at Year-end 1969 (Continued)

Company	Assets (in millions of dollars)	Sector*
137. Borg-Warner	949	I
138. Teledyne	944	I
139. American Metal Climax	941	I
140. CPC International	931	I
141. Great Atlantic and Pacific Tea Company	912	R
142. Martin Marietta	906	I
143. Kimberly-Clark	904	I
144. Textron	895	I
145. National Distillers and Chemicals	889	I
146. May Department Stores	883	R
147. Allied Stores	880	R
148. Coca Cola	871	I
149. Ashland Oil	846	I
150. Columbia Broadcasting System	832.7	O
151. General Tire and Rubber	832.2	I
152. American Smelting and Refining	825	I
153. Scott Paper	812	I
154. Phelps-Dodge	811	I
155. Mead	811	I
156. Kresge, S. S.	798	R
157 Safeway Stores	789	R
158. Hercules	787	I
159. Pfizer	784	I
160. Kidde, Walter	775	I
161. United States Industries	758	I
162. Swift	744	I
163. Northwest Airlines	743	T
164. Eaton, Yale and Towne	736	I
165. Norton Simon	735	I
166. American Home Products	726	I
167. Greyhound	725	T
168. Gamble-Skogmo	714	R
169. Grant, W. T.	713	R
170. General American Transportation	712	I
171. Chicago, Milwaukee, St. Paul and Pacific Railway	705	T
172. Allis Chalmers	703	I
173. Walter, Jim	697	I

TABLE A-1. The 200 Largest Nonfinancial Corporations Ranked by
Assets at Year-end 1969 (Continued)

Company	Assets (in millions of dollars)	Sector*
174. National Lead	695	I
175. Kroger	692	R
176. Ingersoll-Rand	690	I
177. United Merchants and Manufacturers	686	I
178. Ralston Purina	676	I
179. Kerr McGee	668	I
180. Stevens, J. P.	662	I
181. Consolidated Foods	662	I
182. White Consolidated Industries	661	I
183. Diamond-Shamrock	657	I
184. Delta Airlines	634	T
185. Studebaker-Worthington	625	I
186. General Mills	622	I
187. Dayton-Hudson	621	R
188. Ethyl	619	I
189. Wheeling-Pittsburgh Steel	617	I
190. Dresser Industries	610	I
191. Bristol-Myers	606	I
192. Freuhauf	605	I
193. Spartans Industries	604	R
194. Dart Industries	600	I
195. Heinz, H. J.	599	I
196. Babcock and Wilcox	593	I
197. Ogden	591	I
198. Colt Industries	589	I
199. Kaiser Industries	530	O
200. Mississippi River Corporation	226	T

*I — industrial company   U — utility company
R — retailing company   O — other company
T — transportation company

Classification of the 200 Largest Nonfinancial Corporations by Type of Control, 1967-1969

Tables B-1 and B-2 present the detailed results of my study of control over the top 200 nonfinancial corporations during 1967-1969. In Table B-1 control by groups of financial institutions is excluded. Table B-2 presents the changes in classification that result from including control by groups of financial institutions. Table B-3 provides an alphabetical index to the 200 corporations classified in Tables B-l and B-2.

Reliance on External Finance

In Tables B-l and B-2 the following terms are used to indicate the ratio of long-term debt to total assets for a corporation:

Description	*Ratio of long-term debt to assets*
light user of long-term debt	less than 11%
moderate user of long-term debt	11% to 20%
moderate/heavy user of long-term debt	20% to 35%
heavy user of long-term debt	35% to 50%
very heavy user of long-term debt	more than 50%

Any corporation that was a light user of long-term debt had a debt-to-asset ratio of less than two-thirds of the average for all manufacturing corporations. (The average ratio of long-term debt to assets for manufacturing corporations was 16.7 percent in the fourth quarter of 1969 — U. S. Federal Trade Commission, *Quarterly Financial Report for Manufacturing*, 4th quarter, 1969, table 7, pp. 28-33.) No corporation was classified under financial control based on a capital supplier relationship if the corporation was a light user of long-term debt.

Abbreviations

The following abbreviations were used in Tables B-1 and B-2 for sources of information about control relationships:

Abbreviation	*Source*
AR	Annual report of a corporation.
CABR	Annual report to the Civil Aeronautics Board by an airline.
FCCR	Annual report to the Federal Communication Commission by a communications utility.
FPCR	Annual report to the Federal Power Commission by a power utility.
GOCI	U. S., Congress, Senate Government Operations Committee, *Disclosure of Corporate Ownership*, 93rd Congress, 1st Session, 1973, part I.
GOCII	*Ibid.*, part II (by R. Soldofsky).
HBCC	U. S., Congress, House Banking and Currency Committee, *Commercial Banks and their Trust Activities: Emerging Influence on the American Economy*, 90th Congress, 2nd Session, 1968.
HJC	U. S., Congress, House Judiciary Committee, *Investigation of Conglomerate Corporations*, 92nd Congress, 2nd Session, 1971.
ICCR	Annual report to the Interstate Commerce Commission by a railroad.
ISSR	U. S., Securities and Exchange Commission, *Institutional Investor Study Report*. House Document 92-64 (referred to the House Committee on Interstate and Foreign Commerce), 1971.
MI	*Moody's Industrial Manual.*
MT	*Moody's Transportation Manual.*
Pr	Proxy statement issued by a corporation.
S&P	Standard and Poors *Corporation Records.*
SOI	Schedule of investments of a life insurance company.
WSJ	The *Wall Street Journal.*

All data in Tables B-1 and B-2 are for 1969, unless otherwise noted. The percentage of a corporation's voting stock listed as held by a financial institution excludes stock over which the financial institution has no voting authority, unless indicated otherwise by an asterisk(*). Thus, an asterisk indicates that the percentage of a company's stock cited in the table may include stock over which the financial institution has no voting authority.

Definitions of the control categories used in Tables B-1 and B-2 are found in chapter 4.

TABLE B-1. Classification of the 200 Largest Nonfinancial Corporations
by Type of Control Excluding Control by Groups of Financial
Institutions, 1967-1969

A. *Full financial control*

Corporation	Controller(s)	Basis of classification
Aluminum Co. of America	Mellon National Bank	The bank held 20.5% of the voting stock in 1967 (HBCC) and had 2 representatives on the board ('69 AR).
American Smelting and Refining	Morgan Guarantee Trust	The bank held 10.6% of the voting stock in 1967 (HBCC), still had 11.6%* in 1970 ('70 Pr), and had 1 representative on the board ('70 Pr).
Celanese	Chase Manhattan Bank	The bank held 5.19% of the voting stock (GOCII) and had 1 representative on the executive committee ('69 AR).
Chicago, Milwaukee, St. Paul, and Pacific Railway	First National Bank, Chicago	The bank held 89.1% of the voting stock in escrow pursuant to an exchange offer by Northwest Industries ('69 ICCR).
Eastern Airlines	Chase Manhattan Bank	The bank held 6.2% of the voting stock (HBCC, IISR, '69 CABR) and is the second biggest creditor (Equitable Life is first), holding 10.4% of the company's long-term debt ('69 CABR). The company is a very heavy user of long-term debt ('69 CABR).
Goodrich, B. F.	First National Bank of Chicago	Northwest Industries held 16.3% of the voting stock ('70 MI, '70 Pr); Northwest Industries is under full financial control by First National Bank, Chicago (see below).
Gulf Oil	Mellon National Bank	The bank held 14.8% of the voting stock (GOCII) and had 1 representative on the board ('69 Pr).

TABLE B-1. Classification of the 200 Largest Nonfinancial Corporations by Type of Control Excluding Control by Groups of Financial Institutions, 1967-1969 (Continued)

A. *Full financial control (Continued)*

Corporation	Controller(s)	Basis of classification
Kennecott Copper	Morgan Guarantee Trust	The bank held 13.1% of the voting stock (HBCC) and had 1 representative on the executive committee ('69 Pr).
Louisville and Nashville RR	Mercantile-Safe Deposit and Trust	Seaboard Coast Line RR held 33.2% of the voting stock ('69 ICCR); the latter railroad is under full financial control by the bank (see below).
Northwest Industries	First National Bank, Chicago	The bank held 5.1% of the voting stock ('69 ICCR, IISR) and had 1 representative on the executive committee ('69 Pr).
Ogden	Allen and Company	The investment bank and its partners had 13.9% of the voting stock and had 2 representatives on the board ('69 Pr).
Seaboard Coast Line Industries	Mercantile-Safe Deposit and Trust	Atlantic Coast Line Company (a holding company) held 16.5% of the voting stock ('69 Pr); the bank held 51.4% of the voting stock of Atlantic Coast Line Company (HBCC, '69 ICCR for Atlantic Coast Line Co.) and had a representative as chairman of the executive committee of both Seaboard and Atlantic ('69 AR).
Union Pacific	Brown Brothers Harriman	The chairman of the board, chairman of the executive committee, and 1 more executive committee member are representatives of the bank ('67-9 AR); also, historical relationship.

TABLE B-1. Classification of the 200 Largest Nonfinancial Corporations
by Type of Control Excluding Control by Groups of Financial
Institutions, 1967-1969 (Continued)

B. Partial financial control only

Corporation	Controller(s)	Basis of classification
AMK	An investment company complex	An unidentified investment company complex held between 5% and 6% of the voting stock (GOCII).
Boeing	Chase Manhattan Bank	The bank held 6.5% of the voting stock (GOCII).
Burlington Industries	1) Morgan Guarantee Trust; 2) Wachovia Bank and Trust	Morgan Guarantee Trust held 10.8% of the voting stock in 1967 (HBCC); Wachovia Bank and Trust held 11.4% of the voting stock in 1968 ('69 Pr).
Burroughs	Bankers Trust Company	The bank held 5.9% of the voting stock (GOCII).
Chrysler	Manufacturers Hanover Trust	The bank was the lead bank for Chrysler and arranged a $400 million emergency loan in 1970 (N.Y. *Times*, 6/70); the chairman of the finance committee was a representative of the bank ('69 AR). Chrysler was in financial difficulty in 1969 and 1970 (WSJ).
Cities Service	Loeb, Rhoades and Company	The investment bank co-managed (with First Boston Corp.) $200 million in bond offerings in 1967-1969 and had 1 representative on the executive committee ('71 MI, '69 Pr); company was a moderate/heavy user of long-term debt ('71 MI).
Colt Industries	a commercial bank	An unidentified commercial bank held 5.1% of the voting stock (GOCII).

TABLE B-1. Classification of the 200 Largest Nonfinancial Corporations by Type of Control Excluding Control by Groups of Financial Institutions, 1967-1969 (Continued)

B. *Partial financial control only (Continued)*

Corporation	Controller(s)	Basis of classification
Continental Can	Lehman Brothers	Lehman co-managed (with Goldman, Sachs) a bond issue in 1970 representing 20% of the company's long-term debt in 1970 ('71 MI); Lehman had a representative on the executive committee ('69 Pr). Company is a moderate user of long-term debt ('71 MI).
Control Data	Bankers Trust Company	The bank held 6.2% of the voting stock (GOCII).
Crown Zellerbach	Bankers Trust Company	The bank's term loans to the company equalled 23% of the company's long-term debt ('70 Pr); the company is a moderate/heavy user of long term debt ('71 MI). The bank has a representative on the executive committee ('69 AR).
Delta Airlines	Dreyfus Funds	Dreyfus funds held 5.2% of the voting stock ('69 CABR, IISR).
Diamond Shamrock	Mellon National Bank	The bank held between 4.8% and 5% of the voting stock (HBCC, IISR, '72 MI), had a representative on the board ('69 AR) and was lead bank for company, which is a moderate/heavy user of long-term debt ('72 MI).
Federated Department Stores	First National Bank, Chicago	The bank held 8.7% of the voting stock in 1967 (HBCC) and had a representative on the board ('69 Pr).
FMC	Lehman Brothers	Lehman co-managed (with Kidder, Peabody) a $100 million bond offering in 1967 ('71 MI) and had a representative on the executive committee ('69 Pr). Company is a moderate user of long-term debt ('71 MI).

TABLE B-1. Classification of the 200 Largest Nonfinancial Corporations
by Type of Control Excluding Control by Groups of Financial
Institutions, 1967-1969 (Continued)

B. *Partial financial control only (Continued)*

Corporation	Controller(s)	Basis of classification
Great Northern Railway	Chase Manhattan Bank	The bank had 5.2% of the voting stock ('69 ICCR).
Hercules	Chase Manhattan Bank	The bank had 5.6% of the voting stock (GOCII).
Honeywell	Bankers Trust Company	The bank had 7.5% of the voting stock in 1967 (HBCC).
Illinois Central Industries	1) Continental Illinois 2) Seattle First National Bank 3) United Calif. Bank 4) U. S. Trust	Continental Illinois had 5.9% of the voting stock (HBCC, '69 ICCR) and a representative on the board ('69 AR). The other 3 banks each had 5.3% of the voting stock under a voting trust agreement with Union Pacific RR ('69 ICCR, '68 MT).
Inland Steel	First National Bank, Chicago	The bank held 10-12% of the company's long-term debt ('69 Pr) and had a representative on the finance committee ('69 Pr). Company is a moderate user of long-term debt ('71 MI).
International Harvester	a commercial bank	An unidentified commercial bank held between 5% and 10% of the voting stock (IISR).
International Paper	Morgan Guarantee Trust	The bank held 7.4% of the voting stock (GOCII).
International Telephone and Telegraph	1) Lazard Freres and Company 2) Kuhn, Loeb and Company	The 2 investment banks co-managed $435 million in bond offerings, and Kuhn, Loeb managed singly an additional $85 million; the company is a moderate/heavy user of long-term debt ('71 MI, '73 S&P). Both investment banks have representatives on the executive committee ('69 Pr).

TABLE B-1. Classification of the 200 Largest Nonfinancial Corporations by Type of Control Excluding Control by Groups of Financial Institutions, 1967-1969 (Continued)

B. Partial financial control only (Continued)

Corporation	Controller(s)	Basis of classification
Kroger	Central Trust Co., Cincinnati	The bank held 6% of the voting stock in 1967 (HBCC).
Monsanto	Chase Manhattan Bank	The bank held 5.7% of the voting stock in 1972 (GOCI).
National Cash Register	1) Morgan Guarantee Trust 2) Dillon, Read and Company	Morgan held 5.8% of the voting stock (GOCII). Dillon, Read managed $250 million in bond offerings (equal to 50% of long-term debt in 1970) in 1969-1970 ('71 MI); the company is a moderate/heavy user of long-term debt ('71 MI). Dillon, Read had a representative on the executive committee ('69 Pr).
National Distillers and Chemical	1) Chase Manhattan Bank 2) Worth Fund	Panhandle Eastern Pipe Line held 11.7% of the voting stock ('69 Pr) and had 2 representatives on the board ('69 AR). Chase had 5.6% of the voting stock of Panhandle ('69 FPCR, HBCC). Worth Fund had 5.9% of the voting stock of Panhandle ('69 FPCR).
Norfolk and Western Railway	1) U. S. Trust Co. 2) Riggs National Bank, Wash, DC 3) First National Bank, Atlanta	Each bank held 5.8% of the voting stock under a voting trust agreement with a subsidiary of Penn Central ('69 Pr, '69 ICCR).
Northern Pacific Railway	1) Chase Manhattan Bank 2) Investors Diversified Services	Chase held 5% of the voting stock ('69 ICCR), Investors Diversified Services held 5% of the voting stock ('69 ICCR).

TABLE B-1. Classification of the 200 Largest Nonfinancial Corporations
by Type of Control Excluding Control by Groups of Financial
Institutions, 1967-1969 (Continued)

B. *Partial financial control only (Continued)*

Corporation	Controller(s)	Basis of classification
Northwest Airlines	Chase Manhattan Bank	The bank held 7.2% of the voting stock (GOCII).
Owens-Illinois	Lazard Freres and Company	The investment bank co-managed (with Goldman, Sachs) $170 million in bond offerings in 1967-1971; the company is a heavy user of long-term debt ('71 MI). Lazard had a representative on the executive committee ('69 Pr).
Penney, J.C.	Chase Manhattan Bank	Chase had between 5% and 10% of voting stock (HBCC, IISR).
Phillips Petroleum	First National City Bank	The bank held 6.4% of the voting stock (GOCII).
Reynolds (R. J.) Tobacco	Wachovia Bank and Trust	The bank held 7.8% of the voting stock (GOCII, '70 Pr).
Safeway Stores	Merrill, Lynch, Pierce, Fenner, and Smith	The investment bank held 8%* of the voting stock and had a representative on the board; the board chairman of Safeway left Merrill, Lynch to become the chairman of Safeway in 1955 ('69 Pr).
Sperry Rand	1) Chase Manhattan Bank 2) Bankers Trust Company	Chase had 7.7% and Bankers Trust had 6% of the voting stock (GOCII).
Standard Oil (Indiana)	First National Bank, Chicago	The bank held 7.2% of the voting stock (GOCII) and had a representative on the board ('69 Pr).
Standard Oil (Ohio)	National City Bank, Cleveland	The bank held 5.8% of the voting stock in 1967 (HBCC).

TABLE B-1. Classification of the 200 Largest Nonfinancial Corporations
by Type of Control Excluding Control by Groups of Financial
Institutions, 1967-1969 (Continued)

B. Partial financial control only (Continued)

Corporation	Controller(s)	Basis of classification
St. Regis Paper	Metropolitan Life Insurance Company	Metropolitan held 36% of the long-term debt of the company, which was a moderate/heavy user of long-term debt ('69 Pr, '70 Pr, '71 MI). Metropolitan had a representative on the executive committee ('69 Pr).
Textron	Industrial National Bank, Rhode Island	The bank held between 5% and 7.7% of the voting stock (IISR, GOCI).
TRW	Morgan Guarantee Trust	Morgan held 5.4% of the voting stock (GOCII). See Table B-2.
Trans World Airlines	Chase Manhattan Bank	Chase held 7.4% of the voting stock. (GOCII, '69 CABR). See Table B-2.
Uniroyal	Kuhn, Loeb and Company	The investment bank managed $120 million in bond offerings in 1967-1971 for the company, a moderate/heavy user of long-term debt ('73 S&P, '71 MI). Kuhn, Loeb had a representative on the executive committee ('69 AR). See Table B-2.
United Aircraft	Chase Manhattan Bank	Chase held 6% of the voting stock in 1967 (HBCC).
U. S. Plywood— Champion Papers	Fifth Third Union Trust, Cincinnati	The bank held 5.2% of the voting stock in 1967 (HBCC, '69 Pr).
Westinghouse Electric	Kuhn, Loeb and Company	The investment bank co-managed (with First Boston Corporation) $400 million in bond offerings in 1967-1970 ('72 MI) and had a representative on the executive committee ('69 AR). Westinghouse is a moderate user of long-term debt ('69 AR). See Table B-2.

TABLE B-1. Classification of the 200 Largest Nonfinancial Corporations by Type of Control Excluding Control by Groups of Financial Institutions, 1967-1969 (Continued)

B. *Partial financial control only (Continued)*

Corporation	Controller(s)	Basis of classification
Xerox	First National City Bank	The bank held 5.2% of the voting stock (GOCII) and had a representative on the board ('69 AR).

C. *Partial financial control and partial owner control*

Corporation	Controller(s)	Basis of classification
Allis Chalmers	1) Cleveland Trust Co. 2) H. T. Mandeville	White Consolidated Industries held 29% of the voting stock ('69 Pr). White was partially controlled by Cleveland Trust and H. T. Mandeville (see below).
Avco	1) Lehman Brothers 2) Harringtons	Lehman Brothers managed $175 million in bond offerings in 1969-1971 ('72 S&P); Avco is a moderate/heavy user of long-term debt ('70 AR). Lehman had 2 representatives on the board ('69 AR). Three Harringtons held 9% of the voting stock and were directors; one of them was vice-chairman of the board ('69 Pr).
Columbia Broadcasting System	1) Chase Manhattan Bank 2) W. S. Paley	Chase held 14.1%* of the voting stock in 1972 (GOCI). William S. Paley held 6.3% of the voting stock in 1970 and was chairman of the board ('70 Pr).
Firestone Tire and Rubber	1) Cleveland Trust Co. 2) Firestones	The bank held 13.2% of the voting stock and had a representative on the board (HBCC, '70 Pr). The Firestone family owns 21.1% of the voting stock and has 4 members on the board, including the chairman and 2 presidents of divisions ('70 Pr).

TABLE B-1. Classification of the 200 Largest Nonfinancial Corporations by Type of Control Excluding Control by Groups of Financial Institutions, 1967-1969 (Continued)

C. Partial financial control and partial owner control (Continued)

Corporation	Controller(s)	Basis of classification
General Dynamics	1) an investment complex 2) Henry Crown and Associates	An unidentified investment company complex held between 7.5% and 10% of the voting stock (GOCII). Henry Crown and his associates held just below 10% of the voting stock in late 1969 (*Fortune,* 6/70; '70 Pr).
Grace (W. R.)	1) First National City Bank 2) J. P. Grace and relatives	The bank held 11% of the long-term debt of the company and had 2 representatives on the board ('69 Pr); Grace is a moderate/heavy user of long-term debt ('71 MI). J. P. Grace and relatives held at least 6.6% of the voting stock; J. P. Grace was president and 3 relatives were on the board ('69 Pr).
Gulf and Western Industries	1) Chase Manhattan Bank 2) Bluhdorn and Duncan	Chase was the lead bank for the company and had a representative serving as a senior vice-president of the company (HJC), which was a heavy user of long-term debt ('71 MI). C. Bluhdorn and J. H. Duncan held 6.2% of the voting stock; Bluhdorn was chairman and Duncan chairman of the executive committee ('69 Pr).
National Steel	1) Chase Manhattan Bank 2) Pittsburgh National Bank 3) G. W. Humphrey and Associates	Chase held 6.1% of the voting stock in 1967 (HBCC). Pittsburgh National Bank held 8.7% of the voting stock (GOCII). Hanna Mining Co. held 6.3% of the voting stock in 1967 ('68 MI); G. W. Humphrey and Associates held 8.2% of the voting stock of

TABLE B-1. Classification of the 200 Largest Nonfinancial Corporations
by Type of Control Excluding Control by Groups of Financial
Institutions, 1967-1969 (Continued)

C. *Partial financial control and partial owner control (Continued)*

Corporation	Controller(s)	Basis of classification
National Steel (Continued)		Hanna and had 2 representatives on the board of Hanna including 1 serving as chairman, and had 2 representatives on the board of National Steel ('69 Pr Nat. Steel, '69 Pr Hanna Mining).
Olin	1) Morgan Guarantee Trust 2) Olin family	The bank held 6% of the voting stock in 1967 (HBCC). The Olins held between 6.5% and 10.5% of the voting stock and 2 family members were directors ('69 Pr, '69 AR).
White Consolidated Industries	1) Cleveland Trust Co. 2) H. T. Mandeville	The bank was a leading creditor of the company, which was a heavy user of long-term debt ('70 Pr, '71 MI). The bank had a representative on the executive committee. ('69 Pr.) H. T. Mandeville held 8% of the voting stock and was a director ('69 Pr).

D. *Full owner control*

Corporation	Controller(s)	Basis of classification
Amerada Hess	Hess family	Leon Hess and family held 28.1% of the voting stock in 1970, and he was chairman and chief executive officer ('70 Pr).
Coca-Cola	Woodruffs	Coca-Cola International held 20.9% of the voting stock ('69 Pr). Two Woodruff foundations held 27.9% of the voting stock of Coca-Cola International ('69 Pr of Coca-Cola International), and two Woodruffs were directors of Coca-Cola, one of whom was chairman of the Finance committee ('69 Pr).

TABLE B-1. Classification of the 200 Largest Nonfinancial Corporations
by Type of Control Excluding Control by Groups of Financial
Institutions, 1967-1969 (Continued)

D. Full owner control (Continued)

Corporation	Controller(s)	Basis of classification
Dayton-Hudson	Daytons	The Daytons held 47.3% of the voting stock in 1970, and 5 Daytons were directors, of whom one was chairman, one president, and one a vice-president ('70 Pr).
Deere	Deere family	Descendants of Chas. H. Deere held 12% of the voting stock ('69 Pr), and the husband of a Deere (W. A. Hewitt) was chairman.
Dow Chemical	Dow family	Seven Dows and their relatives held 5.7% of the voting stock in 1972 (GOCI). Four Dows or their relatives were directors, of whom one was president and chief executive officer, one chairman of the executive committee, and one secretary ('69 Pr).
DuPont (E. I.) de Nemours	duPont family	Christiana Securities (a holding company) held 28.5% of the voting stock in 1970 ('70 Pr). The duPonts and their associates held at least 16.4% of the voting stock of Christiana; duPonts and relatives held a majority of directorships in Christiana, including president and chief executive officer ('69 Pr of Christiana). DuPonts and relatives held 5 directorships in company, and were chairman, and chairman of the finance committee ('70 Pr).
Ethyl	Gottwald family	The Gottwalds held 11.8% of the voting stock, and 3 Gottwalds were directors, including the chairman, chairman of the executive committee, and vice-president ('69 Pr).

TABLE B-1. Classification of the 200 Largest Nonfinancial Corporations
by Type of Control Excluding Control by Groups of Financial
Institutions, 1967-1969 (Continued)

D. Full owner control (Continued)

Corporation	Controller(s)	Basis of classification
Ford Motor Company	Ford family	Fords and their associates owned all the class B stock, which had 40% of the votes. Henry Ford, II, was chairman, and 2 more Fords were vice-presidents ('69 Pr).
Gamble-Skogmo	Gamble family	B. C. Gamble and his family held 11% of the voting stock, and he was chairman ('69 Pr).
General Tire and Rubber	O'Neil family	The O'Neils and relatives held 11.2% of the voting stock, and three O'Neils were directors, and also chairman, president, and chairman of the finance committee ('69 Pr).
Getty Oil	J. P. Getty	J. P. Getty held 62.4% of the voting stock and was president. Another Getty was executive vice-president ('69 Pr).
Grant, W. T.	Grants	The W. T. Grant Foundation owned 29.2% of the voting stock in 1970 ('70 Pr). W. T. Grant was honorary chairman ('69 AR).
Great Atlantic and Pacific Tea Company	Hartfords	The John A. Hartford Foundation held 33.7% of the voting stock ('69 Pr).
Heinz, H. J.	Heinz family	H. J. Heinz, II, and relatives held 26% of the voting stock in 1970. H. J. Heinz was chairman; another Heinz was a director ('70 Pr).
Kaiser Aluminum and Chemical	Kaisers	Kaiser Industries held 32.7% of the voting stock; Kaiser Industries was under full control by the Kaiser family (see below) ('69 Pr). E. F. Kaiser was chairman of Kaiser Aluminum and Chemical ('69 AR).

TABLE B-1. Classification of the 200 Largest Nonfinancial Corporations
by Type of Control Excluding Control by Groups of Financial
Institutions, 1967-1969 (Continued)

D. *Full owner control (Continued)*

Corporation	Controller(s)	Basis of classification
Kaiser Industries	Kaisers	E. F. Kaiser, his family, and associates held between 43% and 48.8% of the voting stock; E. F. Kaiser was chairman ('69 Pr).
Kerr-McGee	Kerrs and McGees	D. A. McGee held 4.1% of the voting stock and Kerr family members held 3.2%. McGee was chairman and chief executive officer and Kerrs held 3 directorships ('69 Pr).
Kresge, S. S.	S. S. Kresge	Mr. S. S. Kresge held 19.1% of the voting stock and was a director ('69 Pr).
Ling-Temco-Vought	James Ling	James Ling held 9.6% of the voting stock and was chairman and chief executive officer ('69 Pr). See Table B-2.
Loew's Theatres	Tisch family	Tisch Hotels owned 31.5% of the voting stock ('70 Pr). L. A. and P. R. Tisch held 100% of the voting stock of Tisch Hotels; L. A. Tisch was chairman and chief executive officer and P. R. Tisch was president and chairman of the executive committee of Loew's ('69 Pr).
Lykes-Youngstown	Lykes family	The Lykeses held 8.5% of the voting stock in 1970; J. T. Lykes, Jr., was chairman and chief executive officer, J. M. Lykes, Jr., was executive vice-president, and C. P. Lykes was a director ('70 Pr).
McDonnell-Douglas	McDonnells	The McDonnells held 19.3% of the voting stock in 1972 (GOCI). McDonnells held 3 executive positions: chairman and chief executive officer, chairman of the finance committee, and vice-president ('69 Pr).

TABLE B-1. Classification of the 200 Largest Nonfinancial Corporations by Type of Control Excluding Control by Groups of Financial Institutions, 1967-1969 (Continued)

D. *Full owner control (Continued)*

Corporation	Controller(s)	Basis of classification
Norton Simon	Simon family	Mr. Norton Simon and relatives held 11% of the voting stock; Norton Simon was on the finance committee and two more Simons were directors ('69 Pr).
PPG Industries	Pitcairns	The Pitcairn Company, a personal holding company, held 25.9% of the voting stock and had 2 representatives on the board ('69 Pr).
Ralston Purina	Danforths	The Danforths held between 26.1% and 28.2% of the voting stock; 3 Danforths were directors, of whom one was chairman of the executive and finance committees and another was executive vice-president ('70 Pr).
Rapid-American	Meshulam Riklis	Meshulam Riklis held 7% of the voting stock and was chairman and president; one more Riklis was a director ('69 Pr).
Reynolds Metals	Reynolds family	The Reynoldses held between 11.6% and 16.8% of the voting stock in 1970; R. S. Reynolds, Jr., was chairman and three more Reynolds were high executives ('70 Pr).
Spartans Industries	Bassine family	C. Bassine and relatives held 12.2% of the voting stock; he was chairman, and his son-in-law, A. G. Cohen, was on the executive committee ('69 Pr).
Sun Oil	Pew family	The Pews held 41.7% of the voting stock; J. Howard Pew was chairman and 2 more Pews were directors ('69 Pr, '69 AR).

TABLE B-1. Classification of the 200 Largest Nonfinancial Corporations by Type of Control Excluding Control by Groups of Financial Institutions, 1967-1969 (Continued)

D. Full owner control (Continued)

Corporation	Controller(s)	Basis of classification
United Merchants and Manufacturers	Schwab family	The Schwabs held 5.3% of the voting stock; M. J. Schwab was president and treasurer, J. W. Schwab was on the executive committee ('69 Pr).
U. S. Industries	top officers and their associates	The top officers and their associates held 35% of the voting stock ('69 Pr).

E. Partial owner control only

Corporation	Controller(s)	Basis of classification
Minnesota Mining and Manufacturing	1) W. L. McKnight 2) R. Ordway	W. L. McKnight held 8% of the voting stock and was honorary chairman and a member of the executive and finance committees ('69 Pr). R. Ordway held 7.9% of the voting stock and was a director ('69 Pr).
Swift and Company	J. A. Vickers	J. A. Vickers held 5.1% of the voting stock and was chairman of a subsidiary in 1970 ('70 Pr).

F. Miscellaneous control

Corporation	Controller(s)	Basis of classification
Allied Chemical	Solvay and Cie had partial control	Solvay and Cie held 8.2% of the voting stock and had a representative on the board ('69 Pr). Solvay and Cie is a Brussels, Belgium, chemical company.
American Metal Climax	Selection Trust Ltd. had full control	Selection Trust Ltd. held 11.5% of the voting stock ('69 Pr) and had 4 representatives on the board, including one each on the executive and finance committees ('69 AR). Selection Trust Ltd. is a British mining and finance company.

TABLE B-1. Classification of the 200 Largest Nonfinancial Corporations
by Type of Control Excluding Control by Groups of Financial
Institutions, 1967-1969 (Continued)

F. Miscellaneous control (Continued)

Corporation	Controller(s)	Basis of classification
Proctor and Gamble	a self-administered fund had full control	A self-administered fund held between 10% and 15% of the voting stock (IISR).
Sears, Roebuck	the Sears Savings and Profit Sharing Pension Fund had full control	The Sears Savings and Profit Sharing Pension Fund held 22.6% of the voting stock ('69 Pr).
United States Steel Corporation	the U. S. Steel Savings Fund for Salaried Employees had partial control	The U. S. Steel Savings Fund for Salaried Employees held 8.2% of the voting stock (IISR, '69 AR).

G. No identified center of control

Corporation	Suspected controller	Comments
Allied Stores	Lehman Brothers	Lehman managed $50 million in bond offerings in 1967 for the company, a heavy user of long-term debt ('71 MI). Lehman had a representative on the board ('69 Pr).
American Airlines	None	Morgan Guarantee Trust held 6.7% of the voting stock in 1967 but had less than 5% in 1969 (HBCC, IISR). Metropolitan Life held 27% of the company's long-term debt ('69 CABR).
American Brands	None	
American Can	None	
American Cyanimid	None	

TABLE B-1. Classification of the 200 Largest Nonfinancial Corporations
by Type of Control Excluding Control by Groups of Financial
Institutions, 1967-1969 (Continued)

G. *No identified center of control (Continued)*

Corporation	Suspected controller	Comments
American Electric Power	None	
American Home Products	None	
American Standard	a commercial bank	An unidentified bank held between 4.2% and 8.4% of the voting stock (IISR).
American Telephone and Telegraph	None	Chase Manhattan Bank, the leading stockholder, held 1.1%* of the voting stock ('69 FCCR).
Anaconda Copper	1) Chase Manhattan Bank 2) First National City Bank 3) Metropolitan Life	Chase held 12% and First National City Bank and Metropolitan each held 11% of the company's long-term debt ('69 Pr, '70 Pr, '69 AR). The three financial institutions each had a representative on the board ('69 AR). Anaconda was a moderate user of long-term debt ('69 AR). See Table B-2.
Armco Steel	None	
Ashland Oil	None	
Atlantic Richfield	None	Cities Service held 9.2% of the voting stock but must vote the stock as management of Atlantic Richfield directs ('69 Pr).
Babcock and Wilcox	None	
Bendix	None	
Bethlehem Steel	None	
Boise Cascade	None	
Borden	None	
Borg-Warner	None	The chairman, Robert S. Ingersoll, succeeded his father as chairman in 1960. Until 1960 the company

TABLE B-1. Classification of the 200 Largest Nonfinancial Corporations
by Type of Control Excluding Control by Groups of Financial
Institutions, 1967-1969 (Continued)

G. *No identified center of control (Continued)*

Corporation	Suspected controller	Comments
Borg-Warner (Continued)		was reported to be an "autocratically run family affair." (*Fortune,* 3/72, p. 22)
Bristol-Myers	None	
Caterpillar Tractor	None	
Chesapeake and Ohio Railway	Cyrus Eaton	In 1953 Eaton purchased Alleghany Corp.'s holding of 1.3% of the voting stock and became chairman ('70 MT). In 1969 Eaton still had 1.3% and was chairman; his son was on the executive committee ('69 ICCR).
City Investing	None	Chemical Bank had a representative on the executive committee and was a creditor of the company, but Chemical held only 6% of the company's long-term debt ('70 Pr, '71 MI).
Columbia Gas System	None	
Commonwealth Edison	None	First National Bank, Chicago, was the top stockholder, with 2.8%* of the voting stock ('69 FPCR).
Consolidated Edison	First National City Bank	The bank had 2 representatives on the board, was apparently the leading contributor to a $100 million revolving credit in 1968 (about 5% of Con Ed's long-term debt), and held $37.6 million of nonvoting preferred in 1967 ('69 AR, '69 Pr, HBCC). The company was a heavy user of long-term debt ('69 FPCR).

TABLE B-1. Classification of the 200 Largest Nonfinancial Corporations
by Type of Control Excluding Control by Groups of Financial
Institutions, 1967-1969 (Continued)

G. *No identified center of control (Continued)*

Corporation	Suspected controller	Comments
Consolidated Foods	Nathan Cummings	Nathan Cummings held 4.7% of the voting stock and was chairman of the executive committee and honorary chairman; he was board chairman through 1968 ('69 Pr).
Continental Oil	an investment company complex	Newmont Mining Corp. held 4.1% of the voting stock and had a representative on the board ('69 Pr). An unidentified investment company complex held between 5% and 10% of the voting stock of Newmont Mining (IISR). The investment company was probably either Investors Diversified Services or Massachusetts Investors Trust, both of which had representatives on the board of Newmont Mining ('69 Pr).
CPC International	None	
Dart Industries	J. W. Dart	J. W. Dart held 1.3% of the voting stock in 1970 and was chairman and president ('70 Pr). On 22 April 1969 the company changed its name from Rexall Drug and Chemical to Dart Industries ('70 MI).
Dresser Industries	None	See Table B-2.
Eastman Kodak	None	
Eaton, Yale and Towne	None	
El Paso Natural Gas	None	
Fruehauf	None	

TABLE B-1. Classification of the 200 Largest Nonfinancial Corporations
by Type of Control Excluding Control by Groups of Financial
Institutions, 1967-1969 (Continued)

G. *No identified center of control (Continued)*

Corporation	Suspected controller	Comments
General American Transportation	None	Kuhn, Loeb was the investment banker for the company and had a representative on the board; but the company did not raise a substantial amount of capital through Kuhn, Loeb ('69 Pr).
General Electric	Morgan, Stanley and Company	The investment bank managed $225 million in bond offerings for GE Credit Corp. and co-managed $525 million (with Goldman, Sachs) in bond offerings for GE in 1967-1972; GE is a moderate user of long-term debt ('72 MI). Morgan, Stanley had a representative on the board ('69 AR). Also see Table B-2.
General Foods	None	
General Mills	Bell family	The Bells held 1% of the voting stock, and C. H. Bell was chairman of the finance committee, F. Bell was on the executive committee ('69 Pr). Also see Table B-2.
General Motors	None	Morgan Guarantee Trust had 2 representatives on the board, one of them on the finance committee; Mellon National Bank had 2 representatives on the board ('69 AR). Prudential Life held $450 million of GM Acceptance Corp.'s bonds (SOI). GM was a light user of long-term debt ('71 MI).
General Telephone and Electronics	None	

TABLE B-1. Classification of the 200 Largest Nonfinancial Corporations
by Type of Control Excluding Control by Groups of Financial
Institutions, 1967-1969 (Continued)

G. *No identified center of control (Continued)*

Corporation	Suspected controller	Comments
Georgia-Pacific	Cheathams	The Cheathams held 1.9% of the voting stock; O. R. Cheatham was chairman of the executive committee and J. N. Cheatham was a vice-president ('69 Pr).
Goodyear Tire and Rubber	None	
Greyhound	None	
Ingersoll-Rand	Grace and relatives	J. P. Grace and relative J. H. Phipps held 4% of the voting stock in 1970; Phipps was on the executive committee and Grace was a director ('70 Pr).
International Business Machines	None	Prudential Life held 49% of IBM's long-term debt in 1969 (SOI). However, IBM was a light user of long-term debt ('71 MI).
International Utilities	None	
Kidde, Walter	Kidde family	The Kiddes held 2.5% of the voting stock; 3 Kiddes held the position of vice-chairman, secretary and treasurer, and vice-president. ('69 Pr.)
Kimberly-Clark	Schweitzers	The Schweitzers held 2.7% of the voting stock; M. P. Schweitzer was vice-president and on the executive and finance committee, W. P. Schweitzer was on the executive committee ('69 Pr).
Kraftco	None	
Litton Industries	Thornton and Ash	C. B. Thornton and R. L. Ash held 4.7% of the voting stock; Thornton was chairman and Ash was president ('69 Pr).

TABLE B-1. Classification of the 200 Largest Nonfinancial Corporations by Type of Control Excluding Control by Groups of Financial Institutions, 1967-1969 (Continued)

G. *No identified center of control (Continued)*

Corporation	Suspected controller	Comments
Lockheed Aircraft	None	
Marathon Oil	None	
Marcor	None	An unidentified commercial bank held 4% of the voting stock (GOCII).
Martin Marietta	None	
May Department Stores	1) May family 2) Goldman, Sachs and Company 3) Lehman Brothers	The Mays held 1.7% of the voting stock; 3 Mays were directors, of whom one was chairman and another was vice-chairman and treasurer ('69 Pr). For information on the two investment banks, see Table B-2.
Mead	Meads	The Meads reported holding less than 1/4 of 1% of the voting stock in 1969 ('69 Pr) but in 1964 they held 7.5% of the voting stock ('64 Pr). H. T. Mead was chairman of the finance committee, N. S. Mead was a vice-president ('69 Pr).
Mississippi River Corp.	None	
Mobil Oil	None	
National Lead	None	
North American Rockwell	None	
Occidental Petroleum	Armand Hammer	Hammer held 3% of the voting stock and was chairman and chief executive officer ('69 Pr).
Pacific Gas and Electric	None	The Bank of America was the top stockholder, with 3.1%* of the voting stock ('69 FPCR).

TABLE B-1. Classification of the 200 Largest Nonfinancial Corporations
by Type of Control Excluding Control by Groups of Financial
Institutions, 1967-1969 (Continued)

G. No identified center of control (Continued)

Corporation	Suspected controller	Comments
Pan American World Airways	None	Chase Manhattan Bank held 6.6% of the voting stock in 1967 but less than 5% in 1969 (HBCC, IISR). Metropolitan Life, Prudential Life, and Morgan Guarantee Trust were leading creditors ('69 CABR).
Penn Central	1) Morgan Guarantee Trust 2) F. M. Kirby	Morgan held about 3.7% of the voting stock, was a leading creditor, and had a representative on the board (HBCC, '69 Pr, '69 AR). F. M. Kirby and the Alleghany Corp. (controlled by Kirby) held 2.4% of the voting stock; Kirby and an associate were on the board ('69 Pr, '69 AR).
Pfizer, Charles	None	
Phelps Dodge	1) Manufacturers Hanover Trust 2) First National City Bank 3) Morgan Guarantee Trust	The 3 banks were the principal participants in a $125 million revolving credit agreement; each bank had a representative on the board ('69 Pr).
Philip Morris	Cullman family	The Cullmans held 1.8% of the voting stock; J. F. Cullman, III, was chairman and chief executive officer, H. Cullman was executive vice-president ('69 Pr).
Public Service Electric and Gas	None	Morgan Guarantee Trust held 5%* of the voting stock ('69 FPCR).
RCA	None	Metropolitan Life held $201 million of company's bonds ('69 Pr, SOI), and had a representative on the board ('69 Pr).

TABLE B-1. Classification of the 200 Largest Nonfinancial Corporations by Type of Control Excluding Control by Groups of Financial Institutions, 1967-1969 (Continued)

G. *No identified center of control (Continued)*

Corporation	Suspected controller	Comments
Republic Steel	None	
Santa Fe Industries	None	The Missouri Pacific Railroad, a subsidiary of the Mississippi River Corp., held 8% of the voting stock in 1967 ('67 ICCR). The Mississippi River Corp. had no identified center of control (see above).
Scott Paper	1) Morgan Guarantee Trust 2) McCabe family	For information on Morgan Guarantee Trust, see Table B-2. The McCabes held 2.7% of the voting stock; one was chairman of the finance committee and another was a vice-president ('69 Pr).
Signal Companies	S. B. Mosher	S. B. Mosher held 4.1% of the voting stock and was chairman ('69 Pr).
Singer	Clarks	S. C. Clark reported holding 1.2% of the voting stock in 1969 ('69 Pr). In 1964 the Clark family and associates held 25% of the voting stock ('64 Pr).
Southern California Edison	None	See Table B-2.
Southern Company	None	
Southern Pacific	None	Massachusetts Investors Trust held 3.3% of the voting shares in 1968 ('68 ICCR).
Southern Railway	None	Chase Manhattan Bank was top stockholder with 3.6% of the voting stock ('69 ICCR).
Standard Oil of California	None	
Standard Oil (New Jersey)	None	See Table B-2.

TABLE B-1. Classification of the 200 Largest Nonfinancial Corporations by Type of Control Excluding Control by Groups of Financial Institutions, 1967-1969 (Continued)

G. *No identified center of control (Continued)*

Corporation	Suspected controller	Comments
Stevens, J. P.	Stevens family	The Stevenses held 4.4% of the voting stock in 1970; 4 Stevenses were directors, of whom one was president, one chairman of the executive committee, and one a vice-president ('69 Pr).
Studebaker-Worthington	Supervised Investors Services, Chicago	Supervised Investors Services held 4.4% of the voting stock and had one representative on the board ('69 Pr).
Teledyne	None	
Tenneco	None	Houston National Bank was the top stockholder in 1968, with 2.3%* of the voting stock, and had a representative on the board ('68 FPCR, '69 Pr).
Texaco	None	
Union Carbide	None	
Union Oil	None	
United Air Lines	None	Morgan Guarantee Trust held 6.4% of the voting stock in 1967 but less than 2.5% in 1969 (HBCC, IISR). Morgan Guarantee Trust, Prudential Life, and Metropolitan Life were big creditors of the company in 1968 ('68 CABR).
Walter, Jim	J. W. Walter	J. W. Walter held 3.4% of the voting stock and was chairman ('69 Pr).
Weyerhaeuser	Weyerhaeuser family	The Weyerhaeusers held 1.1% of the voting stock; one was president and chief executive officer, another was a director ('69 Pr).

TABLE B-1. Classification of the 200 Largest Nonfinancial Corporations by Type of Control Excluding Control by Groups of Financial Institutions, 1967-1969 (Continued)

G. No identified center of control (Continued)

Corporation	Suspected controller	Comments
Wheeling-Pitts-burgh Steel	None	
Woolworth, F. W.	Knox family	The Knoxs held 1% of the voting stock and two of them were on the finance committee ('69 Pr). See Table B-2.

TABLE B-2. Changes in the Classification of the 200 Largest Nonfinancial Corporations Resulting from the Inclusion of Control by Groups of Financial Institutions, 1967-1969

Corporation	Controller(s)	Basis of classification
Anaconda Copper	Chase group (Partial control)	Chase Manhattan Bank and Metropolitan Life together held 23% of the company's long-term debt ('69 Pr, '70 Pr). Anaconda was a moderate user of long-term debt ('69 AR). Chase and Metropolitan each had a representative on the board ('69 AR).
Dresser Industries	Mellon group (Partial control)	First Boston Corp. co-managed (with Eastman Dillon Union Securities) a $50 million bond offering in 1970 for the company, a moderate/heavy user of long-term debt ('71 MI). Mellon National Bank had a representative on the finance committee ('69 Pr).
General Electric	Morgan group (Partial control)	Morgan, Stanley and Company managed $225 million in bond offerings for GE Credit Corp and co-managed (with Goldman, Sachs and Company) $525 million in bond offerings for GE in 1967-

TABLE B-2. Changes in the Classification of the 200 Largest Nonfinancial
Corporations Resulting from the Inclusion of Control by Groups of
Financial Institutions, 1967-1969 (Continued)

Corporation	Controller(s)	Basis of classification
General Electric (Continued)		1972; GE is a moderate user of long-term debt ('72 MI). Morgan, Stanley and Morgan Guarantee Trust each had a representative on the board ('69 AR).
General Mills	Morgan group (Full control)	Bankers Trust Company held 4.7% of the voting stock in 1967 (HBCC) and Prudential Life held 1.6% of the voting stock in 1969 (SOI), totalling 6.3% of the voting stock. Prudential held 21% of the long-term debt of the company, a moderate/heavy user of long-term debt (SOI, '71 MI).
Ling-Temco-Vought	Lehman-Goldman, Sachs group (Partial control) (Also partial control by James Ling)	Lehman Brothers and Goldman, Sachs managed $185 million in bond offerings in 1967-1968 for the company, a very heavy user of long-term debt ('71 MI). Lehman and Goldman, Sachs each had a representative on the board ('69 Pr).
May Department Stores	Lehman-Goldman, Sachs group (Partial control)	Lehman Brothers and Goldman, Sachs managed $100 million in bond offerings in 1969-1970 ('74 S&P), and Goldman, Sachs lent $202 million (short-term) in fiscal 1968. Each investment bank had a representative on the board ('69 Pr). The company was a moderate/heavy user of long-term debt ('71 MI).
Scott Paper	Morgan group (Partial control)	Morgan Guarantee Trust held 37% of the long-term debt and had a representative on the board ('70 Pr). Smith, Barney and Company co-managed (with Drexel and Company and Merrill, Lynch) a $100

TABLE B-2. Changes in the Classification of the 200 Largest Nonfinancial
Corporations Resulting from the Inclusion of Control by Groups of
Financial Institutions, 1967-1969 (Continued)

Corporation	Controller(s)	Basis of classification
Scott Paper (Continued)		million bond offering in 1968 and had a representative on the board ('71 MI, '69 AR). Scott was a moderate user of long-term debt ('71 MI).
Southern California Edison	Chase group (Partial control)	Chase Manhattan Bank held 2.8% and Equitable Life held 3.2% of the voting stock ('69 FPCR), totalling 6% of the voting stock.
Trans World Airlines	Chase group (Full control)	Chase Manhattan Bank held 7.4% of the voting stock (GOCII). Chase, Metropolitan Life and Equitable Life together held 23% of the long-term debt of the company, a very heavy user of long-term debt ('69 CABR).
TRW	Morgan group (Full control)	Morgan Guarantee Trust held 5.4% of the voting stock (GOCII). Smith, Barney and Company managed $100 million in bond offerings in 1967-1970 and co-managed (with two foreign investment banks) $52 million more in 1967-1970 ('71 MI). TRW is a moderate/heavy user of long-term debt ('71 MI).
Uniroyal	Chase Group (Partial control) (Also partial control by Kuhn, Loeb)	Metropolitan Life held 18% of the long-term debt (SOI); Uniroyal was a moderate/heavy user of long-term debt ('71 MI). Chemical Bank had a representative on the executive committee ('69 AR).
Westinghouse Electric	Mellon group (Partial control) (Also partial control by Kuhn, Loeb)	First Boston Corp. co-managed (with Kuhn, Loeb) $400 million in bond offerings in 1967-1970 ('71 MI). Mellon National Bank was a creditor of the company, and had a representative on the executive committee ('69 Pr).

TABLE B-2. Changes in the Classification of the 200 Largest Nonfinancial Corporations Resulting from the Inclusion of Control by Groups of Financial Institutions, 1967-1969

Corporation	Controller(s)	Basis of classification
Westinghouse Electric (Continued)		The company was a moderate user of long-term debt ('69 AR).
Woolworth, F. W.	Chase group (Partial control)	Equitable Life held 24% of the long-term debt (SOI); the company was a moderate user of long-term debt ('71 MI). Chase Manhattan Bank and Chemical Bank each had a representative on the finance committee ('69 Pr).

Corporation	Suspected controller	Comments
Standard Oil (New Jersey)	Chase group (suspected control)	Metropolitan Life, Equitable Life, and two Rockefeller foundations held 1.9% of the voting stock (SOI, foundation AR's); historical relationship.

TABLE B-3. Alphabetical Index to Table B-1

Corporation	Section of Table B-1	Corporation	Section of Table B-1
Aluminum Company of America	A	American Metal Climax	F
Allied Chemical	F	American Smelting & Refining	A
Allied Stores	G	American Standard	G
Allis Chalmers	C	American Telephone & Telegraph	G
Amerada Hess	D		
American Airlines	G	AMK	B
American Brands	G	Anaconda Copper	G+
American Can	G	Armco Steel	G
American Cyanimid	G	Ashland Oil	G
American Electric Power	G	Atlantic Richfield	G
		Avco	C
American Home Products	G	Babcock & Wilcox	G
		Bendix	G

TABLE B-3. Alphabetical Index to Table B-1 (Continued)

Corporation	Section of Table B-1	Corporation	Section of Table B-1
Bethlehem Steel	G	DuPont (E. I.) de Nemours	D
Boeing Aircraft	B	Eastern Airlines	A
Boise Cascade	G	Eastman Kodak	G
Borden	G	Eaton, Yale & Towne	G
Borg-Warner	G	El Paso Natural Gas	G
Bristol-Myers	G	Ethyl	D
Burlington Industries	B	Federated Department Stores	B
Burroughs	B	Firestone Tire and Rubber	C
Caterpillar Tractor	G		
Celanese	A	FMC	B
Chesapeake & Ohio Railway	G	Ford Motor Company	D
		Fruehauf	G
Chicago, Milwaukee, St. Paul & Pacific Railway	A	Gamble-Skogmo	D
		General American Transportation	G
Chrysler	B		
Cities Service	B	General Dynamics	C
City Investing	G	General Electric	G+
Coca Cola	D	General Foods	G
Colt Industries	B	General Mills	G+
Columbia Broadcasting System	C	General Motors	G
		General Telephone & Electronics	G
Columbia Gas System	G		
Commonwealth Edison	G	General Tire & Rubber	D
Consolidated Edison	G	Georgia-Pacific	G
Consolidated Foods	G	Getty Oil	D
Continental Can	B	Goodrich, B. F.	A
Continental Oil	G	Goodyear Tire and Rubber	G
Control Data	B		
CPC International	G	Grace (W. R.)	C
Crown Zellerbach	B	Grant, W. T.	D
Dart Industries	G	Great Atlantic & Pacific Tea Company	D
Dayton-Hudson	D		
Deere	D	Great Northern Railway	B
Delta Airlines	B		
Diamond Shamrock	B	Greyhound	G
Dow Chemical	D	Gulf Oil	A
Dresser Industries	G+		

TABLE B-3. Alphabetical Index to Table B-1 (Continued)

Corporation	Section of Table B-1	Corporation	Section of Table B-1
Gulf & Western Industries	C	Mead	G
Heinz, H. J.	D	Minnesota Mining & Manufacturing	E
Hercules	B	Mississippi River Corporation	G
Honeywell	B		
Illinois Central Industries	B	Mobil Oil	G
Ingersoll-Rand	G	Monsanto	B
Inland Steel	B	National Cash Register	B
International Business Machines	G	National Distillers & Chemical	B
International Harvester	B	National Lead	G
International Paper	B	National Steel	C
International Telephone & Telegraph	B	Norfolk & Western Railway	B
International Utilities	G	North American Rockwell	G
Kaiser Aluminum & Chemical	D	Northern Pacific Railway	B
		Northwest Airlines	B
Kaiser Industries	D	Northwest Industries	A
Kennecott Copper	A	Norton Simon	D
Kerr-McGee	D	Occidental Petroleum	G
Kidde, Walter	G	Ogden	A
Kimberly-Clark	G	Olin	C
Kraftco	G	Owens-Illinois	B
Kresge, S. S.	D	Pacific Gas & Electric	G
Kroger	B	Pan American World Airways	G
Ling-Temco-Vought	D+		
Litton Industries	G	Penn Central	G
Lockheed Aircraft	G	Penney, J. C.	B
Loew's Theatres	D	Pfizer, Charles	G
Louisville & Nashville Railroad	A	Phelps Dodge	G
		Philip Morris	G
Lykes-Youngstown	D	Phillips Petroleum	B
Marathon Oil	G	PPG Industries	D
Marcor	G	Proctor & Gamble	F
Martin Marietta	G	Public Service Electric & Gas	G
May Department Stores	G+		
McDonnell-Douglas	D	Ralston Purina	D

TABLE B-3. Alphabetical Index to Table B-1 (Continued)

Corporation	Section of Table B-1	Corporation	Section of Table B-1
Rapid-American	D	Swift and Company	E
RCA	G	Teledyne	G
Republic Steel	G	Tenneco	G
Reynolds Metals	D	Texaco	G
Reynolds (R. J.) Tobacco	B	Textron	B
		Trans World Airlines	B+
Safeway Stores	B	TRW	B+
Sante Fe Industries	G	Union Carbide	G
Scott Paper	G+	Union Oil	G
Seaboard Coastline Industries	A	Union Pacific	A
		Uniroyal	B+
Sears, Roebuck	F	United Aircraft	B
Signal Companies	G	United Air Lines	G
Singer	G	United Merchants & Manufacturers	D
Southern California Edison	G+	U. S. Industries	D
Southern Company	G	U. S. Plywood-Champion Papers	B
Southern Pacific	G	United States Steel Corporation	F
Southern Railway	G		
Spartans Industries	D	Walter, Jim	G
Sperry Rand	B	Westinghouse Electric	B+
Standard Oil of California	G	Weyerhaeuser	G
Standard Oil (Indiana)	B	Wheeling-Pittsburg Steel	G
Standard Oil (New Jersey)	G+	White Consolidated Industries	C
Standard Oil (Ohio)	B	Woolworth, F. W.	G+
Stevens, J. P.	G	Xerox	B
St. Regis Paper	B		
Studebaker-Worthington	G		
Sun Oil	D		

+See also Table B-2.

Financial and Owner Control Among Industrial Companies, by Industry

The industrial companies in the sample have been classified by industry, using the Standard Industrial Classification system. Some of the industry categories used here correspond to two-digit major industry groups, such as "chemicals." Some combined two adjacent two-digit groups, such as the "food and tobacco" group. Others comprised only a part of a two-digit group, such as motor vehicles, which form part of the two-digit transportation equipment group. Table C-2 lists the industry categories used and relates them to Standard Industrial Classification categories.

The industry categories used here were defined with two goals in mind. One was a desire to incorporate as many industrial companies as possible into some distinctive industry category, minimizing the use of the "diversified manufacturing" category. Today most industrial companies are quite diversified. A corporation was assigned to a particular industry group if its sales of products within that group were substantially greater than its sales within any other single group, provided that the firm's sales within the group in question comprised at least 30 percent of its total sales. Corporations that did not fit into any normal industry group were assigned to the "diversified manufacturing" category. If for two related two-digit categories, several companies were found to have their sales evenly divided between the two, then the two categories were usually combined, to avoid swelling the diversified manufacturing group. For example, the "wood and paper" category was formed out of the lumber and wood products major industry group and the paper major industry group for that reason.

A second goal in defining industry categories was to avoid too small industry groups. Any two-digit category having fewer than 4 companies out of the sample of 153 industrials was combined with an appropriate neighboring category. An exception to this rule led to the "other manufacturing" group. The stone, clay, glass, and concrete products group and the fabricated metal products group, both two-digit S. I. C. groups, had only two companies each from the sample. It was not appropriate to combine either group with an adjacent two-digit group. Instead, the two groups were combined to form the "other manufacturing" group. In addition, a few quite large two-digit categories were broken up when they contained two well-known subcategories that involved no serious overlap problems for the companies involved.

Table C-1 shows the findings on financial and owner control by industry. Financial control was most frequent for office machinery and professional and scientific equipment, which includes computers; tires and rubber; aircraft; and the small "other manufacturing" category. Financial control was least frequent for food and tobacco, textiles and apparel, steel, and electrical machinery. Owner control was most frequent for textiles and apparel, food and tobacco, tires and rubber, nonelectrical machinery, aircraft, and chemicals. It was least common for office machinery and professional and scientific equipment, electrical machinery, and wood and paper.

TABLE C-1. Financial and Owner Control among Industrial Companies in the Sample, by Industry

Industry	Number in Sample	Financial control*		Owner control	
		Number	Percentage of industry	Number	Percentage of industry
Food and tobacco	15	2	13.3	6	40.0
Textiles and apparel	4	1	25.0	2	50.0
Wood and paper	10	4	40.0	0	0
Chemicals	16	5	31.3	5	31.3
Petroleum	19	5	26.3	4	21.1
Tires and rubber	5	3	60.0	2	40.0
Steel	8	2	25.0	2	25.0
Nonferrous metals	9	3	33.3	2	22.2
Nonelectrical machinery	8	3	37.5	3	37.5
Electrical machinery	4	1	25.0	0	0
Office machinery and professional and scientific equipment	8	6	75.0	0	0

TABLE C-1. Financial and Owner Control among Industrial Companies
in the Sample, by Industry (Continued)

Industry	Number in Sample	Financial control*		Owner control	
		Number	Percentage of industry	Number	Percentage of industry
Motor vehicles	7	2	28.6	1	14.3
Aircraft	6	3	50.0	2	33.3
Diversified manufacturing	29	11	37.9	5	17.2
Other manufacturing+	4	2	50.0	1	25.0
All industrials	152	53	34.9	35	23.0

*Excluding control by groups of financial institutions.
+Includes stone, clay, glass and concrete, and
 fabricated metal products.

TABLE C-2. Industry Categories in Table C-1 and Standard Industrial
Classification Categories

Industry in Table C-1	Standard industrial classification	
Food tobacco	20	Food and kindred products
	21	Tobacco manufactures
Textiles and apparel	22	Textile mill products
	23	Apparel and other finished products made from fabrics and similar materials
Wood and paper	24	Lumber and wood products, except furniture
	26	Paper and allied products
Chemicals	28	Chemicals and allied products
Petroleum	13	Crude petroleum and natural gas
	29	Petroleum refining and related industries
Tires and rubber	30	Rubber and miscellaneous plastic products
Steel	331	Various basic steel manufacturing operations

TABLE C-2. Industry Categories in Table C-1 and Standard Industrial
Classification Categories (Continued)

Industry in Table C-1	Standard industrial classification	
Nonferrous metals	333, 334, 335, 336	Aluminum, copper, lead, zinc, and other nonferrous metal manufacturing
Nonelectrical machinery	35	Except 357 — Nonelectrical machinery except office machinery
Electrical machinery	36	Electrical machinery, equipment, and supplies
Office machinery and professional and scientific equipment	357	Office machinery
	38	Professional, scientific and controlling instruments; photographic and optical goods; watches and clocks
Motor vehicles	371	Motor vehicles; passenger car, truck and bus bodies; motor vehicle parts and accessories; truck trailers
Aircraft	372	Aircraft, aircraft engines and parts
Diversified manufacturing		Not applicable
Other manufacturing	32	Stone, clay, glass and concrete products
	34	Fabricated metal products, except ordnance, machinery, and transportation equipment

Companies Controlled by Groups of Financial Institutions

Tables D-1 through D-4 list the companies in the sample that are controlled by one of the four groups of financial institutions. Companies that are controlled by a single financial institution in a group of financial institutions are listed separately in each table. The last part of each table lists companies that meet the criteria for control by the group of financial institutions but do not meet the criteria for control by any single financial institution in the group.

Tables D-5 and D-6 list the companies controlled by Chicago and Cleveland financial institutions, respectively. Although Chicago and Cleveland financial institutions were not treated as groups of financial institutions, other students of financial control have regarded them as groups.

For an explanation of the classification of companies by industry, see Appendix C.

TABLE D-1. Companies Controlled by the Chase Group

A. Companies controlled by Chase Manhattan Bank

Company	Industry or sector	Other controllers
Boeing	aircraft mfg.	
Celanese	diversified mfg.	
Columbia Broadcasting System	broadcasting	W. S. Paley
Eastern Airlines	airline	
Great Northern Railway	railroad	
Gulf and Western Industries	diversified mfg.	Bluhdorn and Duncan
Hercules	chemicals	
Monsanto	chemicals	

TABLE D-1. Companies Controlled by the Chase Group (Continued)

Company	Industry or sector	Other controllers
National Distillers and Chemical	food and tobacco	Worth Fund
National Steel	steel	Pittsburgh National Bank; G. W. Humphrey and Associates
Northern Pacific Railway	railroad	Investors Diversified Services
Northwest Airlines	airline	
Penney, J. C.	retail trade	
Sperry Rand	office machinery and professional and scientific equipment	Bankers Trust Company
Trans World Airlines	airline	
United Aircraft	aircraft mfg.	

B. Companies controlled by Metropolitan Life

St. Regis Paper	wood and paper	

C. Companies not controlled by any individual financial institution in the Chase group

Anaconda Copper	nonferrous metals	
Southern California Edison	utility	
Woolworth, F. W.	retail trade	
Uniroyal	tires and rubber	Kuhn, Loeb and Company

TABLE D-2. Companies Controlled by the Morgan Group

A. Companies controlled by Morgan Guarantee Trust

Company	Industry or sector	Other controllers
American Smelting and Refining	nonferrous metals	
Burlington Industries	textiles and apparel	Wachovia Bank and Trust
International Paper	paper and wood	
Kennecott Copper	nonferrous metals	

TABLE D-2. Companies Controlled by the Morgan Group (Continued)

Company	Industry or sector	Other controllers
National Cash Register	office machinery and professional and scientific equipment	Dillon, Read and Company
Olin	chemicals	Olin family
TRW	diversified mfg.	

B. Companies controlled by Bankers Trust Company

Burroughs	office machinery and professional and scientific equipment	
Control Data	office machinery and professional and scientific equipment	
Crown Zellerbach	paper and wood	
Honeywell	office machinery and professional and scientific equipment	
Sperry Rand	office machinery and professional and scientific equipment	Chase Manhattan Bank

C. Companies not controlled by any individual financial institution in the Morgan group

General Mills	food and tobacco	
General Electric	electrical machinery	
Scott Paper	paper and wood	

TABLE D-3. Companies Controlled by the Mellon Group

A. Companies controlled by Mellon National Bank

Company	Industry or sector	Other controllers
Aluminum Company of America	nonferrous metals	
Gulf Oil	petroleum	
Diamond Shamrock	chemicals	

B. Companies not controlled by any individual financial institution in the Mellon group

Dresser Industries	nonelectrical machinery	
Westinghouse Electric	electrical machinery	Kuhn, Loeb and Company

TABLE D-4. Companies Controlled by the Lehman-Goldman, Sachs Group

A. Companies controlled by Lehman Brothers

Company	Industry or sector	Other controllers
Avco Corporation	diversified mfg.	Harringtons
Continental Can	fabricated metal products	
FMC	nonelectrical machinery	

B. Companies not controlled by any individual financial institution in the Lehman-Goldman, Sachs group

Ling-Temco-Vought	diversified mfg.	James Ling
May Department Stores	retail trade	

TABLE D-5. Companies Controlled by Chicago Financial Institutions

A. Companies controlled by First National Bank, Chicago

Company	Industry or sector	Other controllers
Chicago, Milwaukee, St. Paul and Pacific Railway	railroad	
Federated Department Stores	retail trade	
Goodrich, B. F.	tires and rubber	
Inland Steel	steel	
Northwest Industries	diversified mfg.	
Standard Oil (Indiana)	petroleum	

B. Companies controlled by Continental Illinois National Bank

Company	Industry or sector	Other controllers
Illinois Central Industries	diversified mfg.	Seattle First National Bank; United California Bank; U. S. Trust

TABLE D-6. Companies Controlled by Cleveland Financial Institutions

A. Companies controlled by Cleveland Trust Company

Company	Industry or sector	Other controllers
Allis Chalmers	nonelectrical machinery	H. T. Mandeville
Firestone Tire and Rubber	tires and rubber	Firestone family
White Consolidated Industries	nonelectrical machinery	H. T. Mandeville

B. Companies controlled by National City Bank, Cleveland

Company	Industry or sector	Other controllers
Standard Oil (Ohio)	petroleum	

Selected Bibliography

BOOKS

Adler, Cyrus. *Jacob H. Schiff: His Life and Letters.* London, 1929.

Alhadeff, David A. *Monopoly and Competition in Banking.* Berkeley, 1954.

Bain, Joe S. *Industrial Organization,* 2nd ed. New York, 1968.

Baran, Paul, and Sweezy, Paul M. *Monopoly Capital.* New York, 1966.

Barron, Clarence W. *They Told Barron: Notes of the Late Clarence Barron.* New York, 1930.

Baum, Daniel J. and Stiles, Ned B. *The Silent Partners: Institutional Investors and Corporate Control.* Syracuse, 1965.

Baumol, William. *Business Behavior, Value, and Growth.* New York, 1959.

Berle, Adolf A. *Power Without Property.* New York, 1959.

————. 1954. *The Twentieth Century Capitalist Revolution.* New York.

Berle, Adolf A., and Means, Gardiner C. *The Modern Corporation and Private Property.* rev. ed. New York, 1968.

Bonbright, James C., and Means, Gardiner C. *The Holding Company.* New York, 1932.

Brandeis, Louis D. *Other People's Money, and How the Bankers Use It.* New York, 1914.

Bullock, Hugh. *The Story of Investment Companies.* New York, 1960.

Burr, Anna R. *Portrait of a Banker: James Stillman.* New York, 1927.

Campbell, Edward G. *The Reorganization of the American Railroad System, 1893-1900.* New York, 1938.

Carosso, Vincent P. *Investment Banking in America: A History.* Cambridge, Mass., 1970.

Chevalier, Jean-Marie. *La Structure financiere de l'industrie americaine.* Paris, 1970.

Clews, Henry. *Fifty Years in Wall Street.* New York, 1908.

Corey, Lewis. *The House of Morgan.* New York, 1930.

Creamer, Daniel; Dobrovolsky, Sergei; and Borenstein, Israel. *Capital in Manufacturing and Mining.* Princeton, 1960.

Crosse, H. D. *Management Policies for Commercial Banks.* Englewood Cliffs, 1962.

Donaldson, Elvin F. and Pfahl, John K. *Corporate Finance.* 2nd ed. New York, 1963.

Douglas, William O. *Democracy and Finance.* New Haven, 1940.

Flynn, John T. *God's Gold: John D. Rockefeller and his Times.* New York, 1932.

Galbraith, John Kenneth. *The New Industrial State.* 1967.

Goldsmith, Raymond. *Financial Institutions.* New York, 1968.

————. 1958. *Financial Intermediaries in the American Economy Since 1900.* Princeton.

Gordon, Robert Aaron. *Business Leadership in the Large Corporation.* Berkeley, 1961.

Grayson, Theodore J. *Leaders and Periods of American Finance.* New York, 1932.

Hammond, John W. *Men and Volts.* New York, 1941.

Harbrecht, Paul P. *Pension Funds and Economic Power.* New York, 1959.

Hickman, W. Braddock. *The Volume of Corporate Bond Financing Since 1900.* Princeton, 1953.

Hilferding, Rudolf. *Das Finanzkapital.* Wiener Volksbuchhandlung. Wien, 1923.

Josephson, Matthew. *The Robber Barons.* New York, 1934.

Kaplan, Gilbert E., and Welles, Chris. *The Money Managers.* New York, 1969.

Karr, David. *Fight for Control.* New York, 1956.

Koch, Albert. *Financing of Large Corporations 1920-39.* Washington, 1947.

Larner, Robert J. *Management Control and the Large Corporation.* Cambridge, Massachusetts, 1970.

Lehman, Robert. *Wall Street: Twentieth Century.* New Haven, 1959.

Mace, Myles L. *Directors: Myth and Reality.* Boston, 1971.

Marris, Robin. *The Economic Theory of 'Managerial' Capitalism,* Glencoe, Ill., 1964.

————, and Wood, A., eds. *The Corporate Economy.* Cambridge, Mass., 1971.

Mason, Edward S., ed. *The Corporation in Modern Society.* New York, 1969.

McDonald, Forrest. *Insull.* Chicago, 1962.

Menshikov, S. *Millionaires and Managers.* Moscow, 1969.

Moody, John. *The Masters of Capital.* New Haven. 1919.

————. 1904. *The Truth about the Trusts.* New York.

Nadler, Marcus, and Bogen, Jules. *The Bank Holding Company.* New York, 1959.

O'Connor, Harvey. *Mellon's Millions: The Life and Times of Andrew W. Mellon.* New York, 1933.

Peach, W. Nelson. *The Security Affiliates of National Banks.* Johns Hopkins University Studies in History and Political Science, Series LVIII, No. 13, Baltimore, 1941.

Pecora, Ferdinand. *Wall Street Under Oath: The Story of our Modern Money Changers.* New York, 1939.

Perlo, Victor. *Empire of High Finance.* New York, 1957.

Prochnow, Herbert V., ed. *American Financial Institutions.* New York, 1951.

Ripley, William Z. *Trusts, Pools and Corporations.* New York, 1905.

Robinson, Roland I. *The Management of Bank Funds.* New York, 1962.

Seltzer, Lawrence H. *A Financial History of the American Auto Industry.* Boston, 1928.

Soldofsky, Robert M. *Institutional Ownership of Common Stock: 1900-2000.* Ann Arbor, 1971.

Studenski, Paul, and Krooss, Herman E. *Financial History of the United States.* 2nd ed. New York, 1963.

Tilove, Robert. *Pension Funds and Economic Freedom.* New York, 1959.

Trescott, Paul B. *Financing American Enterprise.* New York, 1963.

Vance, Stanley C. *Boards of Directors: Structure and Performance.* Eugene, 1964.

_____ . 1968. *The Corporate Director.* Homewood.

Williamson, Oliver. *Corporate Control and Business Behavior.* Englewood Cliffs, New Jersey, 1970.

_____ . 1964. *The Economics of Discretionary Behavior.* Englewood Cliffs, New Jersey.

ARTICLES

Baumol, William. "On the Theory of Expansion of the Firm." *American Economic Review,* December 1972.

Beed, C. S. "The Separation of Ownership from Control." *Journal of Economic Studies,* vol. 1, no. 2, Summer 1966.

Berle, Adolf A. "The Impact of the Corporation on Classical Economic Theory." *Quarterly Journal of Economics,* February 1965.

Chevalier, Jean-Marie. "The Problem of Control in Large American Corporations." *Anti-Trust Bulletin,* Spring 1969.

Dooley, Peter C. "The Interlocking Directorate." *American Economic Review,* June 1969.

Fitch, Robert, and Oppenheimer, Mary. "Who Rules the Corporations?" *Socialist Revolution,* vol. 1, nos. 4-6, 1970.

Gordon, Robert Aaron. "Financial Control of Large-Scale Enterprise." *American Economic Review,* March 1939.

Grabowski, Henry, and Mueller, Dennis. "Managerial and Stockholder Welfare Models of Firm Expenditures." *Review of Economics and Statistics,* February 1972.

Herman, Edward. "Do Bankers Control Corporations?" *Monthly Review,* June 1973.

Kamershen, David. "The Influence of Ownership and Control on Profit Rates." *American Economic Review,* June 1968.

Kaysen, Carl. "Another View of Corporate Capitalism." *Quarterly Journal of Economics,* February 1965.

_____ . "The Social Significance of the Modern Corporation." *American Economic Review*, May 1957.

Larner, Robert J. "Ownership and Control of the 200 Largest Nonfinancial Corporations, 1929 and 1963." *American Economic Review*, September 1966.

Lewellen, W. G. "Management and Ownership in Large Firms." *Journal of Finance*, May 1969.

Lintner, John. "Dividends, Earnings, Leverage, Stock Prices, and the Supply of Capital to Corporations." *Review of Economics and Statistics*, August 1962.

_____ . "The Financing of Corporations." In *The Corporation in Modern Society*, edited by Edward S. Mason, 1969.

Louis, Arthur. "The Mutual Funds Have the Votes." *Fortune*, May 1967.

Lybecker, Martin E. "Regulation of Bank Trust Department Investment Activities." *Yale Law Journal*, April 1973.

Machlup, Fritz. "Theories of the Firm: Marginalist, Behavioral, Managerial." *American Economic Review*, December 1967.

Mason, Edward S. "The Apologetics of Managerialism." *Journal of Business*, January 1958.

Monson, R. J.; Chin, J.; and Cooley, D. "The Effect of Separation of Ownership and Control on the Performance of the Large Firm." *Quarterly Journal of Economics*, August 1968.

Monson, R. J., and Downs, A. "A Theory of Large Managerial Firms." *Journal of Political Economy*, June 1965.

Peterson, Shorey. "Corporate Control and Capitalism." *Quarterly Journal of Economics*, February 1965.

Sheehan, Robert. "Proprietors in the World of Big Business." *Fortune*, 15 June 1967.

Sweezy, Paul M. "Resurgence of Financial Control: Fact or Fancy?" *Monthly Review*, November 1971.

Supple, Barry. "A Business Elite: German-Jewish Financiers in 19th Century New York." *Business History Review*, Summer 1957.

Villajero, Don. "Stock Ownership and Control of Corporations." *New University Thought*, Autumn 1961; Winter 1962.

Williamson, Oliver. "Managerial Discretion and Business Behavior." *American Economic Review*, November 1963.

Zald, Mayer. "The Power and Functions of Boards of Directors." *American Journal of Sociology*, July 1969.

U. S. GOVERNMENT STUDIES

U. S., Congress, House Banking and Currency Committee, *Acquisition, Changes in Control, and Bank Stock Loans of Insured Banks*, 90th Congress, 1st Session, 1967.

U. S., Congress, House Banking and Currency Committee, Subcommittee on Domestic Finance, *Bank Stock Ownership and Control*, 89th Congress, 2nd Session, 1966.

U. S., Congress, House Banking and Currency Committee, Subcommittee on Domestic Finance, *Commercial Banks and Their Trust Activities: Emerging Influence on the American Economy*, 90th Congress, 2nd Session, 1968.

U. S., Congress, House Banking and Currency Committee, *Report of the Committee Appointed Pursuant to H. R. 429 and 504 to Investigate the Concentration of Control of Money and Credit*, 62nd Congress, 2nd Session, 1913.

U. S., Congress, House Judiciary Committee, *Investigation of Conglomerate Corporations*, Staff Report of the Antitrust Subcommittee, 92nd Congress, 1st Session, 1971.

U. S., Congress, House Judiciary Committee, *Study of Monopoly Power*, pt. 1, 1949.

U. S., Congress, House Select Committee on Small Business, *Chain Banking: Stockholder and Loan Links of the 200 Largest Member Banks*, 87th Congress, 1963.

U. S., Congress, Joint Economic Committee, Subcommittee on Fiscal Policy, *Investment Policies of Pension Funds*, Hearings, 91st Congress, 2nd Session, 1970.

U. S., Congress, Senate Banking and Currency committee, *Stock Exchange Practices*, Senate Report 1455, 73rd Congress, 2nd Session, 1934; and *Stock Exchange Practices*, Hearings, 72nd Congress, 1st Session, 1932-1933.

U. S., Congress, Senate Government Operations Committee, Subcommittee on Intergovernmental Relations, and on Budgeting, Management, and Expenditure, *Disclosure of Corporate Ownership*, 93rd Congress, 1st Session, 1973; and *Corporate Disclosure*, Hearings, 93rd Congress, 2nd Session, 1974.

U. S., Congress, Senate Government Operations Committee, Subcommittee on Reports, Accounting, and Management, *Corporate Ownership and Control*, 94th Congress, 2nd Session, 1975.

U. S., Congress, Senate Government Operations Committee, Subcommittee on Reports, Accounting, and Management, *Institutional Investors' Common Stock: Holdings and Voting Rights*, 94th Congress, 2nd Session, 1976.

U. S., Federal Deposit Insurance Corporation, *Trust Assets of Insured Commercial Banks — 1974*.

U. S., Federal Trade Commission, *Report on Interlocking Directorates*, 1951.

U. S., National Resources Committee, *The Structure of the American Economy*, 1939.

U. S., Securities and Exchange Commisssion, *Institutional Investor Study Report*, House Document 92-64, referred to the House Committee on Interstate and Foreign Commerce, 1971.

U. S., Temporary National Economic Committee, *Investigation of Concentration of Economic Power*, Monograph No. 29, "The Distribution of Ownership in the 200 Largest Nonfinancial Corporations," 1940.

Index

NOTE: This index is to text matter only. It does not include references to the appendices.

Abbot, Roy T., 139, 140
Acme-Cleveland Corporation, in antitrust suit, 133-134
Aircraft companies, Chase group and, 113
Airlines: Chase group and, 112, 113; Chase Manhattan Bank and, 124; data source for, 92; financial control among, 105
Alger, Fred, 129
Alleghany Corporation, 57n152
Allen and Company, Ogden and, 137, 138, 143n68
Allis Chalmers, 99n65
Aluminum Company of America: growth of, 51; Mellons and, 38
Amalgamated Copper Company, 37
AMK, 96
American Banker, on overcapitalization, 33
American Society of Corporate Secretaries, as data source, 92
American Telephone and Telegraph: has greatest assets, 74; independence of, 58; Morgan and, 36, 49; size affects control of, 103-104; Western Electric is subsidiary of, 73
American Transportation Enterprises, 138
Anaconda Copper: Chase group and, 120, 135; Chase Manhattan Bank and, 21n15; Stillman-Rockefeller group and, 37, 51
Armour, 73
Assets: summary of control by, 101-103, 110-111. *See also* Trust assets

Atlantic Coast Line Company, 115-116
Automobile industry, bank influence on, 34, 42-43
Avco Corporation, 109, 113, 137

Bain, Joe S., 14
Baker, George F., 35, 41
Bank Holding Company Act of 1956, 82
Bank of America: growth of, 45, 46; trust assets in 1974, 70
Bankers: conservatism of, 42; source of power of, 8
Bankers Trust: in Morgan group, 35, 36, 50, 85, 88, 112, 149n75; number of companies and assets controlled by, 111; Sperry Rand and, 122; trust assets in 1974, 70. *See also* Morgan group
Banking Act of 1933 (Glass-Steagull Act), 54-55, 87, 88
Bankruptcy Act of 1898, Chandler Amendments, 21, 56
Banks, consolidation of, 45. *See also* Commercial banks; Financial institutions; Investment banks
Baran, Paul, 6
Baring family, the, 25n2, 29
Baum, Daniel, 9
Baumol, William, 5
Berle, Adolf A., on financial control, 9. *See also* Berle and Means
Berle and Means: on immediate control, 7; on management control, 2, 4, 14-15, 58, 118; managerial thesis modified, 149
Board of directors. *See* Management

Board representation. *See* Management

Bonds, data sources for, 93; life insurance companies purchase, 20, 62; utility, 46

Borrowing. *See* Commercial banks, as creditors; External finance

Boston interest group, 59

Brokerage firms, effect of depression on, 52

Brown Brothers Harriman, Union Pacific and, 82-83, 119

Burlington Northern Railway, 73n2

Business periodicals, as data source, 92, 93

Chandler Act of 1938, 21, 56

California, growth of banking in, 45

Capital, supplying. *See* External finance; Commercial banks, as creditors

Capitalism, 144-145, 148-149

Carnegie, Andrew, 2, 132; Morgan and, 32, 113-114

Carnegie Steel Company: Mellon and, 38; Morgan and, 32

Carosso, Vincent P.: on bank control of railroads, 30; on decline of banker power, 41n74

Central Trust Company, General Motors and, 34

Chandler Act of 1938, 21, 56

Chase group: Anaconda Copper and, 120, 135; members of, 85, 86-87; number of companies and assets controlled by, 112, 113; power of, 145, 146; types of companies controlled by, 112-113; Southern California Edison and, 107; Standard Oil of New Jersey and, 100

Chase Manhattan Bank: airlines and, 124, 134; Anaconda Copper and, 21n15, 120; Columbia Broadcasting System and, 95; Gulf and Western merger program and, 138-140; number of companies and assets controlled by, 110, 111; Rockefellers and, 87, 112, 149; Sperry Rand and, 122; trust assets in 1974, 70; types of companies controlled by, 113; vertical relationships and, 136. *See also* Chase group

Chase National Bank, Rockefellers and, 50, 87

Chemical Bank, 85, 87. *See also* Chase group

Chemical companies, Chase group and, 113

Chicago, Illinois, financial institutions in: growth of, 46; number of companies and assets controlled by, 111, 112; power of, 59, 145; types of companies controlled by, 113

Chicago, Burlington and Quincy Railroad, 73

Chicago, Milwaukee, St. Paul and Pacific Railway, 105

Chicago and Northwestern Railway, 74

Chile, Anaconda Copper and, 21n15, 120

Chrysler Corporation, 20n12

City Bank of New York, Rockefeller and, 37. *See also* National City Bank

Civil Aeronautics Board: as data source, 92, 93; investigates director interlocks, 124

Clark, S.C., Singer and, 79

Clayton Act, 40

Cleveland, Ohio, financial institutions in: number of companies and assets controlled by, 111, 112; power of, 59, 111, 145; share control with stockholders, 113

Cleveland Trust Company: antitrust suit against, 133-134; Firestone Tire and Rubber Company and, 114-115; number of companies and assets controlled by, 111

Coffin, Charles, 32n33

Colt Industries, 96

Columbia Broadcasting System, 74, 95

Commercial banks: became investment banks, 35; competition among, 45; as creditors, 20, 62-63, 131, 132, 142-143; effect of depression on, 52-53; growth of, 45; informal pressure by, 127; investment trusts sponsored by, 48; mergers and, 138-140; New Deal legislation and, 54, 55; number of companies controlled by, 108-109; postwar activity, 62-63; security affiliates, 45, 48; in World War II, 57. *See also* Commercial banks, trust departments; External finance; Financial institutions; *names of individual banks*

Commercial banks, trust departments, 63; competition among, 45, 84; concentration of, 69, 70-71; data sources for, 89-92; informal pressure by, 128; interest in portfolio companies' profitability, 141-143, 147; power of as stockholders, 20, 63-66, 68, 71, 132, 141-142; regulation of, 69; trust assets, 63, 66-68, 70-71;

voting by, 125-127. *See also* Commercial banks; Financial institutions; *names of individual banks*
Commercial Banks and Their Trust Activities. See Patman Report
"Community of interest," 39; Clayton Act discouraged, 40; railroads and, 132; in steel industry, 32; weakens competition, 39, 135
Competition: conglomerates and, 140; financial control reduces, 132-135, 137; among financial institutions, 26-27, 30, 38-39, 43-47; among railroads, 27, 28, 30; in steel industry, 32; vertical relationships reduce, 137
Competitive bidding, compulsory, 57, 60
Computers, Morgan group and, 113
Concentration, economic: effect of, 145-147; extent of, 145; mergers increase, 140
Conglomerates: reduce competition, 140; in sample of 200, 74-75; types of financial institutions controlling, 109. *See also* Mergers
Consolidated Edison, 37, 78-79
Consolidated Gas Company, 37
Control: basis of, 14, 18-22, 26; categories of, 75; criteria for determining, 6-7, 16, 75-84; defined, 1, 14-16; by groups, 16, 17-18; immediate vs. ultimate, 7, 19n8, 83-84; implications of, 1-2, 15-16; Larner study of, 116-118; managing distinguished from, 16-18; ownership separated from, 3; in sample of 200, 96-108; working definitions of, problems in applying, 93-96. *See also* Financial control; Financial control thesis; Managerial thesis; Owner control
Corey, Lewis, 41n74
Corporations, nonfinancial: control of other corporations by, 19n8: criteria for control of, 75-79; early, 24; goals of, 140-145, 146; in interest groups, 59; large, rise of, 1, 31-35, 60; Larner study of, 116-118; looting of, 28; "mature," 60; New Deal legislation and, 55, 56; "soulfulness" in, 5, 13, 144; sources of external finance for, 57-58, 61-63, 71. *See also* Corporations, sample of 200; Portfolio companies
Corporations, sample of 200: control of summarized, 96-108; described, 72-75; most powerful influences on, 110-113; sources of control over, 109-110; sources of data for, 89-93; types of

controlled by groups of financial institutions, 112-113; types of controlling institutions, 108-110
Creditor relationships, sources of data on, 92-93. *See also* Commercial banks, as creditors; External finance
Crown, Henry, 94
Crown Zellerbach, 134

Depression, effect of on financial institutions, 51-53
Devon Securities, Fifth Avenue Coach Lines and, 21n14
Diamond Alkali, 96
Diamond Shamrock Corporation, 96
Dillon, Reed and Company, 48
Director interlocks: in Chase group, 87; control through, 21-22, 86; implications of, 147; and informal vertical relationships, 135; in Morgan group, 88; regulatory barriers to, 87, 123-124. *See also* Management, control through representation in
Director representation. *See* Management, control through representation in
Disclosure of Corporate Ownership (Metcalf Report): on Columbia Broadcasting System, 95; as data source, 11, 90-92, 95; on Dow Chemical, 91-92; on McDonnell Douglas Corporation, 92; studied combined stockholdings of New York banks, 85
Dow Chemical, sources of data on, 91-92
Drew, Daniel, 28
Drexel and Company, 55n143
Drexel, Morgan and Company: origins of, 25n2; ties with English capital, 26
Dun and Bradstreet, *Million Dollar Directory* as data source, 93
DuPont family: General Motors and, 34n44, 43; independence in, 18n7
DuPont interest group, 59n163
Durant, William C., 34n44
Dutch capital, for American railroads, 26

Eastern Airlines, 134
Eaton, Cyrus, 57n152
Edison General Electric Company, 31-32
Electric bond and Share group, 47
Employee benefit funds: commercial banks manage, 67; concentration of, 69; financial control through, 116; as savings, 71; self-administered, in miscellaneous control category, 75. *See also* Pension funds

Employee Retirement Income Security Act of 1974, 69

English capital, for American railroads, 26, 27; Morgan and, 26, 42, 149

Entrepreneurs, new, 42-43

Equitable Life Assurance Society: in Chase group, 85, 87 89; Morgan and, 36; in Rockefeller group, 50. *See also* Chase group

Equitable Trust, Rockefeller and, 50

Europe, socialism in, 39

European capital: for American railroads, decline in importance of, 41-42

External finance: as basis for control, 20-21, 80-81, 82, 109-110; measuring reliance on, 80-81; reliance on and type of control, 130-132; sources of, 57-58, 61-63, 71. *See also* Commercial banks, as creditors; Creditor relationships, sources of data on

Federal Power Commission, as data source, 92

Federal Reserve Board, approves stock purchases, 82

Federal Reserve System: Banking Act and, 54; weakened New York banks, 40

Federal Steel, 32

Fifth Avenue Coach Lines of New York, 21n*14*

Financial control: basis of, 19-22, 75-77, 109-110, 122, 130; competition and, 132-135, 137; corporate goals under, 141-145, 146; criteria for determining, 75-77, 79-84, 93-96, 121; decline of, 1930-1945, 58-60; development into from owner control, 113-116; early rise of, 24-41; effect of, 130-140, 143, 145, 146; extent of, 63-71, 122; full, 76-77; instance of, defined, 121-122; means of exercising, 14, 15, 119-130; mergers and, 137-140; in 1920s, 49; partial, 77, 98, 99-100; passive, 127, 129; postwar spread of, 61-71, 118; suspected, 78-79; types of, 119-120; vertical relationships and, 135-137

Financial control, summary of results for sample of 200, 97-101; by assets, 101-103; by industrial sector, 105-108; by size group, 101, 103-104

Financial control thesis, 8-13, 148-149; external debt financing and, 131-132

Financial groups, 146-147. *See also* Financial institutions, groups

Financial institutions: abuses investigated, 53-54; competition among, 43-47, 84-85; control by, *see* Financial control; controlling competing companies, 133-135; cooperation among, 51; as creditors, *see* Commercial banks, as creditors, *and see* External finance; depression and, 52-53; growth of, 1948-1965, 61-63; informal pressure by, 127-130; interest in portfolio companies' profitability, 141-145, 147; legislation controlling, 54-56; in managerial thesis, 3; as managers of savings, 71; partial control adequate for, 99-100; personal power declined in, 41; reforms, 1905-1914, 39-41; and sample of 200, 108-113; sources of data on, 89-93; sources of power, 19-22, 71; as stockholders, 10, 19-20, 63-71; voting rights and, 125-127; World War II and, 56-58. *See also* Commerical banks; Commercial banks, trust departments; Investment banks; Investment companies; Life insurance companies

Financial institutions, groups of, 35-39, 77, 84-89; data about, 100-101; economic concentration under, 145; power of, 146, 147; and sample of 200, 112-113

Firestone Tire and Rubber Company, 114-115

First Boston Corporation, New York, in Mellon group, 85, 86, 89. *See also* Mellon group

First National Bank of Boston, as shareholder, 95n*60*

First National Bank of Chicago: number of companies and assets controlled by, 111; trust assets in 1974, 70

First National Bank of New York: in Morgan group, 35-36, 50, 84; power of, 36. *See also* Morgan group

First National City Bank: Consolidated Edison and, 79; informal pressure by, 128-129; number of companies and assets controlled by, 111; in Stillman-Rockefeller group, 112, 149; trust assets in 1974, 70. *See also* National City Bank

Fisk, James, 28

Fitch, Robert, 11, 146-147

FMC, 109, 137

Ford, Henry, 42-43

Ford Motor Company: independence of, 42-43; under owner control, 101

Fortune: as data source, 92; on General Dynamics and Crown, 94

Galbraith, John Kenneth: on corporate "soul," 5; and managerial thesis, 4; on planning and vertical integration, 136

Gary, Judge, 132

Gates, John W., 132

General Dynamics Corporation, 94, 96

General Electric, 100; Morgan and, 31-32, 36, 50

General Motors Company: banks gained temproary control of, 34; duPont and, 43; Morgan and, 42n76, 43

German capital, for American railroads, 26, 27

Getty, J. Paul, 99

Getty Oil, 99

Giannini, A.P., 46

Glass-Steagull Act, 54-55, 87, 88

Goldman, Sachs and Company: in Lehman-Goldman, Sachs group, 85, 86, 89; sponsored investment trusts, 48; types of companies financed by, 35, 86; and utility holding companies, 48. *See also* Lehman-Goldman, Sachs group;

Gordon, Robert Aaron: on control of U.S. Steel, 15; on managerial control, 4, 49n113

Gould, Jay, 28, 30

Government: antitrust actions, 39-41; financed war production, 56; investigated financial institutions, 53-54; New Deal legislation, 54-56. *See also* United States Congress

Gray-Pecora investigations, 53-54

Great Depression, effect of on financial institutions, 51-53

Great Northern Railroad, 26, 73

Greyhound, 73

Guarantee Trust, Morgan and, 35, 36, 50, 88

Gulf and Western Industries, Chase Manhattan Bank and, 138-140

Gulf Oil: growth of, 51; Mellons and, 38; under financial control, 101

H.J. Heinz Corporation, 114

Halsey, Stuart and Company: and competitive bidding struggle, 57n152; rise of, 46, 60; utility holding companies and, 48

Harriman, E.H.: railroad rivalry with Morgan, 38-39; Rockefeller and Stillman backed, 37, 38; Union Pacific Railroad and, 37, 82-83

Harringtons, the, and Avco Corporation, 137

Harris, Forbes and Company, utility control by, 48, 49n112

Harris Trust, trust assets in 1974, 70

Heinz, H.J. II, 114

Heinz, V.I., 114

Herman, Edward, 11-12

Hill, James J., 37

Holding companies: and public utilities, 47-48; and railroads, 48

Hughes, Howard, 108

Illinois Central Industries, 74-75

Illinois Central Railroad, 74

Industrial producer goods, Mellon group and, 113

Industrials, control of, 106, 108

Informal pressure, financial control through, 121, 127-130

Inland Steel v. National Labor Relations Board, 67

Institutional Investor Study Report: on bank power, 11, 131-132; as data source, 11, 89, 90, 91, 95, 100; on groups of stockholders, common interests of, 84; on informal control, 127-128, 129; unidentified institutions in, 96; on voting rights, exercise of by institutional investors, 126-127

Insull, Samuel, and utility empire, 46, 48, 51

Interest groups, 59. *See also* Financial institutions, groups of

International Business Machines (IBM), 113

International Harvester, 36, 96

International Paper, 134-135

International Telephone and Telegraph, 109, 137, 138

Interstate Commerce Commission: as data source, 92; on railroad monopoly, 30; regulations encourage financial control, 105; required competitive bidding for railroad securities, 57

Investigation of Conglomerate Corporations, 137-138, 139

Investment advisors: exercise of voting rights by, 126; informal pressure by, 129

Investment banking, "active," 26. *See also* Investment banks

Investment banks: competition among, 26, 44-45, 46-47; competition with commercial banks, 45; conglomerates and, 109, 113, 137-138; conservatism of, 33; in depression, 52; growth of large corporations and, 31-35; interest in portfolio companies' profitability, 143; as intermediaries, 61-62; investigated, 59-60; investment trusts and, 48-49; New Deal legislation and, 54-60 *passim;* number of corporations controlled by, 109; postwar activity, 62; railroads and, 25-31; rise of, 24-27; sources of power of, 20, 21, 26, 34, 131; "spreads," 57n153; utilities and, 47-48, 107; voting trusts used by, 63-64; as "wholesalers" of securities, 44; in World War II, 56-57. *See also* Financial institutions

Investment Company Act of 1940, 56

Investment company complexes: defined, 70n208; influence of, 108, 109; investment advisors manage, 126

Investment companies: concentration of, 69-70; extent of stockholdings, 65, 68-69, 108, 109; interest in portfolio companies' profitability, 143; manage savings, 71; power of, 66, 131n38; regulation of, 69

Investment trusts: defined, 48; effect of depression on, 53; growth of, 48-49

Kahn, Otto, 44

Kaiser, E.F., 99n65

Kaiser Aluminum and Chemical, 99n65

Kaiser Industries: in sample of 200, 73, 74; under owner control, 99n65

Kaiser Steel, 73

Kaysen, Carl: on corporate "soul," 13, 144; on managerial corporation, 4-5

Kennecott Copper: Morgan group and, 50; Morgan Guarantee Trust and, 135

Kidder, Peabody and Company: effect of depression on, 52; obtained Santa Fe stock, 29; sponsored investment trusts, 48; ties with English capital, 26

Knowles, James C., studied Rockefeller group, 86, 87

Kuhn, Loeb and Company: effect of Banking Act on, 54-55; effect of competition on, 44; effect of depression on, 52; ITT and, 137; number of companies and assets controlled by, 111; origins of, 25n2; power of, 37, 42, 51, 59, 112; railroads and, 29, 37, 112; ties with German capital, 26-27; Westinghouse Electric and, 37

Lamont, Thomas, 50

Larner, Robert J.: on management control, 4; on owner control, criteria for, 83; Sheehan confirmed findings of, 7; study of corporate control compared, 116-118

Lazard Freres and Company: ITT and, 137, 138; number of companies and assets controlled by, 111

"Lead banks," 20

Lee, Higginson and Company, 34, 52

Lehman Brothers: Avco Corporation and, 137; early power of, 112; companies, 35; FMC and, 137; in Lehman-Goldman, Sachs group, 85, 86, 89; number of companies and assets controlled by, 111; types of companies financed by, 35, 86. *See also* Lehman-Goldman, Sachs group

Lehman-Goldman, Sachs group: Avco Corporation and, 113; economic concentration under, 145; Ling-Temco-Vought and, 113, 137; members of, 85, 86, 89; number of companies and assets controlled by, 112; shares control with individual stockholders, 113; types of companies financed by, 35, 86

Life insurance companies: concentration among, 69, 70; data sources for, 92, 93; effect of depression on, 53; exercise of voting rights by, 126; growth of as stockholders, 65; interest in portfolio companies' profitability, 143; New Deal legislation and, 55; number of companies controlled by, 109; source of power of, 20, 62, 64, 126, 131; struggle for control over, 36, 84; in World War II, 57-58. *See also* Financial institutions

Ling, James, 137

Ling-Temco-Vought, 100, 109, 113, 137

Lingua, George M., 128-129

Lorillard, P., 31n29

Magowan, Merrill, 96

Magowan, R.A., 95-96

Management: control through representation in, 21-22, 81, 82, 119, 120, 121-125; defined, 1, 14, 16-17, 121n7; extent of voting against by institutional investors, 125-127

Managerial corporations: corporate goals in, 140-141; implications of, 4-6; mathematical models for, 5; profit rates in, 144

Managerial thesis, 2-6, 148; basis of power in, 19; beginnings of, 58; challenged, 9, 10-11, 13; supported, 7, 8; on corporate goals, 140-141; financing and, 46-47, 53n135, 130, 131; and independence from banks, 46-47; modified, 149

Managing, control distinguished from, 1, 16-18

Mandeville, H.T., 99n65

Manufacturers Hanover Trust: as lead bank for Chrysler, 20n12; trust assets in 1974, 70

Manufacturing companies; diversified, Chase group and, 113; Lehman-Goldman, Sachs influence on, 35, 86

Market behavior: corporate control and, 1-2; effect of financial control on, 12-13, 130-140; managerial corporations and, 5

Marris, Robin, 5

Marxian economics, corporate goals in, 140; social significance of, 144-145

Marxist economists: financial control thesis and, 8-9, 11-12; managerial thesis and, 4

Mathematical models, for managerial corporations, 5

Mayer, J.A., 114

McDonnell Douglas Corporation, 92

McGuirk, William E., Jr., 115

Mead Corporation, 83n18

Means, Gardiner, managerial thesis and, 2. See also Berle and Means

Mellon, R.K., 149

Mellon family: power of, 38, 51, 149

Mellon group: economic concentration under, 145; members of, 85, 86, 89; number of companies and assets controlled by, 112; power of, 59, 146; trust assets in 1974, 70, 71; types of companies controlled by, 113

Mellon National Bank and Trust: Diamond Shamrock and, 96; Heinz Corporation and, 114; Mellon family retains power in, 149; in Mellon group,

85, 86, 89; number of companies and assets controlled by, 111; power of, 38; trust assets in 1974, 70

Menshikov, S., 9, 86-89 passim

Mercantile-Safe Deposit and Trust of Baltimore: number of companies and assets controlled by, 111; Seaboard Coast Line Industries and, 115-116

Mergers: and data collection problems, 94; commercial banks and, 138-140; investment banks and, 31-33, 109, 137-138; waves of, 137. See also Conglomerates

Merrill, Lynch, Pierce, Fenner and Smith, Safeway and, 95-96, 143

Metcalf, Senator Lee, 11, 91, 92

Metcalf Report. See Disclosure of Corporate Ownership

Metropolitan Life Insurance Company: Anaconda Copper and, 120; in Chase group, 85, 87; in Rockefeller group, 50. See also Chase group

Million Dollar Directory, as data source, 93

Millionaires and Managers (Menshikov), 86

Miscellaneous control category, 75; criteria for determining, 78

Mississippi River Corporation, 73, 74

Missouri Pacific System, 73

Monopoly: financial control and, 133-135; government acted against, 31-41, 133-134; investment banks and, 33, 34

Moody, John: on Atlantic Coast Line Railroad, 115; on competition between railroads, 27; on Morgan, 29; on Rockefeller independence, 37

Moody's Industrial, Transportation, and Public Utility Manuals, as data source, 92, 93

Morgan, Henry S., 44n143, 87-88

Morgan, J.P.: Baker and, 35; Bankers Trust and, 88; "community of interest" principle, 132; General Electric merger and, 31-32; power of, 8, 40, 41, 119, 149; railroads and, 28, 29, 30, 31, 149; railroad rivalry with Harriman, 38-39; U.S. Steel and, 32, 114, 132

Morgan, J.P., Jr.: as director of National City Bank, 39; effect of Pujo Committee on, 40; power of in 1920s, 50

Morgan, J.P. and Company: Bankers Trust and, 35, 36; became commercial bank, 55, 87; competition reduced power of, 44, 46; in depression, 52; duPont and, 43; English capital and, 26, 42, 149;

First National Bank of New York and, 35-36, 84; General Motors and, 42n76, 43; Guarantee Trust and, 35, 36, 88; life insurance companies and, 36; National Bank of Commerce and, 35, 36; New Deal legislation and, 55; origin of, 25n2; power of, 35-36, 42, 50. See also Morgan group

Morgan, Stanley and Company: and American Telephone and Telegraph, 58; formed after Glass-Steagull Act, 55n143, 87-88; Morgan descendents in, 149n75; in Morgan group, 85-89 passim. See also Morgan group

Morgan group: competing companies controlled by, 134-135; and competitive bidding struggle, 57n152; economic concentration under, 145; members of, 35-36, 85, 87-89; numbers of companies and assets controlled by, 112; power of, 36, 50, 58, 59, 146; trust assets in 1974, 70; types of companies controlled by, 36, 50, 59, 113; U.S. Steel and, 15; utilities and, 47, 50, 51

Morgan Guarantee Trust: Kennecott Copper and, 135; Morgan descendents and, 149n75; in Morgan group, 85, 88, 89, 112; number of companies and assets controlled by, 110, 111; voting policy, Trust and Investment Division, 125-126; trust assets in 1974, 70. See also Morgan group

Mutual funds. See Investment companies

Mutual Life, Morgan and, 36

National Bank of Commerce, control of, 35-36

National banks, rise of, 35

National City Bank: Morgan and, 39; power of, 37, 42; Rockefellers and, 37, 50, 51. See also First National City Bank

Neoclassical economics, corporate goals in, 140, 144

Neoclassical economists, and managerial thesis, 4

New Deal legislation, 54-56

New York (city) financial institutions: competition and, 46, 51; cooperation among, 51; power of, 41, 110-111, 112

New York (state), life insurance control in, 39

New York Central Railroad, 25, 28

New York Life Insurance Company: Morgan and, 36; in Rockefeller group, 87n32. See also Rockefeller group

Nonferrous metal producers, Morgan group and, 113

Norfolk and Western Railway, 105

Northern Pacific Railway: battle for control of, 38-39; European capital for, 26; subsidiary, 73

Northwest Airlines, 134

Northwest Industries, 75

O'Connor, James, 11-12

Office machinery, Morgan group and, 113

Ogden: under financial control, 109, 137; shareholders' suit against, 138, 143n67

Oppenheimer, Mary, 11, 146-147

Otis and Company, 57n152

Overcapitalization, mergers and, 33

Owner control, 1, 2-3, 6-8; basis of, 19; criteria for determining, 78, 83; defined, 18; development into financial control, 113-116; families and, 18; full, 78, 98-99; partial, 78; profits under, 144; sources of data about, 99; summary of results about, 97-99, 101-108; suspected, 79

Paper companies, Morgan group and, 113

Parkinson, C. Jay, 120

Patman, Wright, 10

Patman Report, 10-11; as data source, 84, 89, 90, 95, 100; group control not noted in, 84, 100; on importance of stock ownership, 79-80, 81-82

Pennsylvania Railroad, 28

Pension funds: bank interest in profit from, 142; extent of stockholdings, 65; commercial banks manage, 66-67; power of, 66, 68; reason for, 67; regulation of, 69. See also Employee benefit funds

Percy, Senator Charles, 128

Perlo, Victor, 9, 88

Personal trust funds: bank interest in profitability of, 141-143; commercial banks manage, 63, 66; distribution of income from, 141-142; example of financial control through, 114-115; power of as stockholders, 65-66; reason for, 66, 71; as savings, 71

Peterson, Shorey, 6

Pew, J. Howard, 99

Pittsburgh, Pennsylvania: Mellons and, 38; financial power of, 111

Place, John M., 21n15, 120

Pneumo-Dynamics Corporation, 133-134

Politics, effect of economic concentration on, 147

Portfolio companies: controlling bank as creditor to, 131, 132, 142-143; defined, 126n19; exercise of voting rights in, 126, 127; financial insitutions' interest in profitability of, 141-144; informal pressure on, 127-130

Proctor and Gamble, 31n29

Profit maximization, as corporate goal, 140-144; social significance of, 144-145; types of control and, 6, 144

Proxy statements, as data source, 91-92, 93, 99

Prudential Life Insurance Company, in Morgan group, 85, 88. See also Morgan group

Public utility holding companies; competitive bidding required for sale of securities by, 57, 60, 105, 107; financial control over weakened, 55-56, 105, 107; growth of, 47-48; investment trusts and, 49; Morgan group and, 47, 50, 51

Public Utility Holding Company Act of 1935, 55-56

Pujo, Congressman Arsène, 40

Pujo Committee investigation, 40-41, 124; on lack of competition among banks, 26n6

Radio Corporation of America, 50

Railroad holding companies, 48

Railroads: adopted corporate form, 24, 108; Chase group and, 113; Chicago financial institutions and, 113; competition among, 27, 28, 30, 132; competitive bidding required for sale of securities by, 57, 60; data source for, 92; financial control among, 28-31, 105, 108, 132; growth of, 27; investment banking and, 25-31; Kuhn, Loeb and Company and, 51; monopolistic rate structure among, 30; Morgan group and, 50

Receivership, threat of, 21

Recessions, postwar, 63

Reconstruction Finance Corporation, 56

Reforms, antitrust, 39-41

Retail trade companies: Chase group and, 113; control of, 106, 107-108; investment banks and, 35, 86

Rockefeller, David, 87, 149

Rockefeller, James Stillman, 149

Rockefeller, John D.: banking activity in 1920s, 50-51; descendents of retain power, 149; independence of, 34, 37; managerial thesis and, 2

Rockefeller, William: descendents of retain power, 149; rivalry with Morgan, 38-39; Stillman and, 37, 50. See also Stillman-Rockefeller group

Rockefeller family: Chase Manhattan Bank and, 112; Standard Oil and, 39. See also Chase group; Rockefeller group; Stillman-Rockefeller group

Rockefeller group, 59; trust assets in 1974, 70-71. See also Chase group; Stillman-Rockefeller group

Rothschilds, the, 25n2

Safeway Stores, 95-96, 143n68

San Francisco, California, growth of as finance center, 46

Santa Fe Railroad, 29

Sarah Mellon Scaife Foundation, 86

Savings, institutionalization of, 71

Schiff, Jacob: on board representation, 25n5; power of, 41

Scientific equipment firms, Morgan group and, 113

Scott Paper, 135

Seaboard Coast Line Industries, 115-116

Seagram and Sons, 73

Sears, Roebuck: bank control of, 35; employee benefit fund controls, 75, 101

Securities, increased sale of, 43-44, 45

Securities Act of 1933, 55

Securities and Exchange Commission (SEC): investment companies and, 56; public utility holding companies and, 56, 57, 105, 107; reporting requirements, 82, 89, 91. See also Institutional Investor Study Report

Security affiliates, sponsored investment trusts, 48

Seligman, J.W. and Company: General Motors and, 34; ties with German capital, 26-27

Shamrock Oil and Gas, 96

Sheehan, Robert, 7

Shell Oil, 73

Singer Corporation, 79

Smith, Barney and Company, in Morgan group, 85, 88. See also Morgan group

Social Security, pension funds and, 67
Socialism, 39
Soldofsky, Robert, 91
Solow, Robert, 6
"Soulful" corporation, 5, 13, 144
Speculation, investment banks and, 33-34
Sperry Rand, 122
Standard and Poors Corporation Records, as data source, 92, 93
Standard Brands, 50
Southern California Edison, 100, 107
Standard Oil of New Jersey, 100, 101, 104
Standard Oil Trust: effect of dissolution on, 39; independence of, 37; power of, 34
Steel industry: Morgan and, 32-33, 34, 132; competition in, 32, 132
Stiles, Ned, 9
Stillman, James: descendents of retain power, 149; power of, 41; William Rockefeller and, 37, 50. See also Stillman-Rockefeller group
Stillman-Rockefeller group, 37; Harriman and, 37, 38, 119; power of, 42, 50-51; rivalry with Morgan, 38-39
Stockholders: beneficial vs. of record, 19; competition among, 84-85; control by, 1, 6-8, 18; financial institutions as, 10, 63-71; groups of financial institutions as, 84-89; in managerial thesis, 2-3, 4; as representative democracy, 125; in sample of 200, defined, 76. See also Owner control
Stockholdings, control through, 19-20, 63-71, 79-80, 81-82, 109-110, 130, 132; data sources on, 89-93; and interest in portfolio companies' profitability, 141-143, 147; voting rights and, 19, 94-96, 121, 125-127
Stuart, Charles, 57n152
Subsidiary corporations, in sample of 200, 73-74
Sun Oil, 99
Supreme Court, antitrust action, 39
Sweezy, Paul: on financial control thesis, 8-9, 11-12; on managerial corporations, 6

Temporary National Economic Committee: investigated investment banking, 59-60; on owner control, 6-7; study criticized, 83

Tenneco, Inc., 75
Thompson-Houston Company, 31-32
Tobacco trust, effect of dissolution on, 39
Trans World Airlines, 108, 134
Transamerica Corporation, 46n93
Transportation companies: Chase group and, 112-113; type of control over, 105, 106, 108
Trust assets: as source of financial control, 114-116, 118; regulation of, 69; of ten largest commercial banks in 1974, 70-71; voting rights for, 125-127
Trust banks, source of data on, 90
Trust departments, See Commercial banks, trust departments

Unincorporated businesses, structure of, 1
Union Pacific Railroad: Brown Brothers Harriman and, 82-83, 119; European capital for, 26; Harriman and, 37, 82-83, 119; Jay Gould and, 28
United Cigar Manufacturers, 35
United Corporation group, Morgan and, 47
United Founders Corporation, 49n112
United States Congress: House Banking and Currency Committee, see Patman Report and see Pujo Committee investigation; House Judiciary Committee, investigated conglomerates, 137-138, 139; Senate Government Operations Committee report, see Disclosure of Corporate Ownership; Senate Gray-Pecora investigations, 53-54
United States Department of Justice, antitrust suit by, 133-134
United States National Resources Committee, studied interest groups, 59
United States Steel Corporation: employee benefit fund controls, 75; Morgan and, 15, 32-33, 50, 113-114; stability of financial control of, 34
United States Trust Company: number of companies and assets controlled by, 111; trust assets in 1974, 70
Utilities: bond issues for, growth of, 46; data sources for, 92; in sample of 200, 72-73; types of control among, 105, 106, 107, 108. See also Public utility holding companies

"Valuation ratio," 5
Vanderbilt, Cornelius, 2, 25
Van Sweringen brothers, 48

Vertical relationships, 135-137
Villard, Henry, 31
Villejero, Don, 7
Voting rights: control through, 121, 125-127; and criteria for determining control, 80, 95-96
Voting trusts, 29-30, 63-64

Wachovia Bank and Trust, 111
Wall Street Journal, as data source, 92
Walters, Henry, 115
Warner and Swasey Corporation, 133-134
Western California Canners, 138
Western Electric, 73

Western Union, 36
Westinghouse, George, 37n57
Westinghouse Electric: incorporated, 31n29; Kuhn, Loeb and Company and, 37; Mellons and, 51
White Consolidated Industries, 99n65, 133-134
Who's Who in America, as data source, 93
Williamson, Oliver, 5
World War I, foreign capital declined during, 41
World War II, effect of on financial institutions, 56-58

Young, Robert R., 57n152